Legen

of

Brittany

...from the dawn of history to the nuclear age...

Wendy Mewes

Legends of Brittany
published by Red Dog Books
ISBN 978-0-9568699-2-0

© Wendy Mewes 2012

Red Dog Books is based in Somerset and in Brittany.
Enquiries should be addressed to the editorial office at
Red Dog Books, 29410 Plounéour-Ménez, France.

email: reddogbooks@orange.fr

www.reddogbooks.com

Printed by imprint*digital*.net

This book is dedicated
to the memory
of my beloved father

A.W.R.Thomas

who gave me the key
to the world of legends

About the author

Wendy Mewes has lived in Finistère for many years, finding the Monts d'Arrée a good fit for her Welsh background. She has a research degree in ancient history from the University of Wales and was Head of Classics at Godolphin & Latymer in London before concentrating full-time on writing.

The author of eight books about Brittany, including Discovering the History of Brittany, a guide to the Nantes-Brest canal and Walking the Brittany Coast, she also produces E-books on the region such as town guides to Quimper and Rennes, Megaliths, Parish Closes and Food and Drink.

She created the Brittany Walks organisation in 2004, and works to promote Breton heritage, landscape and products to anglophones through walks, talks, courses, guided visits and tourist projects. She has also written articles on Brittany for the national press in the UK, been filmed for French TV and broadcast a series on the history of Brittany for Spotlight radio.

ACKNOWLEDGEMENTS

With thanks to all those historians, folklorists, bards and musicians who over centuries have kept alive the illuminating fire of Breton legend, and especially the abundance of story-tellers and singers in Brittany today, making contemporary sense of the oral tradition so important in Celtic societies. Special thanks are due to all those who have shared their childhood stories with me and urged their favourites forward for this book.
Many thanks also to Isabelle Berthou at the Bibliothèque bretonne, Abbaye de Landévennec.

CONTENTS

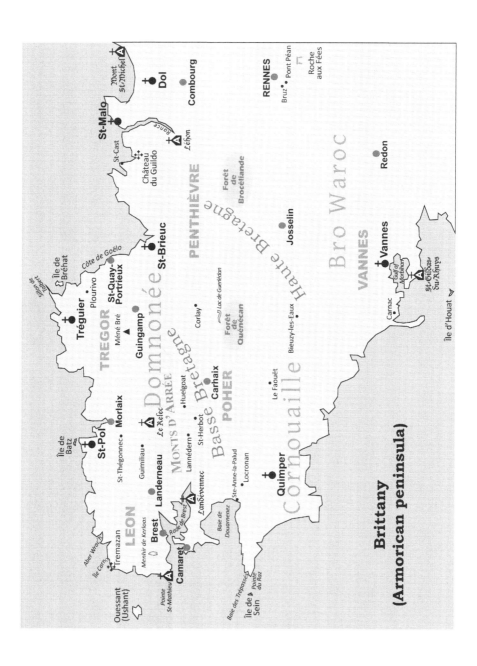

Brittany
(Armorican peninsula)

FOREWORD

The purpose of this book is to make the world of Brittany's legends accessible to English-speaking readers, and to present the historical context in which these traditions originated. Many places are mentioned, as often legends are inextricably connected to landscape, and these sites provide rewarding exercise for the imagination even today. Plenty of reference is given to Breton and French sources for those who would like to pursue the subject further. For anyone who is more interested in stories than history, sections of analysis are clearly distinguished from legends in the text.

My research and reading on the subject of legends as well as lots of 'listening experiences', either from professional story-tellers or simply tales told to me by friends and acquaintances, had to be put into some sort of orderly form to realise this book. With such a vast jumble of material, including variations of almost every story, I have divided the content into themes, incorporating what seem to me to be interesting and important aspects of Brittany's past.

This personal selection still covers a wide range from the most obscure of tales, whose origins are shrouded in mist, to famous stories of saints and miracles recorded in early written documents, right through to more recent events well-studied by historians. After all, the events of today are often the legends of tomorrow.

Brittany's legends spring from oral tradition, with stories passed down by word of mouth for generations before being documented in any way. I have tried to reflect the immensely varied form in which they have survived with reference to sayings, songs and theatrical works as well as dramatic narration.

Legends come in all shapes and sizes, serious, funny, gruesome, puzzling, easily explicable. They represent the world of imagination linked to the realities of everyday life and significant events. Legends enshrine what we believe about ourselves, our origins and social values; they add up to a sense of belonging to something larger and more meaningful than the individual.

No book on the subject can hope to compete with the powerful experience of live story-telling, so easily accessible in Brittany today. The tales of oral tradition were created for performance and entertainment, but they were passed down through generations because they meant more than that to their audiences. It is worth thinking about what the legends have to tell us about the popular imagination of Brittany, how Bretons see their past and the intrinsic character of that chameleon often referred to as Breton identity.

Wendy Mewes

THE LEGENDS OF BRITTANY

We may think of legends as tales of an imaginative world, but they can also lead us to the realities of the past. Stories enshrine a collective memory from distant times right up to recent events, and they indicate what people today believe about their own origins and about themselves as a community. In this way, legends are stories from yesterday for today and even for the future.

Introduction

Brittany's landscape and history are imbued with tales of saints, sinners, monsters, giants, mischievous imps, knights and ladies, products of a vast rich oral culture stretching back over many centuries. These stories go further than mere entertainment. They uphold beliefs about Breton identity that continue to exist in the present day, kept very much alive by the deeply-layered resource of traditional legend.

Through the efforts of folklorists in the last 150 years, the legends of Brittany have been preserved by collecting oral testimony - particularly from the older generation - all over the region, from Haute Bretagne in the east, where Gallo was the local language, to the Breton traditions of Basse Bretagne further west[1].

Old tales (*contes*) are now told in innovative ways, as each individual story-teller processes often well-known material through their own personal filter. Music and drama are important elements of the presentation of legends, as chants and theatrical pieces also present stories from the past. The *gwerz* (plural *gwerziou*) or dramatic ballad is today widely performed in Breton and French with songs based on popular traditions.[2]

Story-tellers (*conteurs/conteuses*) perform in village halls and in churches, at festivals and across the landscape throughout the year

---

[1] See Map, page xx.

[2] For example, those performed by well-known artists like Denez Prigent and Yann-Fañch Kemener whose work is widely available on CD.

to large audiences of young and old. They create evocative scenes through patterns of words and music, through gestures, facial expressions and that most versatile of instruments, the human voice. So the tale begins:

> *Eur wech a oa, eur wech 'oa ket,*
> *Mez me ya da gonta deoc'h bepred*

> There was a time, there was not a time,
> But I'm going to tell you anyway...

What is a legend?

The word 'legend' comes from the Latin *legenda* – meaning literally 'things that must be read'. On the face of it that seems an odd way to signify the products of oral tradition, which were rarely written down until many centuries after their original promulgation, but the term has developed through the medieval medium of the *Légende dorée* (Golden Legend), a work produced in Latin in the 1260s by a Dominican monk, Jacques de Voragine, in Genoa. This seminal collection and monumental work of the Lives of Saints was originally called *Legenda Sanctorum* – Things that must be read about Holy Men, the imperative being to learn from their examples of goodness and morality. So influential was the book that it was soon known by its more familiar name of The Golden Legend, and the term 'legend' was henceforth applied to exemplary stories of many kinds.

The subsequent connection between the word 'legend' and the lives of saints is certainly an important one in any study of Brittany's past. The early religious and political development of Breton society revolved significantly around the foundation of monasteries, which frequently became a focus for the growth of secular settlements. Legends describing their origins could even be used to endorse the property rights and moral authority of these early religious institutions. The holy men and monks responsible for their establishment were part of the wave of immigration from Britain – especially Cornwall and Wales – during the 4th-6th centuries.[1]

---

[1] See pages 24 & 27.

Legends often have many versions, a result of their transmission via oral means and their application to different locations. Today it may be possible to discern a double or even multiple context: the time in which the tales are set, the period in which they were first written down, and then future adaptations to suit later periods of history. There are many examples in the world of legends of this kind of inevitable re-interpretation and potential manipulation. A well-known example relevant to Brittany is the story of King Arthur.[1]

Elements of legend

A legend is a story told as if it were an event that actually happened. It is set in real time, with named characters (who may have actually existed) and often specific locations. These elements tend to separate legend from the timeless nature of myths and the fanciful world of fairytales, although traditional stories cannot be expected always to fit neatly into categories of genre. Certainly some magical and miraculous elements are common in legend, but the link with reality or perceived reality is an important factor.

Historical and topographical echoes are highly significant for anchoring a society's cultural origins. Place names in Brittany are redolent of the past, of people and events preserved in a toponym over centuries and through the memories of generations. A place called Folgoët or Folgoat (fool + wood in Breton) or Toul ar Sarpant (hole + serpent) require an explanation, and legends may provide it or, on the other hand, stories may be created to furnish one.

Localised stories relating to topographical detail and even man-made structures are legion. Why are there lines of several thousand standing-stones at Carnac, or extraordinary granite boulders, bigger than houses, at Huelgoat? In the eras before the development of scientific principles and detailed historical knowledge, legends provided explanations that are easy for us to dismiss as irrational or fantastical, but which could have made perfect sense at the time. The story of giants throwing enormous rocks at each other can be used to

---

[1] See Chapter 8

account for the Chaos phenomenon. Megaliths which we know to be the work of man are given names like 'Fairies' house' and 'Giant's tomb' because they once seemed to come from another age, immense structures created when men were physically larger or nature spirits had magical powers.

Legends are essentially popular tales – that is to say stories of the people, reflecting a life lived close to nature, to the fearsome power of the sea and vagaries of the weather so crucial to an agrarian existence. Despite the underlying presence of a whole host of Little People, Breton tales are anchored firmly in the world of real people in a real landscape, and the sense of their lives often emerges powerfully in details large and small. At the other end of that life is Death – that rite of passage so prominent in the Celtic consciousness – and the importance of securing an afterlife in heaven rather than hell. This theme figures widely in the canon of legends that have survived in popular imagination.

Oral tradition

Legends were originally the work of oral composition, tales told around the hearth and passed down through families from generation to generation, or performed by specialists, often in song, to entertain wider audiences. This is said to be one of the characteristics of 'Celtic' society, which has left no written documents despite a remarkable level of achievement in the art of craft-work. The Druids were the repositories of the collective memory, creating or telling and re-telling ancient stories in their role as bards. Such an ability was and still is regarded as a special gift.[1]

These traditions reflect a stage in the long history of human story-telling, like epic poems which have survived in later manuscripts but were originally vast bodies of poetry preserved and transmitted in oral form. The Iliad and the Odyssey are well-known European epics of this type, conserved in Homer's texts in about 750BC, but referring to events of the earlier Mycenaean age.[2] Experiments in rural cultures

---

[1] The Welsh festival called an *eisteddfod* is a good example of contemporary events involving competitive compositions and performances.

[2] They describe the exploits of heroes at the Trojan War and its aftermath.

in modern times have shown that a skilled story-teller can recite for hours on end, constructing a story as he goes along, using basic 'building blocks' of repeated or standard sections of text (such as descriptions of the dawn or heroic appearance) to underpin his own creative contributions.

The number of surviving versions of many legends reflects this disparate composition. A local story-teller may adapt the core narrative to create a connection with his own place, or fuse an external story with a well-known local tale to please his audience. Medieval bards and minstrels housed in palaces were employed not only to entertain a king or noble but to give a good account of the status and achievements of their patron's family and ancestors. It was a form of social imaging and political propaganda well-used by leaders in a pre-print age. That legends and stories could influence the minds of the people and help form their opinions was undisputed. Powerful men were often on the move, for reasons of war, alliance-seeking or simply putting in an appearance to reinforce loyalty in their territories. Their escort certainly included bards and musicians ready to sing their praises and achievements loud and clear and so leave a lasting oral legacy of the visit.

It is clear that early Brittany was particularly rich in oral literature. Marie de France, a female poet of the 12th century claimed to have drawn on Breton songs and legends in her work. These sources, although unknown directly, are usually referred to as the *matière de Bretagne*' or Breton material, a general term for early stories that pre-date the Saxon and Norman invasions of Great Britain, especially from Wales, and the Armorican peninsula or early Brittany.[1] This is the idea of 'Celtic' literature, as opposed to that of the French or English, who developed different traditions.

Brittany has certainly preserved an incredible range and variety of tales, songs, hymns, canticles, drama and poems, many of which originated long before the age of written documents.

---

[1] As Brittany was not an established name or place until later than the origins of many legends, the term Armorican peninsula is often used in this book. The Romans took their name for this area - Armorica - from the older Aremori or land by the sea.

Written Sources

We cannot say with any certainty where or when individual legends began, as our information comes mainly from later written traditions, long after the stories had been circulating by word of mouth. The earliest of these are accounts of saints' lives, piously recorded by monks labouring in the scriptorium, or writing room, of abbeys and monasteries. From the 9th century onwards, these books are fertile sources of miracle-working, healing and triumphant Christian tales. They are more hagiography than history, elevating the status of their subjects, but drawing on various genres for their content. The similarity of many of the tales told of saints indicates a sort of pattern book for some of these *Vitae* (Lives), but they can emerge with a sense of individuality and the ring of truth to certain episodes.

Collections of 'biographies' of saints have been of seminal importance in preserving legends from the formative period of Breton history. A work of hagiography *La vie, gestes, mort et miracles des Saincts de la Bretaigne Armorique* by Albert le Grand, a Dominican monk in Morlaix, in the 17th century, became in itself something of a bible of the genre. This was followed in the early 18th century by the efforts of Dom Lobineau, a Benedictine monk from Rennes, who took a rather more historical approach in his *Histoire des saints de la province de Bretagne*.

In medieval times stories of courtly love and the tales of King Arthur's court dominated the literary scene. The work of Geoffrey of Monmouth had presented Arthur as an historical figure, but it was Chrétien de Troyes, writing in the second half of the 12th century who developed the concept of heroic ideals surrounding Camelot. He is thought to have drawn on Breton sources with the first appearance of Lancelot du Lac. The other figure closely associated with Brittany is Merlin, who seems to have developed his role through Welsh sagas, and Druidic notions.

The Breton nobility were highly conscious of the powerful role legend could play in forming public opinion and creating allegiances. Duchess Anne at the end of the 15th century carefully orchestrated the patronage of writers who presented her Montfort family in a positive light. The great Rohan family, bitterly disappointed at being kept out of the ducal power, exploited the legend of Conan Meriadec[1] to vaunt their superior claims via descent from the first 'kings' of Brittany.

A sense of identity

The 19th century saw a great blossoming of interest in oral tradition, in 'Celticism' and in the history of Brittany. **Arthur de la Borderie** (1827-1901) from Vitré in eastern Brittany produced the hugely influential *Histoire de Bretagne*. This work sought to minimise the influence of France and present the history of Brittany as an independent state. It was an inevitable reaction to the post-Revolutionary and post-Napoleonic situation where conformity and uniformity were promoted at the expense of regional powers, languages and traditions. In such a climate it is not surprising that interest in Brittany's past burgeoned through historical research, early archaeology, studies of folklore and traditional customs.

As in other parts of France where collections of local songs and legends were becoming the subject of research, Brittany was looking for its own unique identity and ways to preserve and revive it. The notion of things 'Celtic' was an important part of this, as it made the distinction between Brittany and France, and nurtured a sense of connection and solidarity with other places of similar cultural, linguistic and political heritage like Cornwall, Wales and Ireland.

La Borderie's work sounded a rallying call to defenders of Brittany's past and future, and in the later part of the 19th century serious research into legends and folktales began. Four names dominate the process of preservation and dissemination of traditional stories into published prose at this time. Many of the stories told in this book are drawn from their collections.

Théodore Hersart de la Villemarqué (1815-1895) from Quimperlé began his studies in Rennes before going to Paris to study law. He soon became side-tracked by an interest in Breton and medieval Brittany, greatly inspired by a book on Welsh medieval literature *The*

---

[1] See page 89.

Myvynan Archaiology by Edward Williams (also known by his bardic name of Iolo Morganwg).[1] He made an intense study of the Breton language which he only knew imperfectly before, and began work on what was to become his greatest achievement, the *Barzaz Breiz*. This involved collecting and writing down the words and music of popular Breton songs, particularly in the area around his home and Nizon in southern Finistère. These are in effect dramatised legends, recorded as they would have been performed by bards and story-tellers.

In 1838 La Villemarqué made a trip to Wales (where he was welcomed as the Bard of Nizon) as part of a cultural delegation to a Celtic festival organised by neo-Druids. These groups in turn had been highly influenced by Edward Williams, who founded the Gorsedd, or Druid gathering. This experience underlined La Villemarqué's fascination with the working of oral traditions in poetry.

The French establishment rejected publication of the Barzaz Breiz, so the author undertook it at his own expense and the first edition appeared in 1839, followed by another in 1845. Challenges to the authenticity of the material began in the 1860s, with allegations that La Villemarqué had made his own adaptations to notes taken from bards and story-tellers, and that he had exaggerated the antiquity of some texts. It was not until the 1960s when some of La Villemarqué's research notebooks became available for study that he was to a great extent vindicated and his reputation restored in most quarters. The *Barzaz Breiz* remains the most important repository of the riches of the Breton oral tradition that we possess.

François-Marie Luzel, also known by his Breton name Fanch an Uhel (1821-1895) came from Côtes d'Armor (or Côtes du Nord as it was then) and went to college in Rennes, where he was a contemporary of the future historian Arthur de la Borderie, and met Adolphe Orain (see below). He became a folklorist and poet in his own right, specialising initially in collecting songs, legends and dramatic works from the Trégor area. He published *Chantes et Chansons populaires de la Basse-Bretagne* in 1869. After an unclear career path and various stints of research, aided by the influential thinker Ernest

---

[1] It is something of an irony in the light of La Villemarqué's later problems with the critics that some of Williams' texts turned out to be clear forgeries.

Renan, Luzel became the departmental archivist of Finistère, based at Quimper, where he encouraged the work of Anatole Le Braz (see below). He was a critic of La Villemarqué's lack of scientific research methods in the Preface of his own work *Contes Populaires de Basse-Bretagne* which came out in 1887.

Adolphe Orain (1834-1918) was from Ille-et-Vilaine and specialised in the study of folklore in eastern Brittany (Haute Bretagne). He had a successful career in public service in the Prefecture in Rennes and as mayor of his home town, Bain-de-Bretagne. He collected and published the stories, songs and customs of Haute-Bretagne, and was instrumental in the promotion of the language Gallo[1], used in that area of Brittany where Breton was not spoken. His numerous publications included *Folk-lore de L'Ille-et-Vilaine: de la vie à la mort* (1898) and *Chansons de Haute Bretagne* (1902).

Perhaps the best known today is the great Breton writer **Anatole Le Braz** (1859-1926), a follower of Luzel, who researched and recorded the memories of the elder generation, particularly peasants and sailors, through painstaking interviews, which he later translated from Breton into French. His determination to preserve for the future their store of legends handed down through families over centuries resulted in a remarkable collection, *La Légende de la Mort* (1893). This work is still easily available in print today and is highly recommended to those interested in studying Breton legends further. Le Braz was also a prolific author of poems, short stories and novels on Breton themes.

In more recent times many writers have recreated the old tales, or invented stories that fit the pattern and prolific themes from the past. With writers such as Pierre Jakez Hélias it has been an important aspect of preserving the Breton language, the original medium for these legends. They have also added their own imaginative offerings and new interpretations, in the time honoured way preserving and transmitting legends to new generations.

---

[1] Gallo derived ultimately from Latin and the days of Roman occupation

The Evolution of Legend

As in all cultures the legends of Brittany have evolved over time. Distant collective memories may well reach back to the very earliest ages. The basic elements of earth and water appear in creation legends of giants piling up mountains and cities vanishing beneath the waves. The power of fire is portrayed in Aerouant the red dragon.[1] The religion of Celtic people added the animation of nature, with springs, trees and hill-tops gaining their own identities and hence the sort of powers that attract stories, which turn into legends to be handed down. The structures of society, including the position of women,[2] began to change during the period of Roman rule, as old clan systems broke down to be gradually replaced by civic organisation, the political power of the state and, later, the social dominance of the priests.

These changes are reflected in the type of stories told. The arrival of Christianity was something of a turning point. Paganism became the *bête-noire* of the Breton saints and tales focused more and more on the basic polarity of good (i.e. in line with church teaching) and bad (breaking these rules). In medieval times bards and minstrels brought alive traditions like the Arthurian legends, a fertile source of chivalric and heroic values, and the competitive nobility sought to establish the antiquity of their family trees.

With the Age of Enlightenment, rationalism and the growth of scientific principles and historical analysis begin to occupy the minds of the educated, but Romanticism flourished in the increasing attention paid to nature and the landscape.

The 19th century's energetic spirit of enquiry into Brittany's past led to the desire to establish a distinct national identity. An important part of this was to preserve the wide-ranging oral tradition which had survived in popular songs and *contes*.

Here the themes of the sea and its spirits, the rocky landscape and the Little People who inhabit it, the Devil, death and salvation are all

---

[1] A widespread symbol used for example in the Welsh flag or the recent flag of the Trégor region of Brittany.

[2] See Chapter 10.

strongly represented, together with the rich imagination so characteristic of 'Celtic' cultures.

Connections

Breton legends also reflect the close connection between Great Britain and 'Little Britain' over the ages. Many of the saints have sacred sites across the water too – St-Guénolé is Winwaloe in Cornwall and the place-name Lannédern, sacred place of Edern, can be found in both Wales and Brittany. The same stories are told of different places, and genealogies link heroes and saints on both sides of the channel.

The Arthurian tales show that travel between the two places was common, and that support might be sought in Brittany for battles in Britain. Did immigrants bring the story of Arthur to the Armorican peninsula in the Dark ages or did Breton supporters of William the Conqueror return full of a great hero who had fought the pagan Saxons? The story of Conomor too,[1] with evidence from both sides of the channel, suggests close ties between Cornwall and Brittany during the 6th century.

This perceived 'Celtic connection' between Brittany and the fringe areas of Ireland, Wales and Cornwall is an important element in notions of Celtic identity, still important today in the modern world. One has only to think of the *Festival Interceltique* held annually in Lorient and many other musical and cultural ties between the lands where Celtic languages are still spoken and traditions upheld. Modern versions of Druids still meet and compete for bardic crowns.

Conclusion

The legends of Brittany offer much to those seeking to scratch beneath the skin of this region. The stories themselves provide endless entertainment, especially in the hands of a skilful *conteur*, and to enjoy this experience is something to be recommended to all visitors, regardless of nationality and language. In such a performance you can see traditions passed down over many centuries still alive and proudly kicking in the modern world. In mainly illiterate

---

[1] See page 96.

societies, the emphasis lay on the spoken word in a way we can hardly imagine today.

There is also the powerful glimpse of Brittany in its formative years provided by many Dark Age tales and the sense of individual identity so important in a region that does not have total autonomy over its own destiny. It is true to say that legends are a line of self-defence in these days of growing globalization. In addition, some knowledge of legends can help a visitor to appreciate much of what they see, from place-names to iconography in churches and chapels.

And there is no need to restrict an idea of legends to the past: society is constantly revising its own image and creating new legends for new situations and experiences. In Brittany, the Parc d'Armorique held a competition in 2010 for the creation of a legend to explain the moment when the decommissioned nuclear power station in the Monts d'Arrée will disappear from the landscape.[1] Legends are of their time and yet acquire fresh significance in the light of future events. There is always room for a new good story and some examples of 'recent legends' are given in this book.

That legends 'sell' places has been true throughout history from the massive following of the Compostela Trail in northern Spain to the monks of Glastonbury conveniently 'finding', at a time in the 12th century when pilgrim numbers were declining, the bodies of King Arthur and his queen buried in the abbey. The entertaining anecdotes of the tourist guide are a major attraction for modern visitors, who perhaps care little about historicity, but it's worth remembering that legends often have much deeper roots than a superficial ghost or gore story, and much greater significance to the people to whom they actually belong.

---

[1] See Chapter 12.

CHAPTER 1
BRETON SAINTS

The Religious Context

The Breton saints and their legends are of the greatest significance in the origins of Breton language, society and cultural traditions. They are not 'official' saints of the Roman Catholic church but their legacy is no less powerful for that.

Brittany's religious heritage is one of the most striking aspects of the region for visitors today. Roadside crosses, rural chapels, parish closes with their elaborately sculpted *calvaires* and simple *fontaines* with a statue of a saint above the spring water can be seen in every nook and cranny of the countryside, not to mention the impressive cathedrals in places as different as Quimper, Rennes, Vannes, St-Brieuc, Tréguier, St-Pol-de-Léon and Dol-de-Bretagne. The traditional Pardons or celebrations of saints' days with mass, a procession carrying the images and banners and a blessing are another enduring expression of custom, faith and affection that has continued through centuries.

For those unfamiliar with the trappings of Catholicism and perhaps used to the more austere décor of Protestantism, the lavishly decorated churches in Brittany can come as something of a surprise with their colourful statuary, sumptuous altars and a rich hoard of gold and silver in the treasuries. But there is a further dimension to be aware of in Breton churches: beside the conventional line-up of Catholic luminaries officially sanctioned by the Pope, like St-Anthony and St-Margaret, sit the statues, altar-pieces and stained-glass windows of the unofficial Breton saints. This vast

fontaine

23

pageant of locally revered figures has never received the papal sanction or been recognised by the church in Rome. They are largely honoured for their powers of healing and transformation rather than for gory martyrdom or persecution, yet they hold their constant place in Brittany's distinctive heritage.

This juxtaposition is neatly illustrated in a corner of Quimper's beautiful Gothic cathedral. A statue of St-Anthony, traditional Catholic patron of lost things, stands near to the wall-mounted figure of Santig-Du (Little Black Saint), who is the preferred choice of *Quimperois* in search of help to find missing items. In fact, Santig Du is not a legendary personage at all, but a well-documented Franciscan friar who lived in the city in the 14th century and ministered to plague victims before succumbing himself to the disease. Local tradition and allegiance compete with the authorised version of Catholicism in this way all over western Brittany.

The issue is more pronounced in the west (Basse Bretagne, the Breton-speaking part of Brittany) because this is where the immigrants from mainly Wales and south-west England arrived in the 4-6th centuries, driven by Irish raids, Anglo-Saxon expansionism, over-population and an outbreak of plague to seek a new life overseas. Many of these were holy men, bent on evangelism, bringing a few relatives and followers (or sometimes a couple of hundred), looking for land to settle or found religious establishments.

Many already had family connections in the Armorican peninsula. Some became hermits, others gained reputations for wisdom, healing or other miraculous powers. Some were drawn into more political roles as spiritual advisors to kings and counts. They shared a simplicity of devotion and

Chapel of St-Hervé, Méné Bré

24

a strength of faith in the power of Jesus Christ that was an example to all who witnessed their prayers and privations in the name of God. Fasting and endurance of severe living conditions were often part and parcel of their chosen way of life. These men were exponents of what is often today called Celtic Christianity, although the extent to which this was a well-defined and identifiable phenomenon is debated by academics.[1]

In eastern Brittany (Haute-Bretagne), where the influence of Rome and the Franks was much more directly and strongly felt, not least because of its geographical connections to the rest of France and Europe, things were very different. Here the church was more developed, more formalised and had been more intimately connected to the Church of Rome from the time of the Roman occupation in the 1st-3rd centuries. There were bishops in Rennes and Vannes by the end of the 5th century at the latest. It had a longer tradition of administrative structure and the complex rules and regulations of a large-scale organisation in a more urbanised area. In this zone the Pope's word, the Church of Rome and official Catholicism kept a firmer grip on the focus of faith. The metropolitan bishop of Tours, well outside Brittany, held religious authority over the eastern Breton churches. This outside control was something which became a political issue in the 9th century,[2] just at the time when many Lives (Vitae) of earlier Breton saints were being written down by monks in monasteries, the Breton language was in common usage and an independent Breton state was forming.

An example of this east/west contrast may perhaps be glimpsed in the legend of St-Hervé, one of the western Breton saints. When he was late for a meeting convened by important religious and political figures on Méné Bré, near Guingamp, a bishop asked scathingly why this glittering gathering was waiting for a blind itinerant monk.[3] Here is the split between the worldly east of official events and formal

---

[1] For a pragmatic and often mordant view of the issues, see *The Quest for Celtic Christianity* by Donald E. Meek (Edinburgh, 2000).

[2] See page 52.

[3] See page 44.

procedures, and the simple spiritual demeanour of the western religious figures.

An historical document of the early 6th century also lends weight to the proposition. It comes in the form of a letter written by the bishops of Tours, Angers and Rennes to two Breton priests, berating them for celebrating mass in an itinerant way using portable tables. Going to the people rather than the people coming to church was not the accepted way in official echelons. And even worse perhaps was the temerity of these two priests in allowing women to participate in the ritual of distributing the eucharist by carrying the chalice and 'daring to administer the blood of Christ'. The shock and the outrage of undermined authority is clear in the bishops' demand that such practices cease in the name of unity in the church. To allow women to perform such roles is to 'defame the priesthood' and bring discredit on 'our sacred religion'. The attempt by the Church of Rome to control and to impose unity of regulation in religious worship is clear. So is the contrast between east and west.

The acquisition of relics – limbs and bones of dead saints, thought to be imbued with the individual's miraculous powers – was important and competitive from the earliest days of the Church.[1] Many relics had to be taken out of Brittany for safe-keeping at the time of the 9th century Viking raids and many never returned or were the subject of claims, counter-claims and ecclesiastical negotiation. It was an economic calculation as much as a religious one: relics attracted pilgrims, who brought large and regular sums of money to abbey and church coffers.

Such practices became crucial targets of criticism during the Protestant Reformation of the 16/17th centuries. The cults of saints in Catholicism were regarded by Luther as a form of pagan idolatry, and the ridiculous trade in holy relics – how many heads or fingers can one saint have? – brought nothing but the shame of venality to the Catholic Church.

---

[1] According to legend, the Abbaye de Sainte-Mathieu in its striking location on the Atlantic coast at the entrance to the Rade de Brest was founded after Breton sailors brought back the Apostle's relics from Egypt.

The Catholic Counter-Reformation had to respond to these issues, and adapt to survive in the circumstances of major new religious developments. An offensive in the early 17th century saw the Catholic Church aim to strengthen the cults of saints – to do otherwise would be to swim against the tide of their fundamental support base amongst ordinary people – but to tighten up existing practices and get rid of dangerously 'pagan' trends in religious art and decoration. Emphasis was placed on official Catholic saints and acceptable portrayals, with bishops required to report on their dioceses to the Vatican. In this new climate of scrutiny and regulation, the patronage of some Breton saints fell by the wayside. A chapel near Pleyben, formerly dedicated to St-Tugdual, one of the founding saints of Brittany, changed to the charge of St-Laurent, a favoured official saint of Rome.

The Arrival of the Saints in the Armorican peninsula

There were already close ties of trade, kinship and language between Wales and south-west England and the Armorican peninsula just across the Channel before the main time of migrations in the 5th and 6th centuries. It was after all only a day's journey by sea in good weather. Many of the saints were from the upper levels of society, well-connected and well-educated, bringing their families or small groups of followers. St Brieuc is said to have come over and made contact with a cousin, Riwal, who was already established as an important political leader, being lord of Domnonée.[1]

As far as can be assumed from what little Dark Age source material exists, the in-comers were generally well-received. Although some 5th century fortifications may have been constructed to defend territory from immigrants, there is no reason to assume large-scale or organised opposition. Certain legends, however, hint at localised hostility. St-Ronan was driven off by angry women on arrival after he berated their wrecking practices. St-Ké was beaten with gorse by women on the beach at St-Quay-Portrieux[2] Refusal of help was

---

[1] An area across the north of the Armorican peninsula, its name taken from that of Devon.

[2] See page 203.

Stone boats...

Many legends of saints include reference to their arrival in 'stone boats'. St-Ronan is said to have glided on his stone vessel between the boats of fishermen in the Bay of Douarnenez. St-Budoc's 'boat' remains near his chapel at Porspoder today and is illustrated in a gilded panel inside the church. Near the Pointe du Milier on Cap Sizun can be seen what is said to be the stone boat of St-Conogan.

One obvious explanation for such stories is that it gives the saints miraculous powers before they have even arrived. Making a large stone not only float but skim the waves right across the Channel and out into the Atlantic in some cases is no mean feat by any standards. There may be a much simpler explanation, lying as so often in language and human error. It would not be too far-fetched to imagine a scribe inadvertently associating the Latin *cumba*, a small boat of the coracle type doubtless used by the immigrants, with the old Breton word *'koum'* meaning a valley or stone trough. The mistake once made would have been repeated and accepted because of its marvellous implications, which added to the exceptional profile of the saints – such are the workings and purposes of legend. Simpler still, the story was created under the inspiration of large rocks naturally hollowed by sea waters to a boat-shape and found on beaches as if someone had landed in them.

St-Budoc in his stone boat

28

experienced by various saints even if there was no violent reception, as was the case with St-Herbot.[1] Many of the monks who arrived in Brittany from 'Outre-Manche' (across the channel) with bands of followers were initially seeking, not to proselytize, but to replicate the secluded life of a hermit they had left behind.[2] A little hut in a forest or an oratory by the shore was all they required, for days based solely on prayer and fasting. Their followers remained nearby, grubbing a living from rough plots of land to keep these small units alive. But the future saints, as their written Lives relate, had been marked out by God early on for a purpose. Angelic visitations telling them (or their parents) what to do are commonly related. They were to evangelise the population and bring the light of the true God to a new land, something that could not be done from a life of isolation. Events often recalled them to their wider religious duties, although many, like St-Pol[3] remained torn between worldly status and a longing for solitude.

The Armorican peninsula was not suffering from the same land pressures as parts of Great Britain, and territory was readily granted to the newcomers. Some amusing legends spring from the ritual of deciding the boundaries.[4] These new communities contributed greatly to the clearance of land in early Brittany, an activity mentioned, for example, in the Life of St-Brieuc, and the consequent increase of prosperous farming.[5] We also see many examples of monks engaged in routine agricultural duties like harvesting or even tending grapes.[6] Settlements soon grew up around monasteries to provide services, and the miracle-working of saints attracted many followers to live and

---

[1] Who responded with a curse, see page 85.

[2] The Desert Fathers in 3rd century Egypt had strongly influenced the hermetic tradition.

[3] See page 63.

[4] See page 75, for example.

[5] Later the Cistercian monks were to be major *'defricheurs'* in Brittany, cutting down trees and clearing scrub or moorland to establish small agricultural units under the *quévaise* system in the Monts d'Arrée.

[6] Life of St-Malo.

work in the same neighbourhood. In these ways the migrations were of economic benefit to the society they joined.[1]

The arrival of the saints from Britain across the water was a seminal step in the formation of Brittany, although it would be centuries later before that could be called a recognisable entity. In addition to their faith, these Britons brought their language and a desire to settle permanently in the Armorican peninsula. The intermingling of these incomers with the indigenous population was to produce the Breton language (with its close similarities to Cornish and Welsh) and the beginning of a structured society based on communal groups. The word *'plou'* so commonly seen as a prefix in place-names in Brittany today comes linguistically from the Latin *plebs* (people) and signified a 'parish', the community growing up around what was often originally a religious settlement. The same goes for the prefix *Gui(k)* (from the Latin *vicus*), and *Tré* at the beginning of a name indicates a parish district. The prefixes *'Lan'* and *'Loc'* (Lanmeur, Lampaul-Guimiliau, Locquenolé) indicate a holy place. The Breton saints are still ever-present in this form today, their legacy written all over the map of western Brittany.

Struggles with the paganism which still exerted a strong influence over the people of the peninsula are recorded in many legends of the saints, often through symbolic stories. Most famously of all, St-Pol repelled the ferocious dragon which terrorised the Île de Batz.[2] Power over other wild animals is frequently used to demonstrate the superiority of Christianity over the world of nature. Philosopher Ernest Renan (1823-1892) pointed out that the Breton saints often seem more Druidic than Christian, with their staffs used like magic wands and the invocation before miracles of 'in the name of Jesus Christ...' rather like the formula of a spell. They also ape the powers of God himself, showing power over life and death, with many tales of resurrection.

It is clear that attempts of the new bishops to impose rules and religious practices were not always willingly accepted by the native population. A man who ignored St-Pol's decree and continued cutting

---

[1] For a legend symbolising this, see page 116.

[2] See page 73.

his hedges on a Sunday received a dire punishment, finding his sickle inextricably wedded to his hand. Only the saint could release him from this ordeal. A washerwoman was paralysed for similar temerity in getting on with her work regardless of a holy day. Sometimes the saints went to even greater lengths: St-Herbot was ill-treated by the women of Berrien for distracting their menfolk from working the fields by his preaching, so he cursed them, asking God to ensure that forever more the land of Berrien would be nothing but stones.[1]

These little nuggets of information gleaned from legends of the saints reflect the teething problems of new settlements and the arrival of formalised Christianity.

Most of the figures of Breton saints can be said to be only legendary, although a few, like Saint Samson, peep into history with references in accounts of church councils or political gatherings. They were often shown in boyhood by remarkable events or angelic visitations to be marked out for glorious destinies in the service of God. In general their stories sit firmly in a recognisable period of history, often called the Dark Ages, a reference to the lack of contemporary written documents, their stories being preserved through oral tradition and only later being written down by monks So whereas Albert Le Grand, for example, in his seminal work of saints' Lives quotes solely ecclesiastical sources for his work, as one would expect from a scholarly monk in the 17th century, other stories about the saints probably come from popular tradition, preserved in family tales and the songs and stories of local story-tellers, the early *conteurs*.

The essential humanity of the Breton saints and the all-too-human inter-action with their followers is another aspect of their distinctive character. There was a distinct whiff of reciprocal expectation in the relationship between saint and suppliant. The following incident from 1902 when the terrible sardine shortages began to play havoc with the lives of many Bretons who depended on the catch is a good instance.

A thirteen-year-old found his mother at the church in Ploaré with several other women. He saw them bring out the statue of St-Pierre,

---

[1] Berrien is known even today for its extensive quarries.

patron saint of fishermen, and put it face down in the grass. They prayed over it and then beat the statue with branches of broom, exhorting the saint to bring the sardine shoals back. Then they returned the statue to the church.[1]

The lofty reverence of the conventional church is missing here, but this only serves to forge closer, warmer feelings of loyalty towards the Breton saints from their local followings. They were essentially men who belonged to their communities, who represented in their persons expressed in legends, the importance of God's will in the locality.

The true significance of these Breton saints is that they enshrine in popular tradition the origins of Brittany, the formation of its society and the beginning of its language. From these men with their courage, fearlessness in faith and God-sponsored powers are derived the strengths of Breton society, staunch through allegiance to their faith over many centuries when the church and the role of the clergy contributed greatly to the solidarity of society.

The Lives of the Saints

We know so much about the Breton saints because of many written records, despite the fact these were produced usually several hundred years after the deaths of their subjects. These Lives ('*Vitae*') would have been penned in Latin by monks who had an interest in publicising such material to promote the power of Christianity, the status of the abbeys and holy places associated with the saints and the importance of behaviour in accordance with the prescriptions of the Church. They are designed to be edifying rather than entertaining, a record of God's work through his chosen representatives.

Many of the surviving manuscripts recordings saints' lives are in the genre of hagiography, lavishing unstinted praise on the miraculous deeds and feats of their subjects. Hagiographies are also rather formulaic, with the same stories told about different people and repetitious healings and miracles. They are unlikely to be read for

---

[1] This incident is related in *L'Epopée de la Sardine* by Jean-Claude Boulard. St Peter is of course not a Breton saint, but this incident illustrates a general attitude. Other statues of saints in Brittany have been draped in seaweed and put away in cupboards for not producing the goods.

their riveting entertainment value, but a sense of individual character – St-Brieuc's fondness for singing hymns, St-Ronan's reclusive tendencies and St-Samson's aversion to women - and many small details of contemporary interest do emerge from a more homogenous whole.

The Lives also have a strong metaphorical significance expressed through the processes of agriculture so familiar to all in those days – the sowing of seeds (of faith) and harvesting (of souls), getting rid of weeds (sin) and things harmful to crops (pagan practices). The old biblical image of separating wheat and chaff springs even to the modern mind.

Such allusions were not lost on a rural peasant society: it was the language of their everyday lives. Hence also the emphasis on powers over the elements of nature implied in miracles like saints striking rock with their staff to produce spring water. Feats such as these were very impressive to early societies so dependent on the caprices of nature for precarious survival.

That original information about the saints comes from the oral tradition is apparent in the frequent confusion or inconsistency of chronology and the many different versions of almost every story. It is often not possible to make geographical or rational sense of tales in the *Vitae*. Future records in Breton or French or English, with all the possibilities of mistranslation and misunderstanding across languages add to the melting pot.

It is also not unknown for saints to be confused with each other - is Saint Tugdual St Tudy in another form? – and the same story to be told of several different people, like the oxen drawing the burial carts in relation to St-Herbot and St-Ronan. Whether saints were born in Wales or Brittany and whether they landed here or there on the peninsula with few or many followers are the sort of details open for speculation, but the gist of the most famous stories associated with each saint does emerge.

A saint's biography

Guénolé was the son of Fracan, an immigrant from Great Britain.[1] He was one of the brightest stars in the Breton saintly firmament, and the *Life of Saint Guénolé* illustrates a great number of these characteristic details in his personality and religious devotion. It relates a few strange individual incidents as well as the healings and miracles he performed. The stages of his progress towards founding a vitally important place of worship, the Abbey of Landévennec, said to have been the earliest such foundation on the Armorican peninsula,[2] are also described. Here we can see the characteristic elements of hagiography but also small touches of historic realism from Dark Age Brittany.[3]

The main life of St-Guénolé was that written by the monk Gurdisten at Landévennec in the 9th century. In it he refers to an earlier short life and there is certainly overlap in Gurdisten's work with a manuscript in the British Museum also outlining the life of Guénolé, but the sequence and inter-dependence of the two is not clear. Another monk, Clement, composed an early hymn to the saint and could be the author of the *Vita brevis* (Abbreviated Life) given in detail here to provide the full flavour of these early documents.

---

[1] Fracan (also written Fragan), probably came from Wales.

[2] Remains of the later medieval monastery can be visited today, and a modern abbey was founded on the hillside above in the 1950s.

[3] Notably in the horse-racing of Fracan and an early reference to what was probably cider.

The Life of St-Guénolé

racan, cousin of king Catovius, with his twin sons Wethenic and Jacut and his wife Gwen,[1] together with a few others, came by boat to Armorica, which was still an undeveloped and peaceful place. They reached a port called Brahec and found a river valley[2] surrounded by wooded slopes where Fracan decided to settle with his family. The little community began to grow and he soon longed for another son to reflect the idea of the Holy Trinity. His wife conceived at once and soon everyone was celebrating the great day on which Guénolé,[3] destined to be a shining beacon for western Armorica, was born.

From the earliest age, Guénolé was spiritually devout and a student of religious texts. As a child he wanted to become a monk, but his father was against the idea. One day whilst working in the fields with his animals, Fracan was struck down during a terrible storm. He prayed to God for safety and vowed all three of his sons to God should he survive. Once safe, he told his wife what had happened, and seven days later, entrusted young Guénolé to Budoc[4], a monk of great reputation for wisdom and learning. On the boat journey to the island monastery, the sun was suddenly mysteriously blotted out and darkness fell. Fracan was terrified and wondered if it was a sign that he was doing the wrong thing. But Guénolé reassured his father, saying one must always have faith and trust in God without fear. At these words, the sun reappeared and all was well.[5]

---

[1] Meaning 'white'. She was said later to have three breasts because of her three sons. Her daughter is not mentioned here, nor included in the later iconography

[2] This was the Gouët river, in an area today called Pays de Goëlo, north of St-Brieuc. The commune name Ploufragan today means parish of Fragan.

[3] Also written Winwaloë, as he is known in Cornwall, England.

[4] Budoc's community was based on the Île Lavret, part of the Bréhat group of islands.

[5] From this story, St-Guénolé is a patron saint of mariners.

Budoc received Guénolé with kindness and recognised at once his special qualities and the evidence of divine wisdom even in one so young. Fracan went home again early the next day, happy that his son was where he should be. Indeed Guénolé was soon a prodigy of learning, learning the alphabet in a single day and progressing rapidly as time went by to master all religious law and scriptures.

It was not long before his first miracle was attested. One day when Budoc had left the island, one of Guénolé's young companions broke a leg fooling about when he should not have been playing. No-one knew what to do and all were in a state of fear and despondency when Guénolé came on the scene and began to reassure them, urging them to pray. He himself raised his hands to heaven and begged Jesus Christ to heal the young man. He then made the sign of the cross over the broken leg and told the boy to get up in the name of the Lord. He did so and was completely healed. When Budoc returned and heard what had happened, he rejoiced in his heart at this evidence of divine favour for Guénolé.

After this, jealousy among his peers led one to accuse him of pride as a motive for helping the poor. Guénolé bore the criticism humbly, but after he restored sight to a blind man, he became worried by the praise he received from some of his companions. Budoc urged him to recognise and accept his great gifts as God had intended.

A curious incident happened soon after this. Guénolé's sister, Clervie, was attacked by a goose which pecked out and swallowed her eye. The disfigured girl ran home in agony. In Guénolé's sleep an angel appeared and told him what had taken place, saying he must go to his family and save his sister. The angel persuaded him that this rather personal act of mercy would indeed be the work of God. On awakening he went to his parents' house and then in search of the goose. Picking out the fattest one from the flock, he retrieved the eye from its stomach, restoring Clervie to perfect sight.[1]

The miracles continued. One of Guénolé's companions was bitten by a snake whilst sleeping outside and lay in danger of death. Guénolé called the snake out of the crevice where it was hiding, saying "Show yourself and acknowledge the victorious sign of Christ" and then confronted it with the sign of the cross. The snake perished at once, and the man was cured. Fracan then urged his son to pray to God that no snake should dwell in that area again, which he did. It was said that if ever a snake came to that place, it died immediately.

One day a terrible storm came as a shepherd was guarding his sheep. The flock scattered and he fell to the ground in terror. When he came round it was dark and he was surrounded by wolves. The petrified shepherd prayed to Saint Guénolé and saw the saint appear to stand between him and the wolves until darkness dispersed. In the morning the shepherd was able to gather his sheep safely again. He then ran to tell Saint Guénolé what he had experienced. Guénolé was reluctant to take credit for what had happened but the shepherd was quite convinced.

Another marvel followed at a horse-race where his father's horses were competing with those of count Riwalon. They used young boys for jockeys so the light weight would increase the speed of the horses. Sure enough, they flew like the wind, but one of the boys lost control and was thrown onto jagged rocks and died. Mourning was in full spate when Guénolé arrived and brought the boy back to life.

All these things increased the strength of his reputation. Despite his youth, the miracles, his discourses on the scriptures, his wisdom and moral example all contributed to the high esteem in which he was held. But

---

[1] From this strange story, the saint is sometimes given a goose symbol (or the story may explain the symbol)

Guénolé was not destined to remain on the Côte de Goëlo – a greater call was imminent.

Guénolé had conceived a wish to go to Ireland to visit St Patrick. But one night he had a vision of the Irish saint himself telling him not to do this as Guénolé was to remain in Armorica but not in the place where he currently lived. When Guénolé related this to Budoc, the old man realised that this was a divine command and gave Guénolé eleven disciples and his blessing, saying "Happy will be the land where you are sent. I rejoice that God has chosen you, though it will be sad to lose a well-loved disciple. Farewell and go in peace."

God guided the small party through Domnonée and then to the edge of Cornouaille around the Rade de Brest. Here they found a wild, uninhabited semi-island and decided to settle.[1] They built an oratory and cabins and tried to work the soil for a vegetable garden. For three years they struggled here, enduring harsh weather and savage winds, finding the earth unfruitful. Every day they went to a higher point for prayers and looked across the expanse of water to what seemed an idyllic place, a river valley clad in thick forest. They watched the morning mist rise like smoke, and felt the powerful allure of such a peaceful place.[2]

After prayers one day Guénolé asked his companions if they still had a desire to go to that place. They said it was up to him as the chosen one of God to decide and they would abide by whatever he wished to do. He urged them to prayer before striking the shore with his staff. The waters parted, and singing the hymn of Moses crossing the Red Sea, they walked across without getting their feet wet.

---

[1] This was at Tibidy.

[2] This wondrous site was what is now Landévennec, where the great river Aulne flows into the Rade de Brest. Here Guénolé founded his first church. This would later give rise to the abbey which stands on the spot today in ancient ruins.

One of the problems as the monks set about establishing their new settlement was the lack of a fresh-water source. Guénolé prayed: "Jesus Christ, you who had the power to get water from dry stone to relieve the thirst of your followers in the desert, please grant to this little band of monks a source of clear water." Then he traced his staff on the ground where a spring appeared at once.

Soon after their arrival Guénolé was praying by night in an oratory they had built by the mouth of the river. Suddenly the Devil appeared to him in monster form, with eyes of flame, black feathers, a hundred eyes, tongues and ears. Guénolé did not hesitate to admonish the beast without fear, reminding it of the superior power of Christ. And so he dismissed the evil vision. Although Guénolé did not mention it to others, another monk in a hut nearby had overheard the whole thing and reported it to his companions.

Guénolé was absolutely committed to an austere and devout lifestyle. He dressed only in goat-skin and had a stone for a pillow. He said fifty psalms three times a day and prayed constantly. He was always humble and kind to all, never miserable, nor angry, nor agitated, remaining gracious and serene at all times. He ate a simple diet of barley bread and vegetables, but no fat, and drank water mixed with apple juice. Often he fasted for two or three days.[1]

As his fame spread far and wide, queues of those hopeful of healing grew – the blind, lame, deaf, lepers and those possessed by evil spirits. All wanted to lay eyes on the angelic face of this saint – in fact he was no longer a monk but an angel among men.

One of the monks named Rioc got news that his mother was sick. He was given permission to go to her, but Saint Guénolé knew that the woman had already died. He gave Rioc a phial of Holy Water. On arrival he found his mother

---

[1] This was common practice in the Desert Fathers tradition.

dead and was mocked by the mourners when he attempted to revive her with the water and by prayer in the name of his master Guénolé and Jesus Christ. But then they saw the woman get up as if from a little sleep and marvelled at the miracle. The woman then described how after death she saw herself surrounded by tiny figures, black like coal and ice-cold, who wanted to devour her, starting with her hands and feet. But then Guénolé appeared and admonished them, claiming her as his own. From the time of this incident, the mother of Rioc devoted her life to good works.

One day he was going to another church with a young deacon named Ethbin. They met a leper in a field that was being harvested. Guénolé asked how he might help the man and offered to lay hands on his nostrils where the worst infection was contained. "No," the leper replied, "it would be too painful, but you may take them in your mouth." The saint was prepared to do anything to alleviate the man's sufferings and so he did, but the man's nose immediately turned into a small stone in his mouth, and a vision of Jesus appeared, commending Guénolé for his piety and promising him a place in heaven. Neither Guénolé nor Ethbin ever told a soul about this event.[1]

One night the sons of Catmael, believing that such a reputed man must have riches, came to Landévennec to steal any treasures they could find. All they found was a barn full of barley and so they decided at least to fill their sacks with this commodity. Meanwhile Guénolé was at service in the church, although he knew full well what was happening. He alerted the others, but told them to leave it in God's hands. As the robbers went off towards their waiting boat, one was suddenly struck to the ground, another rooted like a tree and the third blinded so that he wandered off along the river bank. Their comrade in the

---

[1] And yet it is recorded in this manuscript!

boat called urgently but there was no reply. Finally Guénolé and the monks came out, and the saint released the men from their afflictions in the name of Jesus Christ, and adjured them not to repeat their bad deeds. If they were truly in need, he told them, God would provide. The robbers vowed to remain Guénolé's followers and to do his bidding.

Towards the end of his life, Guénolé cured a noble woman of blindness. She was weary of her plight, but had a vision of an angel telling her to go to Saint Guénolé, who touched her eyes with his right hand and cured her.

His death[1] came after an angel appeared to tell him his time was near and to prepare himself.[2]

He spoke to the monks with tears and joy, telling them to choose a new leader – as sweet as honey and sharp as absinthe. He says he would take mass later, then be received by Jesus. He begged them not to strive for ease in this life but to concentrate on the sublime tranquillity of the next. So he died by the altar, supported by two monks, after he had taken on the strength of the mass.[3]

Although it is not mentioned in this text, Guénolé later appears as the advisor of Gradlon in many versions of the famous legend of the city of Ys and downfall of Dahut (see page 105).

---

[1] c.532

[2] The death of a saint is always significant and usually elevated by legends. Guénolé is no exception. He had earlier had an angelic vision about the death of older monks in the community. Guénolé said he was not ready himself as he still had imperfections to work on. So another monk was taken. In fact they passed away in order of age.

[3] This is an echo of the death of St Benedict, whose rule had been established in Landévennec in 818 under the influence of Louis Le Pieux, king of the Franks.

OTHER IMPORTANT BRETON SAINTS

Saint Hervé

Saint Hervé is one of the most ubiquitous of the Breton saints. He was born in Brittany, his father being a famous bard from Great Britain. Despite being clearly marked for greatness in the circumstances of his birth, Hervé refused to be drawn into official structures of the church, preferring an itinerant and simple lifestyle. To this extent he may be said to personify a purer religious tradition. Blind from birth he was yet a traveller, honoured today in many places, renowned for his wisdom and for his musical talents, being traditionally regarded as the composer of the canticle *Ar Baradoz* (Paradise).

The father of Hervé, Hoarvian, was a bard well-known for his musical and linguistic abilities. He came from his native Great Britain to the court of Childebert, emperor of the Franks, in Paris, where his talents made him an instant success. He was however devoutly religious and not one for the pleasures of court life, soon asking the emperor to let him return home. Childebert reluctantly agreed and gave him letters to return via the territories of the count of Léon.

So Hoarvian travelled to western Brittany, and all went well in his preparations for departure across the channel. But on the eve, he had a curious dream. An angel told him he must stay in Brittany and that he would meet and marry a girl called Riwanon. This was not welcome news to Hoarvian who valued his chastity and purity of life, and had no thought of marrying.

He began his journey as planned the following day, but soon encountered a young woman by a *fontaine*. When he discovered her name was Riwanon and that she too had had a similar dream, he accepted the will of God, at least for a short time. They were married, and Riwanon became pregnant but they never lived together, each preferring to be alone. The mother-in-waiting prayed that her child would never see the cruel vices of the world; the father hoped that the child would see only the glories of heaven. In the fullness of time, a boy was born. He was blind.

Hervé remained with his mother until the age of seven, before being entrusted to a monk for his education. He soon was familiar with all the scriptures and holy texts, but he had no desire to become a regular priest, preferring to wander in the countryside around his base at what is now Lanhouarneau.[1] He lived in a hermitage in the woods where he attracted many followers. Most loyal was his constant guide, young Guiharan, said to be something of a simpleton. On an occasion when Guiharan was using a cart

---

[1] Holy place of Houarne, a Breton form of Hervé.

drawn by a donkey, this animal was killed by an attacking wolf, which then fell down in penitence when reproached by St-Hervé. The saint made the wolf take the donkey's place, and it was later said to be another of his faithful companions.[1]

At the time of Conomor's ill-deeds, a conference of important religious and political leaders was summoned on the top of Méné Bré to decide his punishment. Hervé was to attend in the company of the bishop of St-Pol-de-Léon, but the party was late as he travelled more slowly than the others. One of the waiting dignitaries exclaimed indignantly about such great matters waiting for a mere blind itinerant monk. This man was immediately struck down and lay, eyes open but unseeing, as if dead. On arriving St-Hervé agreed to revive him, but as there was no fresh water he had to strike his staff on the ground to miraculously produce a bubbling spring. When the meeting finally got underway, the decision was to excommunicate Conomor.[2]

St Hervé lived to a great age and was forewarned of his death by a vision so he had time to prepare and to die joyfully in prayer.

---

[1] Blind Hervé led by a young man and escorted by a wolf is a theme of the saint's iconography – see cover illustration.

[2] The Chapel of St-Hervé on top of the Méné Bré is still visible from afar. The Pardon of St-Hervé takes place there on the third Sunday in June (the 17th being his sacred day) and on August 15th the Festival of the Breton Horse takes place on the hill. This event was originally started by the monks of Begard in the 12th century. St-Hervé is a patron of horses (see page 71).

Saint Ronan

The story of St-Ronan is especially interesting for the potential conflict it suggests between incomers to Brittany in the 5/6th century and the native inhabitants. The clash between paganism and Christianity, and the assimilation of the former by the latter is another aspect of the same issue. Ronan's territory,[1] which he ritually walked each day in prayer, is said to be on the same site as an earlier 'nemeton' or Celtic sacred space, where Druids had worshipped.

Ronan's personality is also somewhat distinct, and the way he confronted the women wreckers in one version of the legend suggested at least a lack of diplomacy in a new land, and stories that he had to leave after more trouble later in his life do not suggest much personal development! One gets the sense of a true solitary.

t-Ronan came from Ireland, possibly at the turn of the 5th century or early 6th. Whether or not he travelled in a stone boat and made an initial stop on the island of Molène, most traditions say he first tried to settle in Léon, where the town of St-Renan (Ronan) stands today. After a short time, an angelic visitation encouraged him to move on, so Ronan continued to the shores of the Bay of Douarnenez. The local men were all away fishing, but he was immediately set on by their womenfolk, who were long-practised as wreckers, luring boats onto the rocks and seeking plunder from their victims. They soon realised that Ronan had nothing worth taking, but he found their aggression so reprehensible that he caused a great light to shine on the sea so that no more ships would be wrecked on that shore.[2] This action made the local people very angry and Ronan was forced to withdraw inland into the forest of Nevet.

Here he established a hermitage and devoted himself to quiet prayer and contemplation, taking the same regular long walk each day as a fasting ritual and keeping away

---

[1] Around what is now Locronan – holy place of Ronan.

[2] In another version he asked God for a great bell to use as a warning noise for ships that land was near.

from the company of others. All was calm until he attracted the wrath of a woman named Keben.

One day as Ronan stood at the door of his humble cabin, a wolf ran past carrying a sheep in its mouth. In pursuit was the peasant owner of the sheep. Ronan prayed at once that the sheep would be saved, and sure enough, the wolf dropped his prey unharmed. The peasant gave thanks to Ronan and often came to him afterwards for conversation. This incurred the anger of the peasant's wife and she tried to turn all the people against the monk.[1]

Direct hostility had no effect on Ronan, so Keben went to King Gradlon of Quimper to accuse the monk of terrible crimes. She claimed he was a sorcerer who had spirited away her daughter. Ronan was summoned to answer the charge and protested his innocence, but Gradlon decided to conduct a test by setting savage dogs on him.[2] Ronan was unafraid and made the sign of the cross, upon which the dogs cowered before him. He then told Gradlon that Keben had hidden the girl in a large coffer in her own house. When they checked on this, they found the girl dead, but Ronan was able to bring her back to life. He then went back to his hermitage and devoted himself to solitary

---

[1] Another tale makes Keben the wife of the local chief, a man who was attracted by the teachings of Ronan, thus stirring her jealousy and resentment against Christianity taking over the old ways.

[2] Presumably before his conversion to Christianity!

prayer. Keben's punishment is not known and it did not prevent her from returning to attack the saint again later on.[1]

When Ronan died his body was placed on a cart drawn by two oxen to wander at will. Where they stopped would be his burial place. It is said that Keben mocked the body as it passed and struck off an ox's horn[2] before she herself was struck down in retribution for abusing the saint. The cart came to rest where the church of Locronan[3] stands today, and there he is buried.

The *Petite Troménie* (literally in Breton *tro minihi* – journey around monastic land) is held at Locronan in Finistère each July, involving a 6km walk. Every six years it becomes the *Grande Troménie*, with a circuit of 12 kms followed by thousands of pilgrims and walkers.

On the route of the latter (but on private property and inaccessible at other times) is a large stone called the Jument de Pierre or La Chaise de Saint-Ronan. It is an ancient lying stone marked by a deep groove and has a local legend that it was the stone boat Ronan arrived in, or the place he sat on his regular walks to gaze out over the bay. It is also associated with fertility rituals, for women used to lie on the stone and rub their bellies against it. This aspect has naturally not found favour with religious officials, but it may connect to earlier times when the site was part of very different types of worship.

---

[1] Some said he had to leave the area because of her continuing threats, or because he had upset others, and made his way across Brittany to Hillion on the Bay of St-Brieuc.

[2] This is clearly a topographical detail to explain the place name Plas ar Horn at Locronan.

[3] Some of the events of his life can be seen carved on the pulpit panels in the impressive church.

Saint Gildas[1]

Gildas is something of a split personality. There are two surviving *Vitae*, one from Brittany (9th century) and one a little later from the monastery of Llancarfan in Wales. In the latter, Gildas is a friend of King Arthur, and strongly connected with Street and Glastonbury in Somerset, but there is no mention of his life in Brittany.[2] There is some overlap between the two accounts of his early years, but it is hard to reconcile the different stories and personas convincingly.

He was known as Gildas the Sage for his writing, including '*De Excidio et conquestu Britanniae*' written in Latin about 530. In it he says he was born in the year of the battle of Mont Badon[3], which is thought to be about 490. The text lambasts the kings of Britain for their veniality and moral corruption.

In Brittany Gildas/Gweltas has a clear role as the founder of the abbey now called St-Gildas-de-Rhuys. He is also associated with other places and more unusual tales, one of which indicates a rather irascible and vindictive nature...

Gildas' connection with Waroc, Count of Vannes, led to his involvement in the tragic story of the count's daughter Tréphine.[4] In most versions of the Conomor legend it is said to have been St-Gildas who revived and restored Tréphine after her husband cut off her head.[5]

Chapelle de St-Gildas, Bieuzy, Morbihan

---

[1] His Breton name is Gweltas.

[2] Gildas' own written work never mentions Arthur.

[3] This is supposedly the battle in which King Arthur received his fatal wound, but there is no mention of him as leader in Gildas' text.

[4] In Caradoc's *Life of St-Gildas*, he is also involved in the King Arthur story.

[5] There is also a story that his prayers brought down the castle walls and killed Conomor. See page xx and 100.

t-Gildas was the son of a king from the north of Britain. His religious education was with the illustrious abbot Ildut at the monastery of Llanwit in Wales. He later studied in Ireland and went on a trip to Rome before deciding to leave Britain altogether in search of a place of solitude.

He came to the small island of Houat off the south coast of the Armorican peninsula. Here he lived as a hermit, eating only the fish he caught himself and drinking water from a spring he had caused to flow. Many came to visit him as his fame as a holy man spread, but he never accepted the presents they offered in the hope of special favour. He told them to take the gifts away, and when they refused, Gildas threw the objects into the sea as there were no poor people on the island who were in need.

Many more people wanted to see him than could make the journey over the sea, so eventually he reluctantly agreed to go to the mainland. Crowds gathered to see him and hear him speak, hoping to see miracles performed, and he decided to build a monastery. Gildas chose a few companions to escort him to Vannes, where he asked the lord of the area, Count Waroc, for a small piece of land. Waroc was much taken with the monk and pressed on him extensive holdings for his foundation.[1]

He still felt the need for times of solitude and returned to Houat when he could, as well as later building an oratory on the banks of the Blavet river with his disciple Bieuzy, where many came to hear him speak.

There is also an Île Saint-Gildas off the north coast of Côtes d'Armor, accessible at low tide at certain times, where the saint is said to have dwelt.[2] On his little island Gildas used to preserve fish by drying and salting it. He got

---

[1] This was built on the site of what is today called the Abbaye de St-Gildas-de-Rhuys

[2] Riders traditionally took their horses to eat bread that had touched the foot of the statue of Saint-Gildas at a little chapel there. Today there is a Pardon with horse blessing on the first Sunday in June, with the procession leaving from Buguélès.

supplies of salt either from the producers of Buguélès who carried it out on foot at low tide nice and dry, or those of Crec'h Morvan who came by a rotten old boat and often left damp salt or failed to produce any at all. The saint got fed up with this poor service and fired them. Without any means of earning their living these men began to act like bandits to survive and finally asked the bad fairies of Gwragez[1] to help them destroy the business of their rivals to get Gildas' salt order again. The fairies agreed in return for daily salt and lay in wait for the salt-carriers making their precarious way at night over the rocky trail which was full of chasms and old shafts. At any opportunity they lured the unlucky men to their downfall in a terrible fall.

Gildas was angry about the non-arrival of his supplies and warned the men of Buguélès that the Devil would punish them. Finally St-Nicolas advised them to send women instead. This they did, the women walking in single file each carrying a basket of salt. In the darkness one suddenly fell into a great hole. The others went on with their precious charge and arrived safely to the delight of the saint. The next day the women were amazed to see their companion, whom they thought lost, safe and sound. She was surprized at their concern and said she had not moved from her house the previous night. So they went back to the place of the accident and found women's garments on the rocks. They were those of the bad fairies of Gwragez – one of them had fallen in whilst trying to attract the salt-carriers. Now it was known who was behind all the mischief.

Gildas punished the fairies by turning them into little silver fish.[2] One of them went mad, snatched off his mitre and put it on her head, but he turned her, hat and all, into stone on the spot. As for the salt-makers of Crec'h Morvan, he drove them from the district and made them lepers.

---

[1] Women's island in Breton.

[2] Sand eels.

CHAPTER 2
THE FOUNDING SAINTS OF BRITTANY

Introduction

The Bretons have honoured their seven founding saints since the end of the Dark Ages, when monks in monasteries began to record the lives of holy men in documents that are an inextricable mixture of historical fact and legendary elements. These seven – not to be confused with the *Sept Saints* or Sleeping Saints[1] - are regarded as the great standard-bearers of formalised Christianity in the early church of Brittany.

Like the other Breton saints, the Founding Saints have a social and political significance in the settlement and development of early Brittany. Because of their important positions as bishops of early

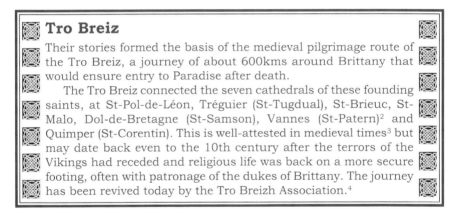

Tro Breiz

Their stories formed the basis of the medieval pilgrimage route of the Tro Breiz, a journey of about 600kms around Brittany that would ensure entry to Paradise after death.

The Tro Breiz connected the seven cathedrals of these founding saints, at St-Pol-de-Léon, Tréguier (St-Tugdual), St-Brieuc, St-Malo, Dol-de-Bretagne (St-Samson), Vannes (St-Patern)[2] and Quimper (St-Corentin). This is well-attested in medieval times[3] but may date back even to the 10th century after the terrors of the Vikings had receded and religious life was back on a more secure footing, often with patronage of the dukes of Brittany. The journey has been revived today by the Tro Breizh Association.[4]

---

[1] This special group of Seven are 3rd century martyrs from Ephesus, buried alive for refusing to renounce their faith. They are honoured in Brittany with a chapel at Vieux-Marché.

[2] St Patern's church is separate from the cathedral in Vannes today.

[3] An example of evidence for the Tro Breiz includes a statement in support of claims made to canonise Yves Helori in the 14th century. St-Yves, from Tréguier, was made an official Catholic saint in 1347 and became the patron saint of Brittany. One of the witnesses records that he was away carrying out this sacred journey at the time of Yves' death..

[4] See the website www.trobreiz.com for details and practical guides to the routes.

cathedrals, they were often involved in decision making with the secular leaders of their territories. So Saint-Corentin is said to have been a spiritual advisor of King Gradlon in Quimper, and Saint-Samson participated in the Council of Paris during the reign of Childebert, king of the Franks. Such worldly involvement often went against their individual inclinations towards quieter lives: St-Pol in particular was reluctant to obey the call of the public stage, preferring a peaceful, contemplative life on the Île de Batz.

Five of the seven saints concerned in the religious foundations of Brittany between AD450 and 650 probably came from Wales, the other two being native to the Armorican peninsula, although one of those may have been a first generation immigrant. All seven were associated with the first 'cathedrals' which were presumably very simple structures serving as monastery churches, but destroyed during the Viking incursions of the 9/10th centuries and rebuilt in stone on a grander scale. Some remain to this day patron of the later buildings, others have to share the honours with official Catholic saints.[1]

The notion of the Founding Saints is an important one in the perception of Breton identity, an issue still of significance in contemporary Brittany. In the 9th century Nominoë, leader of the nascent Breton state against the aggression of the Franks, tried to establish Dol-de-Bretagne as an archbishopric with responsibility for cathedrals in Brittany to replace the bishop of Tours in his role of Metropolitan. This attempt to Bretonise religious control was an on-going issue of debate until 1199 when the Pope made a definitive pronouncement in favour of Tours.

Apart from the efforts the Founding Saints made and their wondrous powers which elevated the early creation of Breton society, the connections with Wales and south-west England also represent an important cultural origin which separates Brittany firmly from the French. It is this difference and this uniqueness that lends fuel to the image of Celticism cultivated in various ways today, with varying degrees of historicity and credibility.[2]

---

[1] The cathedral at St-Malo is dedicated to St-Vincent and that at Vannes to St-Pierre.

[2] For notions of 'Celtic Christianity', see page 25.

St Brieuc (Cathedral of St Brieuc)

Various dates are given for Brieuc, ranging from 409-502 to 524-614. His noble birth, youthful prodigy and family connections discovered in Armorica are common themes in the lives of the Dark Age saints. The account below is largely from the version of Albert Le Grand, except that he claims St-Brieuc was born in Armorica and went to Wales as a young boy for his education. Details of his early life before coming to Brittany are included to show a typical pattern for the founding saints, with the common elements of hagiography.

The cathedral in St-Brieuc today is dedicated to St-Etienne rather than the founding saint.

Brieuc was born in the 5th or 6th century in Wales into a rich and noble pagan family. When his mother Eldruda was pregnant she had a visitation from an angel who told her she was carrying a child who would be dear to God and who would shine the light of Christianity through the land. It was therefore important that she and her husband turned from their pagan idols and worshipped the one true God.

When the baby was born he was called Brieuc in accordance with the angel's instructions. As a very young child he seemed to have the manners and assurance of a much older person, showing no interest in the games and pleasures of his peers, but only in study. His mother wanted to entrust the boy to the care of St-Germain[1] but her husband Cerpus was reluctant, not wanting his son to

---

[1] Probably Saint Germain, bishop of Auxerre in the 5th century, who was famous for combating the Pelagian heresy which claimed man was not automatically corrupted by original sin and could choose good or evil deeds for himself.

end up by becoming a monk.[1] Another visit from an angel, who lectured him on the folly of obstructing God's will, resulted in agreement to the project, and off Brieuc went.

When he reached St-Germain and fell at his feet in reverence, a white dove descended and rested on the boy's head, confirming the instinct St-Germain had had about the significance of this new arrival. Brieuc was indeed a prodigy of learning, mastering Latin in a day and absorbing all the religious texts with alacrity. He was also of a noticeably charitable inclination, constantly giving away whatever he had to the poor and needy.

At the tender age of twelve he began fasting, sometimes for three days at a time, and declared his desire to go into the desert and focus completely on God, but the abbot refused as he was too young. He remained in the monastery until the age of twenty-four when he was made a priest. It was said that at the ceremony a column of fire descended on his head.

Eventually Brieuc had yet another angelic prompting to cross the sea to the Armorican peninsula and evangelise the people there. He set off with a large group of monks. The Devil tried to stop the boat on the way but he was no match for Brieuc's strength of faith and prayers. They arrived via the river Jaudy to where Tréguier stands today, and were well-received by the inhabitants. A monastery was founded, but when Brieuc himself was called back to Wales because of a terrible plague, he left his nephew Tugdual in charge. On return he was so impressed with the arrangements and leadership of Tugdual that he himself decided to move on elsewhere with eighty-four companions.

They sailed into the Léguer estuary and landed where St-Brieuc stands today. In the forest they stopped by a spring to rest and were spotted by one of the local lord's men. He ran off to his master and spoke of a large group of

---

[1] This paternal opposition is a motif of many saints' Lives.

54

people in strange clothing who were surely spies and a threat to security. Count Riwal, lord of Domnonée, immediately gave orders for a party of soldiers to go and destroy the invaders. No sooner had he given this order than he was struck down by violent illness. Realising that this must be a punishment for his reaction to the incomers, he rescinded the order and had the monks brought before him. When they arrived, he recognised Brieuc as his cousin. He asked for pardon and Brieuc released his body from its torment.

Brieuc had a small oratory built at the spot where he had first halted by the spring.[1] He was also encouraged to start a monastery adjoining the manor of Riwal, on the Champ du Rouvre, which in turn led to the development of a town alongside. Later Brieuc was inspired by God to construct a cathedral and to take the role of bishop for himself.

Much later at the age of ninety, he had a revelation of his own impending death and said prayers with all the monks before dying as he spoke the name of Jesus Christ. Two monks from other lands had visions at the time of this event. Marcanus saw the soul of Brieuc as a white dove ascending to heaven with four angels. Simanus came to Brittany to witness that he had seen a ladder ascending to heaven for Brieuc. Simanus related how the Devil had tried to strangle him on his journey, but calling on the name of Brieuc had been enough to save him. He also recorded later that a young man whose skin was not supported by bones and nerves and who had spent all his money on doctors with no avail was cured at the tomb of Brieuc and went home in robust health.

News of such miracles led to the body being uncovered and relics taken. During the dangers of the Viking invasions of the 9th century, king Erispoë had these sent to Angers for safety. It was not until 1210 that the bishop

---

[1] Today this adjoins the Chapelle Notre-Dame de la Fontaine in St-Brieuc.

of Saint-Brieuc cathedral went to ask for them back. The night before he left Angers, Bishop Pierre had a vision of Brieuc thanking him for honouring his relics. Arriving at Saint-Brieuc the relics were carried in solemn procession by none other than the great lord of the region, Alain de Penthièvre himself.

Albert Le Grand's account has no room for the wolf story that gave rise to later iconography of St-Brieuc, a simple allegory reflecting the repentance of sinners, symbolised by the savage animals made docile in the face of faith.

In old age St-Brieuc is said to have been travelling in a cart, singing hymns together with a group of monks walking alongside, when suddenly they were surrounded by a pack of wolves. His companions fled, but Brieuc confronted the beasts fearlessly with the sign of the cross offered in benediction and they knelt before him humbly.

St-Brieuc Cathedral

Saint Samson (Cathedral of Dol-de-Bretagne)

The Life of Samson is claimed to have been one of the earliest, written down within a century of the saint's death. In Geoffrey of Monmouth's text, Samson was a contemporary of King Arthur. Later Lives certainly added to the picture, particularly under the influence of politics in 9th century Brittany, when the status of Dol-de-Bretagne as an archbishopric was of great political significance.[1] Because of his connections with Wales, Cornwall and possibly the north of England, his trips to Paris and his historically documented participation in political events, Samson is one of the major figures of Dark Age Brittany.

Samson was born in Wales to relatively old and previously barren parents, but his mother Anne had a vision that the child she bore would be dear to God. The boy showed a remarkable thirst for learning, begging to be sent to school at the age of five to study the scriptures. His mother supported this spiritual bent, but his father Amon (or Amonius) was opposed to it, as he wanted Samson to be able to take his place in the everyday world. But Amon soon received an angelic vision telling him that he was blocking his son's destiny. It was therefore decided that Samson should go to the monastery of Abbot Ildut at Llanwit Major in Wales.[2] The abbot greeted the child as one destined for special things in the service of God.

Samson was a contemporary of Pol and Gildas, with whom he formed lifelong friendships. A prodigy of learning, he was said to have assimilated the alphabet in a day, and Latin in a month. As soon as he was old enough, he was ordained, but Samson was of solitary inclinations. He indulged in excessive fasting and prayer, rarely lying down to sleep. He ate no meat or fish and barely enough

---

[1] See page 52.

[2] The Aber-Ildut on the west coast of Finistère is said to have been named for this illustrious monk by some of his followers on their arrival.

vegetables to stay alive. He also studiously avoided the sight of women. He asked the abbot for permission to go to an island monastery, and spent some time in retreat, before returning to more active service. When a great plague came on the land because of sins of the people, many fled but Samson stayed to tend the sick as best he could. Then he had an angelic visitation, telling him to go to Armorica, where God had work for him.

He finally arrived at the mouth of a river in the east of the peninsula where he met a man named Privatus grieving loudly. When asked the matter, Privatus replied that he was awaiting a holy man who would cure his wife of leprosy and his daughter of possession by evil spirits. Samson immediately offered his services and cured them both. Privatus was so grateful that he offered the saint land to settle and remain in the area,[1] so Samson built a new monastery at what is now Dol-de-Bretagne. An early miracle came when the lamps went out during a service of Matins and no fire could be found to rekindle them. Samson spoke a prayer and all the candles in the church burst into flame.

After establishing this major religious foundation, Samson was asked by a group of nobles to go to the court of Childebert at Paris to ask the king to support Judual against the tyrant Conomor.[2] He agreed, and on arrival soon demonstrated his power by performing an exorcism on a senior official, which impressed everyone. He spoke at length to Childebert about the crimes of Conomor and persuaded the king to send Judual back to Brittany with financial backing and a large troop of soldiers. But the queen was very fond of the young man and did not want him to go, so she persuaded a courtier to offer Samson a cup of poisoned wine. Samson knew his own danger and made the sign of the cross above the cup, which caused it

---

[1] This story is shown in a stained-glass window in Dol cathedral.

[2] For details, see page 101.

to break. The wine splashed the courtier's arm and immediately began to burn up his whole body. He would have died had Samson not healed him, and would then have been thrown into jail had not the saint interceded for him with the king.

But the queen was implacable and when Samson was intending to ride off to visit Judual in his residence a few miles away, she had him given a wild, vicious stallion from the king's stable. Samson however made the sign of the cross before mounting and the horse went off docilely. The queen made a final attempt on Samson's life by having a lion released into the garden where he was walking, but this time such was Samson's power that the animal fell dead at his feet. The queen herself died soon after of a mysterious seizure, which caused excessive bleeding from her nose. No-one intervened to save her.

Samson then returned to Brittany with Judual and the French soldiers Childebert had promised.[1] In addition, the king gave him the islands of Jersey and Guernsey as possessions for the monastery at Dol. Samson was present at the final battle between Judual and his step-father Conomor in the Monts d'Arrée[2], praying in the hills nearby and then congratulating the victor.

Many examples of exorcism and healing illuminated Samson's remaining years at Dol. He also made a trip to the Channel Islands, given to him by Childebert, because he heard the locals were still making sacrifices to the pagan god Janus on the first of January. He soon taught them the error of their ways and built a church to ensure future education in the ways of God.

Samson lived to a great age[3] and had enough awareness of his approaching death to gather all the monks together

---

[1] That was not the only time that Samson visited the French court, as his signature can be found on a document relating to the Acts of the Council of Paris in 557.

[2] See page 101.

[3] 112 or 120 according to Albert Le Grand.

and encourage them to continue in their work, appointing Magloire as his successor. When he died in the church during a service, heavenly music drowned the singing of the choir, and after his burial his tomb was illuminated by a bright shaft of light and gave off beautiful perfume. It soon became the source of many miracles of healing.

Albert Le Grand includes the story that Judual asked the Pope in 555 to recognise the bishop of Dol as Archbishop, with jurisdiction over the other Breton bishops, and that this was agreed.[1] He goes as far as to say that the ceremony at Dol was attended by the other founding saints.[2] Samson is usually shown in statues in archbishop's garb, for its serious political significance in the history of Brittany.

Dol Cathedral

---

[1] For this contentious issue, see page52.

[2] In that case, we should maybe add time-travel to the extraordinary powers of these saints!

St Tugdual[1] (Cathedral of Tréguier)

Tugdual is a rather confusing figure in legend, as many and varied accounts have grown from the Lives recorded in the 11th and 12th centuries. He also seems to have distinct traditions in Cornouaille and Trégor, much depending on whether he and St-Tudy are one and the same, as has been strongly argued. No less than three major *Vitae* were devoted to Tugdual but none survive for Tudy. He is also unusual for being seen in a family context in some versions of his legend. Then there is the rather strange political connection, when he sought the confirmation of the King of the Franks for his position, and is even said by some to have become Pope in Rome. This story can be used to explain the title Pabu (Father) associated with him in many place names today,[2] although this could simply be a term of respect for an ordinary priest.

Tugdual was born in Wales (or Devon) about 490. He was a pupil at the monastery of Llanwit Major and came over to Armorica with a large family group including his mother and followers, one of whom was Saint Briac. He had good connections: he may have been the cousin of Saint Brieuc, and was said to be the nephew of Riwal, first king of Domnonée (brother of his mother Pompaea) and cousin of Deroch, Riwal's successor.

He is said to have landed near Le Conquet, where he established a monastery at Trébabu, or in the south of Finistère, where he has a cult at Combrit[3] or indeed in the Aber Wrac'h. In fact his later travels were so extensive that he is associated with many places, but the main one is Tréguier, where he established his monastery[4] and later became the first bishop of the cathedral.

---

[1] His real name in original documents is Tudgual (meaning 'of value to the people'), but a medieval scribe transposed the 'dg' into 'gd', an error perpetuated in later works.

[2] Examples include Trébabu near Le Conquet and Saint-Pabu on the Aber Wrac'h.

[3] Île Tudy is part of that parish.

[4] If Saint Brieuc didn't, see page 54.

According to one story, Tugdual's family were threatened by Conomor, acting in typical aggressive fashion towards those who criticised his actions. At that time Conomor was still supported by the king of the Franks, Childebert,[1] which reinforced his authority. The monk fled to Angers and then, accompanied Saint Aubin, to Paris to see the king. Childebert confirmed Tugdual's episcopal status[2] and he was able to return to Tréguier.

Late in his life, an astonishing tale relates that Tugdual made a journey to Rome. The Pope had just died and another was about to be chosen when a white dove descended and settled on Tugdual's head, so this was taken as a sign from heaven and he was consecrated Pope Leo V. After two years he returned to Brittany when a white horse appeared and miraculously carried him though the skies to Tréguier.

The magnificent cathedral at Tréguier is dedicated to its founder Tugdual, and St Yves, patron saint of Brittany, an historical figure of the early 14th century. Statues of Tugdual often show him as Pope, wearing a special mitre, or with a dove on his shoulder.

Tréguier Cathedral

---

[1] Childebert ruled from 511-558.

[2] This looks like a politically motivated attempt in later centuries to imply the authority of the Franks over the Brittany.

St-Pol (St-Pol-de-Léon cathedral)

The very famous story concerning Pol and the dragon is one which encapsulates the early conflict between paganism and the new religion of the Breton saints.

Pol came from Wales, a disciple of St Ildut from the monastery of Llanwit Major. He was from a noble background, perhaps even with royal connections. He arrived in Brittany in 517, firstly on the island of Ouessant, where the main town is still called Lampaul. He later moved onto the mainland[1] and travelled towards the area north of Morlaix, where St-Pol-de-Leon now stands. Here he met the local lord Withur and they recognised a family connection making them cousins. St-Pol was given land on the Île de Batz where he built a monastery.

Before leaving Britain, St-Pol had asked King Mark of Cornwall for one of his seven special bronze bells, which made a remarkably resonant sound, to take to his new land. The king refused. But at Withur's court a huge fish was brought in and on being cut open, was discovered to contain in its stomach an identical bell,[2] a miracle giving early indication of the importance of St-Pol.

The most famous story about St-Pol tells how he drove out a marauding dragon – said to consume both men and animals - on the Île de Batz. Led to its lair, he demanded that the beast come out and made the sign of the cross. He was then able to use his bishop's stole as a lead to take the dragon to a rocky cove and order it to leap into the waves.[3]

Later pressure was put on a reluctant Pol to come back to the mainland, establish a church and become bishop of what is now the cathedral in St-Pol-de-Léon.

---

[1] Lampaul = the holy place of Pol. Current place names like Lampaul-Ploudalmezeau and Lampaul-Guimiliau reflect his progress eastwards.

[2] A bell purporting to be this one can be seen in the cathedral at St-Pol-de-Léon today.

[3] See page 73 for more detail.

He had already refused this role in Britain, describing it as a weighty burden, and saying he would rather be a sea-bird wandering forever above the waves. But Withur sent him off to the court of Childebert, king of the Franks, in Paris, apparently to confirm the arrangements for the Île de Batz monastery, but unknowingly carrying a message that Pol should be consecrated as a bishop. He could hardly refuse at the royal court and so he was raised to office.

Back on the spot, St-Pol had to clear the area for his new foundation. It was the site of a former fortresses, and inhabited by many wild animals, including a bear, but these were no match for the saint and left the area never to be seen again.

St-Pol was never happy with the public life of a bishop, and after some years in the role begged to be allowed to retire to the Île-de-Batz, where he passed the remainder of his days in prayer and contemplation.

Pol's iconography is easy to spot as he is splendidly displayed in the red robes of office, holding a bishop's staff and with a dragon curled beneath his feet.

St Corentin (Quimper cathedral)

St-Corentin's cult is strong in Quimper where the luminous Gothic cathedral is dedicated to him. He is said to have been born in Armorica (c460) of immigrant parents. He became a hermit on the slopes of Menez Hom, and was only reluctantly drawn into the political life of the growing settlement of Quimper by King Gradlon. As spiritual advisor to the king, Corentin sometimes has a supporting role in the legend of Ys.[1] The famous 17th century missionary Père Maunoir wrote a Life of St-Corentin.

orentin lived the secluded life of a hermit on the slopes of Menez Hom, where miracles provided him with the means to live. He had struck the rock with his staff to produce a spring of fresh water by his hut, and a single fish lived in the pool this had created. Everyday, he would catch the fish and cut off what he needed for sustenance before throwing it back into the water where its flesh was regenerated. When fellow-bishops Malo and Patern came for a visit the pool produced tasty eels, and wine instead of water!

One day a hunting party led by King Gradlon of Quimper arrived at the hut of Corentin. One of the men is said to have sneered at the idea of such a humble dwelling entertaining the king himself, but the hermit received his distinguished guest warmly and somehow managed to feed them all with his single fish. One of Gradlon's men secretly tried the same trick, but his action left the fish wounded and Corentin had to heal it.

The king was impressed by the miracle of the fish, and also by the hermit's humility despite such remarkable powers. He begged the holy man to come back to the new settlement of Quimper and found a great church there. After some resistance, Corentin agreed and the first 'cathedral' of Quimper was set in motion, although he

---

[1] See page 105.

continued to spend time when he could in isolated contemplation.

Corentin devoted much time to instructing young men in the ways of the Church and divided up the area of Quimper into parishes for them to administer. He travelled around encouraging a life lived in accordance with the will of God, setting an example to everyone in his own zeal and simple lifestyle. He finally died in his own church after receiving the divine sacrament, surrounded by his followers. Huge crowds turned out to pay respects to his body and many wonders of healing were witnessed among the lame, blind, deaf and dumb.

Long after his death St-Corentin was still performing miracles. A young woman who had prayed to him for help promised to make a donation if her prayers were heard. She kept her vow and came to the church with a quantity of fine wax for candles. Just as she was about to lay her gift on the altar, the Devil appeared and tempted her to change her mind and keep the precious commodity for herself. She succumbed and left with the wax, but as soon as she got home she found her hand was clenched shut and she could not release it. She prayed fervently to St-Corentin who appeared to her in great splendour and reminded her that promises to God must be kept. He told her to go to his tomb the next day. There she fell into a deep sleep and St-Corentin came to heal her, for on awakening, her hand was restored to normal.

Corentin's iconography is usually a fish or a model of the cathedral at Quimper.

St Patern (Vannes)

Patern's life[1] is well-documented in later sources - such as a mid-19th century work by William Rees on Welsh saints - although he was actually born in Armorica in other traditions. Curious tales like an encounter with King Arthur, and a visit to Jerusalem mingle with his role as first bishop of Vannes.

Patern's name appears in historical documents. The Acts of the Council of Vannes which took place between 465 and 470, under the auspices of the Metropolitan bishop of Tours, Perpetué, record the participation of five other bishops including Patern of Vannes, Athenius of Rennes and Nunechius of Nantes. The purpose may have been to consecrate Patern as first bishop of Vannes.

atern was born in Armorica of noble parents, but soon after his birth they separated because his father wanted to devote himself to God and left for Ireland. The young Patern vowed to follow his father's example in holiness. As an adult he sailed to Wales and founded a monastery there before going on to visit his father. Before returning to Brittany he is said to have travelled to Jerusalem and received gifts including a cross and priest's tunic with gold thread. Years later King Arthur on his travels in Brittany spotted this garment and demanded it, but Patern refused as it was only appropriate for a priest. Arthur came back intent on seizing the tunic by force but Patern prayed and the ground opened up before the king, who recognised his sin by this miracle and begged Patern's forgiveness.

Patern is also said to have been kept in Britain by king Caradauc for many years before being allowed to return to Armorica, by popular demand of the inhabitants. Once back he founded his monastery and became bishop of Vannes.

---

[1] He is not to be confused with St-Padarn of Wales (100 years later), or St Patern of Avranches (later still).

When Saint Samson went on a tour of Brittany to get tribute from other cathedrals in deference to the superior status of the cathedral at Dol,[1] a monk wanted to cause trouble for Patern and suggested that a message was sent to bring him at once because he needed a lesson in humility. Patern arrived obediently, half-dressed and with only one shoe on. The monk laughed and was immediately possessed by an evil spirit. Samson realised what had happened and apologised to Patern, who cured the mean-spirited monk.

But Patern was plagued by jealousy and quarrels and finally went off into the kingdom of the Franks where he died. Soon after, drought and famine hit the area of Vannes because of the way Patern had been treated. An attempt to raise the body for relics was unsuccessful. A noble in Vannes said he had previously refused land Patern had requested for a church and he now granted it. At that, the problems disappeared and the bones of Patern were lifted and brought back to his own special church in Vannes.[2]

So Patern does not have patronage of a cathedral, but of the church that was built over his shrine. This led to some medieval disputes about who should get the pilgrims' offerings – the cathedral or the church of the founding saint. An image of this latter building is often used in iconography for the saint. It stands just outside one of the gates of the former walled city of Vannes, in an area of exceptional medieval houses.

---

[1] See page 52.

[2] The cathedral there remains dedicated to St-Pierre, who today shares the patronage with St-Vincent Ferrier, the 15th century Spanish missionary, who died in the town and became an official Catholic saint.

St Malo[1] (St Malo)

St-Malo is said to have accompanied the Irish St-Brendan on his marvellous voyages of adventure, before arriving in Brittany. Details of his subsequent ministry at Aleth show once again that all did not always run smoothly for evangelists in Armorica.

St Malo was born in Wales and became a pupil of St-Brendan at the monastery of Llancarfan, which had been founded by Saint Cado. He later accompanied Brendan on his seven-year quest to find the Isles of the Blessed. Finally they stopped on what appeared to be a small, uninhabited island and celebrated mass. It was in fact the back of a whale, and the huge sea-creature led them to the island of Cézembre, just off the coast of Brittany.[2] Malo arrived on the island[3] where he was welcomed by the hermit Aaron who lived there. But Malo wanted to evangelise not to be isolated, so he moved onto the mainland nearby at Aleth. He preached there and soon performed miracles, resuscitating a body waiting to be buried and offering water from a marble cup which he then turned into a crystal glass of wine. These marvellous deeds brought him such renown that Malo was able to establish a monastery there which attracted many seeking the religious life.

But the Devil was jealous of the wealth and fame St-Malo had brought to his settlement and sought to undermine him. First, he influenced the local lord to threaten to destroy the monastery, but this man was immediately struck blind and fell on his knees to beg Malo's pardon. Afterwards he became a great supporter of the monk and petitioned Hoël, duke of Brittany, that Malo should be made bishop of Aleth, an event which took place soon after, with the Pope's blessing.

---

[1] Also called Maclou or Maclow.

[2] There are many other versions of the location of the whale incident.

[3] This is now the ville close or famous walled city of St Malo.

The Devil persisted, however, by instigating various people to spread lies about St-Malo and sow discord in the congregation. The saint finally decided to get away from all the intrigue, but he ex-communicated the perpetrators before he left to take refuge at Saintes. A famine and plague in Aleth was taken as a sign of divine punishment for his opponents, and the saint was called back to repeal the sentence he had passed. As soon as he set foot in the area, the pestilence died away and all was well again.

Later St-Malo retired to Saintonge in Charentes and died there in about AD620. His relics were brought back to Brittany, although they were dispersed again like so many others during the Viking invasions.

The cathedral of St Malo was transferred in 1144 by bishop Jean de Chatillon to what is now the walled city of St-Malo. Since the French Revolution it has been dedicated to St-Vincent of Saragoza, a 4th century Spanish martyr. St-Malo's iconic symbol is usually a whale.

Saint-Malo

CHAPTER 3
SAINTS & OTHER ANIMALS

It is not surprising that animals figure strongly in the legends of Breton saints, with stories stemming from a time when the connection between man and the natural world was much more integrated than today. These men were largely settlers, requiring the help of beasts of burden to clear and plough land or carry building materials.

The nature of Breton society has always been traditionally rural, and in the Dark Ages prosperity or even basic survival of a family often depended on the health and safety of livestock.[1] With a lack of scientific and medical knowledge, any means of protecting animals from harm took on a real importance, so the patronage of particular saints was thought to be of the greatest value. Prayers could be directed to saints for the healing of sick animals or their safety and protection.

A chant from the Pardon of St Hervé at Langoëlan includes the verse:

> *"O blessed Saint Hervé*
> *Protect us and our horses*
> *From evil and sickness."*

These associations between holy men and beasts remain celebrated to the current day in many Pardons in western Brittany (and a few in the east), which preserve age-old popular traditions. These may include rituals like horse blessing. Physical offerings such as tufts of hair from cows' tails to St-Herbot or pigs' ears to St-Anthony were once common. These ceremonies were a way of acknowledging the value of work done by animals.

Sometimes the reasons for links between individual saint and animal are obscure, as in the case of Saint Nicodeme and horses or pigs. Sometimes they may arise from particular legends in the saint's life, as in the case of St Hervé and the wolf, or even reflect some older

---

[1] The Celtic tribes may have assessed value in livestock rather than land which tended to have communal ownership overseen by the leader

connections with pre-Christian traditions, as seems possible with St-Cornely. Some great events like the horse Pardon of Ste-Anne-La-Palud may have no obvious connection at all between patron and pageant.

In contrast with domesticated beasts, wild ones are also of great significance in the legends. Savage creatures like dragons and wolves usually have a symbolic interpretation. The animal world is used as a metaphor for paganism and the powers of nature. The control of Christian monks over untamed and frighteningly vicious creatures is symbolic of their superior powers over earlier gods and spirits.

The story of Saint-Hervé and the wolf is a clear message of the triumph of the true God over the destructive wild predator, of order over chaos and unpredictability.

> St-Hervé was blind from birth and was accompanied each day by a young guide named Guiharan. This boy one day called frantically to the saint for help when a donkey pulling the cart carrying stone for a building project was attacked and killed by a wolf. St-Hervé sternly commanded the wild animal to take the donkey's place. Not only did the wolf obey at once, but it remained forever in Hervé's service.[1]

The same tale is told of St-Thégonnec, who is well known for the glorious Parish Close in the village named after him.[2]

> St-Thégonnec was a follower of St-Pol, and came to the Armorican peninsula in the 6th century. He wanted to found his own church and went to fetch building stone from Plounéour-Ménez on a cart drawn by a stag. On the way back a wolf killed the stag and Thégonnec then ordered the wolf to take its place. It obeyed him docilely.[3] He acquired a large following through this miracle and was able to start the settlement that bears his name to this day.

---

[1] For St-Hervé, see page 42.

[2] His name has many variant forms from Coneg to Toqounoc.

[3] Iconography shows St-Thégonnec with his cart in reference to this legend.

Another tradition has him born here, founding a hermitage at Plogonnec and becoming a follower of St-Guénolé at Landévennec. He did not always have such power over animals – according to Albert Le Grand, he was the monk bitten by a snake and then cured by St-Guénolé.

The wolf motif is in fact a common feature of saints' Lives, although it's worth remembering that real wolves lived in Brittany until the beginning of the 20th century and many tales of human encounters with these animals are still told.[1] Representations of saints and wolves are also allegorical, with the beasts symbolic of sinners, their taming the equivalent of seeing the light and submitting to the power of Christ. St-Brieuc is often portrayed with a wolf symbol from a story that he was attacked by a pack of wolves which then knelt at his feet when he made the sign of the cross.

The dragon[2] embodies a ferocious destructive strength which can yet be overcome by the superlative power of Christian faith. The biblical association with the Garden of Eden presents the snake as temptor, linked with evil, the symbol of sin.[3] When the saints destroy dragons or serpents, it is a clear triumph of Good over Evil, the victory of Christianity over paganism, one true god over polytheism.

Nowhere is bestial significance as an expression of paganism more implicit than in the tale of St-Pol and the dragon, a symbolic story of ridding the land of pagan practices.

One of the founding saints of Brittany, St-Pol arrived in the territory of Léon, where he was given land on the Île de Batz by Count Withur. This lord confided in St-Pol that the inhabitants were suffering the ravages of a terrible serpent, and begged him for help in ridding the island of its tormentor. A local man offered to escort the saint to the dragon's lair.

Once there, Pol demanded that the dragon show himself and the beast came out hissing and flashing fire. Without

---

[1] The Musée du loup or Wolf Museum in Cloître-St-Thégonnec preserves their story in graphic forms. www.museeduloup.fr.

[2] In legends there is often a confusion between dragon and serpent or snake.

[3] In world mythology, also of sexuality.

fear the saint made the sign of the cross to render the dragon harmless, and then wound his own episcopal stole[1] around its neck like a dog's lead. He thus led the dragon, unresisting, to the rocky western edge of the island at a spot called Toul ar Sarpant (Dragon's Hole) to this day. Here he ordered it to leap into the sea, where it vanished for good.

The church was naturally fond of stories demonstrating the superiority of the powers of their representatives, which encouraged the locals to offer allegiance to the Christian God. The same motif appears again later in St-Pol's story. When he moved back to the mainland to found his monastery on an old fortress site where St-Pol-de-Léon stands today, it was occupied by many wild animals, including bears and buffalo. St-Pol commanded them to leave and they were never seen again. There was no place for unharnessed brutality in the new order of Christianity.

Of course it is not necessary to believe that dragons actually existed at that time, but perhaps their appearance in legend is directly connected with the form of expression of pagan gods. We know that animalistic representation existed: the Celtic god Cernunnos is said to have worn the antlers of a stag, and serpents are carved on the menhir at the burial site of Le Manio (Carnac) as well as on the pillars of the crypt in Lanmeur church, which probably dates back to not much later than the age of the saints in Brittany. Claims have been made for a serpent cult in pre-Christian times.

Other animals have specific Christian associations, and are therefore of particular significance in the lives of some saints. The fish was a standard symbol for Christianity because the Greek word for fish ICHTHUS also formed the initials of Jesus Christ, son of God.[2] It had a metaphorical importance too, with Jesus and the disciples being 'fishers of men'. Saint Corentin's miraculously regenerating fish is also a reminder of baptism, where new life comes from contact with

---

[1] In the island's church of Notre-Dame de Bon-Secours, a piece of ancient decorated material in the form of a stole is displayed in a glass case. Dated to the 8-9th century, it is too late to be St-Pol's, but it is possible that more ancient relics were once wrapped in it.

[2] *Iesus Christos Theou Uios Soter.*

holy water. His feeding of King Gradlon's party from a single fish recalls the Feeding of the Five Thousand in the New Testament.

Stags figure in the legends of various saints, sometimes offering their labour[1] and often providing the means of establishing a territory. This theme of setting the boundaries of land in the course of a single night is a universal one, being found in the legends of many countries. 'Foundation legends' where land-holding is established are important, giving a sort of special sanction to property ownership. Many valuable rights and privileges could have been attached to such land held by religious groups. Practices such as the Troménie[2] may thus have once held more than religious significance. Such an event in honour of St-Thélo has a history at Landeleau,[3] but several saints have almost the same story

St Thelo[4] came from Wales and may already have been a bishop in his own land. He is said to have made a journey to Jerusalem before deciding to leave Britain for Armorica. On arrival, he first visited his former companion Samson at Dol-de-Bretagne. The search for his own settlement led him to Lan ar Loch where he built a dolmen-like house from long stones.[5] But he could not settle. The noise from the toads in the marsh was continuous and unbearable, as they told him repeatedly to move on.

The next place he found was in a wood by a spring and here he built a house of wood, and later a church.[6] Wanting to form a parish, he asked the local lord of the Château Gall for land and was granted as much as he could cover in a night. The condition was that he must stop when the cock crowed.

---

[1] See below in the story of St-Lunaire.

[2] A ritual journey around monastic land.

[3] And at Locronan in honour of St-Ronan, see page xx.

[4] Also called Télo and Theleau.

[5] The Dolmen of St-Thélo, actually a Neolithic burial place can be seen today. The five small impressions in the stone are said to be the imprint of the saint's fingers, where they rested so often in prayer.

[6] At what is now Landeleau, a name meaning the holy place of St-Thélo.

He went back to his hut and told his sister, who had travelled with him, and although she pretended to be pleased, in fact she fumed with jealousy that Thélo should have this boon of land granted so easily.

As he pondered his task in the doorway of his house, Thélo began to whistle and immediately a large white stag appeared and knelt before him. When night fell Thélo climbed on the stag's back and they began to gallop across the land. But when they passed the château, they were heard and the hounds were let loose to the chase. Thélo had to hide in a tree[1] and the stag plunged into the forest for cover.

They continued their endeavour later, but it was brought to an untimely end by the actions of Thélo's sister, who stuffed a live cock up a chimney and lit a fire of green wood to smoke it into loud cries of alarm. So the cock's crow was heard all over the area and her brother had to halt as promised.

A white granite sarcophagus outside the church at Landeleau is often called the 'Bed of St-Thélo'. It was revered as such in medieval times. St-Yves is known to have spent the night in it in 1303 when he visited the village.

There is no 'official' Life of St-Edern. A *gwerz* recorded by Anatole le Bras gives an outline, and at the end of the 19th century, Dom François Plaine wrote an article on Saint Edern in the Bulletin of the Archaeological society of Finistère. He is associated primarily with Lannédern where he is shown on the calvary riding a stag, and where there is a painted panel of his legend and his tomb. Other places bearing his name include Edern and Plouédern.

Saint Edern came to Brittany from Ireland in the 9th century as a monk seeking to settle in a rural hermitage. He arrived near Douarnenez and lived in the Forêt de Quistinit, three leagues from Quimper.[2] The local

---

[1] The ancient oak 'of St-Thélo' where he hid can still be seen today at Keravel.

[2] This location fits Edern better than Lannédern, which is further away.

lord, however, became angry with the wanderings of the saint's little cow on his land and set the dogs on it. It was left for dead, but the saint came and restored the cow to life. What the lord had failed to notice was that wherever the cow passed, the grain grew stronger.

Edern moved on to build another hermitage further inland. One day he heard a commotion and came to the door of his hut. A stag being chased by hounds raced up and sought sanctuary with St Edern, who protected it when the hunters arrived. The stag remained his companion for life, and is the symbol evoked in imagery of the saint.

St-Edern

One day the Duke of Brittany and his entourage were passing through the forest. One man was sent to ask the way of the saint, but Edern, in prayer, was slow to respond and the man struck him across the face. Edern said not a word, but turned his other cheek, as the bible decrees. God, however, showed his displeasure by striking the entire entourage of the Duke blind, and thus unable to continue their journey until the saint intervened. They all recovered their sight and the Duke honoured the saint as he deserved.

Another version echoes the story of St Thélo. Saint Edern, apparently now based where Lannédern stands, rode a stag through the night, having until cock-crow to establish the boundaries of the area for his settlement. His sister Jenovefa had settled at Loqueffret and did not want to lose territory to her brother, so she dunked a cock in a trough of water to make it crow and bring Edern's ride to a premature end. In the resulting quarrel, they cursed each other's establishments, so Edern's church would never have a high bell-tower, and the bells of Jenovefa's church would never ring true.

The curious trio of **St-Envel, St-Envel and Ste-Yuna,** two brothers of the same name and their sister, are said to have come to Armorica in the 6th century.[1] They settled near Belle-Isle-en-Terre, each with a separate chapel, the elder Envel at LocEnvel, his brother at the Chapel ar Choat at Belle-Isle, and Juna in the commune of Plounévez-Moëdec. Envel devoted himself to agriculture and both he and Juna are invoked in the context of livestock. Animals were brought to drink at the *fontaine* for protection against wolves and disease. Envel was said to have control over the wildest of beasts, including a wolf who menaced his working stag or horse, according to different versions. The wolf was obliged to pull the harrow in its victim's stead afterwards. Another story, shown in a beautiful stained-glass window in the superb church at Loc-Envel, tells of a thief stealing St-Envel's horse, forcing him to recruit stags to do its work. An even more enviable power of the saint was that of scaring crows and ravens from the fields to protect the newly sown crops.

Domestic animals held an important place in family life, primarily practical, but not without its emotional bonds. Their worth was a monetary one, but accommodation was often closely shared by humans and their four-legged companions, including even horses and cows.[2] The warmth provided by beasts in the house was also not an insignificant factor.

Horses have strong traditional importance in Brittany, which is famous for its own breed of sturdy working animals.[3] Horse blessings are held in many places even today and various saints, most notably Saint Eloi (Alar) are associated with their protection. The story of Fracan's horserace[4] which provided an opportunity for a miracle by

---

[1] The twin motif might explain the duality in the landscape here: at LocEnvel there is a Wood of the Night and the Wood of the Day. There is also the parallel of summer and winter festivals, with the holy days of the two brothers relating to the solstices, as if they may have echoes of earlier pagan activities. At the June ceremony, the tantad (literally 'father fire') or ceremonial bonfire is lit as part of the ritual.

[2] The Maison Cornec in St-Rivoal, a well-preserved farmhouse from 1702, shows the living room divided by slate barriers between the family hearth and the hay-racks and troughs of the animals in close proximity.

[3] Landivisiau and Callac are two places still linked strongly with horses.

[4] See page 37.

Saint-Guénolé, suggests an appreciation of the sporting possibilities of horses at a very early period, and certainly many horse-fairs were held throughout medieval times.

The fair at Méné Bré, originally established by the monks from Bégard abbey, is famous and a link between horses and St Hervé, whose chapel sits on the top of the hill. A votive plaque in the church at St-Eloi in Finistère, written in Breton and dated 1920, gives thanks to Sant Alar (St-Eloi) and the Virgin Mary for the safe return of a lost horse.

Eloi is said to have been a blacksmith. Luzel records a version of the legend he was told at Landerneau.

The sign outside Eloi's premises read: "Ironmonger and blacksmith, master among masters, master of all." One day a stranger arrived asking for work. Eloi asked him to demonstrate his skills in shoeing a horse. The stranger calmly cut off the foot of the horse. "What are you doing?" yelled Eloi in horror, but the stranger quietly continued his work. He skilfully fixed a new shoe on and then re-attached the foot to the horse's leg, working with extraordinary speed and precision. Eloi was dumbfounded.

Before he could react to this extraordinary event, a peasant came puffing up asking for the blacksmith to visit his sick horse urgently. Eloi gestured to the stranger and assured the peasant that his new assistant was more than qualified to take his place. When the two men had left, Eloi was keen to try out the amazing new method he had witnessed. A regular customer arrived opportunely at that moment, wanting his horse shoed and the blacksmith set to work. First he cut off the foot of the horse, ignoring the protests of the horse's owner. Then he fixed the shoe with no problem. The trouble came when he tried to join the severed foot back onto the leg. He couldn't do it, and worse still, by now the horse was faint with loss of blood. The beast tumbled over onto a bed of straw in the smithy, and lay as if dead. Fortunately the stranger returned at that moment, Eloi told him in despair what had happened. "I don't know where I went wrong," he said. "You must help me." The man immediately gave his attention to the horse and revived it. He was then able to replace the severed foot so that it was as good as new.

Having finished his task, the stranger simply walked off, leaving Eloi open-mouthed in amazement. But when he saw a halo appear above the retreating head, he realised to his shame that Christ himself had come to teach him humility. His new sign read: "Eloi, blacksmith".

In 1780 Jean-Baptiste Ogée, an engineer and map-maker who wrote extensively about Brittany, described an annual festival of St-Eloi:

"People from ten parishes round about bring their horses along. After prayers, they fill a bowl of water from the sacred spring and wash the ears and womb of their mares and the testicles of the stallions, convinced it will be efficacious. So engrained is this belief in the souls of these good people that nothing in the world could change their minds."

In the iconography of statues and stained-glass windows, Eloi is often represented, dressed either as a bishop or

St-Eloi - St-Alar
(Brasparts, Finistère)

a blacksmith, with a suitable tool in one hand, a horseshoe in the other, whilst the severed foot is on an anvil and the three-footed horse stands beside him, held by an attendant. A window from 1550 in the chapel of Notre-Dame du Crann at Spezet shows the scene in the smithy with the severed foot.

The cult of St-Eloi appears in other parts of France such as Limousin where he was born. Eloi or Eligius (the chosen one) was a goldsmith originally and later by extension a general saint of metalwork. Dagobert, king of the Franks, used him to negotiate an accord with Judicaël, duke of the 'Bretons' in 636. In Brittany, however, there is a not uncommon confusion of identities. Alar is his Breton form, but no life story of Alar is known, except that he was an evangeliser/hermit, and he seems from medieval times to have been replaced in name by St-Eloi.

Donkeys were also important beasts of burden, but their determined and sometimes troublesome nature is the subject of this tale from the life of St-Suliac.[1]

Saint Suliac was a Welsh monk, son of a king, who had chosen the religious life over his father's preference of soldiering. He came to Armorica in the 6th century and arrived on the shores of the Rance, near Dinan. The local lord welcomed Suliac and gave him the peninsula called Montgarrot to settle. Here he founded a monastery and set about cultivating the land, including a plot of vines. All went well for a time, but as soon as the plants were well-established they attracted the unwanted attentions of a group of donkeys. These animals were actually reared in the village of Rigourden, across the river, but at that time the estuary was much narrower and shallow, so that it was easy for the hungry animals to wade across at low tide.

Suliac tried everything to keep the donkeys out and protect his crops, but they pushed through every type of

---

[1] The village of Saint-Suliac on the Rance near Dinan is named after the saint. He also has echoes in many place-names elsewhere. The Parish Close at Sizun in Finistère is dedicated to St-Suliau, and there is a chapel of St-Sulian near Saint-Nic. The hamlet of Kerzulien in the commune of Cleder was recorded as Kersulian in 1419, and the name Plussulien comes from Plou-Sulian.

fence and barrier. Finally, he resorted to more extreme measures, rooting them to the spot (as evidence of their crimes) and turning all their heads backwards. When the owners of the animals finally appeared in search of the missing beasts, they were horrified to see the donkeys, still as statues with twisted heads, and feared that they were lost for good.

But Suliac agreed to release them on condition that the donkeys never bothered the monastery again. Their owners agreed eagerly, but just in case, Suliac took the precaution of widening the river between his land and the village so that crossing on foot was no longer a possibility...

A story from the Life of St-Malo tells how a wolf killed a donkey and was made by the saint to work in its place, proving to be much more willing and providing a much better quality of service than the donkey!

Sheep and pigs do not figure largely in legends, but they have their patrons among the saints. Saint-John traditionally is portrayed with a lamb (from the biblical reference Ecce Agnus Dei – Behold the Lamb of the Lord) and St-Jugon, a shepherd, was honoured in La Gacilly and invoked against the disease of sheep pox (ovinia).

Jugon was a young shepherd, who lived with his widowed mother in the valley of the Oust in eastern Brittany, some time in the 11th century. He was devout and keen to study the scriptures, helped and encouraged by the rector of the church at St-Martin-sur-Oust. He had to leave his flock of sheep together with one cow some distance away to graze when he went daily to the presbytery. Each day he drew a large circle around them with a holly branch and no animal strayed outside this virtual boundary and were safe from all predators there.

But one day he forgot this ritual and a wolf came and attacked the cow. Jugon's mother saw what was happening and gave a loud shout, so loud that Jugon miraculously heard it at a great distance and came running. He comforted his mother and promised that God would restore the cow to them. He prayed and touched the carcass of the beast with his holly branch. The cow immediately revived and went back to grazing with the sheep.

So Jugon became the patron of these animals and the waters of his *fontaine* were said to be a way of preventing and curing the disease of sheep pox. He had a strange death at the tender age of 16 – accidentally struck by his uncle's spade, and this implement is often his symbol.[1] Despite burial his body kept being found uncovered, so it was put on a cart drawn by oxen to find its desired resting place, which turned out to be near La Gacilly at what is now Forêt de St-Jugon.

Saint Antony, one of the Desert Fathers (not the Saint Anthony of Lost Things), is a patron of pigs for no known compelling reason. Possibly the religious order of the Antonines had permission for their pigs to run free, wearing collars with bells. Statues of Saint Antony in Brittany are sometimes accompanied by such an animal, such as those at St-Fiacre (Le Faouët) and the magnificent church at Kernascleden.

St Samson turned the pigs of a woman who was causing trouble in the monastery into billy-goats until she desisted.[2] Saint Gildas is also a patron of pigs, with hams and piglets being offered right up to the 20th century at his shrines in Gueltas and Guegon in Morbihan. Saint Nicodeme had his pig association in the area around Vannes, with offerings of piglets which were sold after the religious ceremonies at Guenin. The animals were brought along in sacks and their squeaking punctuated the church service.

Oxen have their place in many legends, perhaps most famously in providing a strange hiding place for St-Cornely.

---

[1] In the same way as the twelve Apostles in church porches in Brittany carry the thing used to kill them in their martyrdom.

[2] See page 247.

Legend has it that St-Cornely was a Pope in Rome in the 3rd century and either persecuted by the emperor, or forced to flee from Italy by the barbarian invasions. He travelled across Europe in a cart drawn by two oxen, which carried all his possessions.

When he got to Morbihan in southern Brittany, he was closely pursued by soldiers, and had to stop when he reached the shores of the Gulf. But miraculously he was able to hide in the ear of one of the oxen and then turned his pursuers into stone with a curse.[1] Another version says he fled on foot and hid in the ear of a local ox, later rewarding these animals with semi-cult status for saving him.

Some believe that Cornely may be linked with the traditions of the Celtic horned god Cernunnos, or an even earlier cult based on horned beasts from the late Neolithic period, as suggested by archaeological finds in the area around Carnac, such as tomb engravings.

This saint has become the traditional patron of horned beasts. His statue on the exterior of the church in Carnac is flanked by two pictures of cows grazing among the famous megaliths. At the Pardon in Carnac on the second Sunday in September, animals of all sorts are blessed.

A much more recent story is a reminder of the connection between cattle and their fond patron St-Herbot.

St-Herbot[2] was one of the immigrants from Britain who came to Armorica at an early age, St Herbot first settled in Berrien, but was driven away by the women, jealous of the time their husbands spent listening to his teachings.[3] He then sought out a quieter spot to settle and moved on to the bank of the river Elez in the south of the Monts d'Arrée. Here he asked at a nearby manor-house for the

---

[1] This legend is often given as the origin of the lines of standing-stones at Carnac.

[2] Also called Herbaut or Herbault.

[3] A parallel with the story of St Ronan.

loan of oxen to carry building-stone, but was refused as he was a stranger. Herbot responded with a curse that only oxen unfit for labour should be bred in future on the manor farm.

He was luckier at Rusquec where the lord of the manor gave him leave to choose any two beasts from the herd to transport materials for the hermitage he wanted to establish. The white oxen worked hard for the saint and yet were transformed into magnificently strong and healthy beasts by their labour. They stayed with him afterwards and never strayed far from the holy man, even remaining near the hermitage after his death.

St-Herbot certainly preferred the company of animals who honoured and protected him to that of men. He was said to understand their language and to be able to converse with them, and he performed many acts of healing for sick animals. He so loved cows and oxen that he asked to become their patron when he entered heaven, according to the popular tradition.

St Herbot

So recorded Anatole le Braz, who heard the stories of this saint from a sacristan at the church of St-Herbot, where the saint's tomb can be found. It is thought to predate the current building. Two stone tables on entry to the chancel are still used to place offerings of cows' tail hairs.

So Herbot became the patron saint of bovines and also by association the focus of prayers for good butter and generous milk yields. In the late 18th century Jacques Cambry recorded a saying in the area around Lesneven '*si le beurre se forme lentement on a recours à Saint Herbot'* (if the butter is slow to form, call on Saint Herbot). Part of the canticle of St-Herbot contains a plea for blessing on the milk and a good head of cream.

An eye-witness told Anatole le Braz that at a time when the saint was neglected and no pardon held, animals came of their own accord to pay homage to their patron at the village of St-Herbot.

> "I saw a heifer and a bull with my own eyes arriving from the Loqueffret direction, unaccompanied. The bull stopped at the entrance to the cemetery, facing the porch. He stayed there stock-still, his muzzle directed at the saint's tomb whilst the heifer entered the enclosure and went three times round the church. When they had finished their devotions, they bellowed three times and went off in a leisurely fashion in the direction of the mountain."[1]

In iconography, St-Herbot is usually shown with a bovine or sometimes a pat of butter. A famous *Fête du Beurre* (butter festival) is held at St-Herbot (commune of Plonévez-du-Faou, Finistère) on the 4th Sunday in September each year.

And finally, a little bird makes its appearance in the legend of St-Lunaire.

According to tradition, St-Lunaire prayed to God to provide sustenance for him and his companions as they wanted to form a settlement. At that moment a little bird appeared carrying a stem of wheat in its beak. St-Lunaire rejoiced and urged his companions to follow the bird, whilst calling on the bird to lead them to the source of the grain. Sure enough, plunging deep into the forest they finally found themselves in a clearing where there was a little patch of wheat growing. At first they were daunted by the task as they began clearing such an overgrown site, but then suddenly twelve large stags appeared and showed themselves ready to be used as labourers, bowing their heads readily to receive the yoke of the plough.

---

[1] Account by Hervé Ricou.

Overall animals are seen in an unromantic light in many legends. They are the servants of men or in need of mastery by human powers. A rare story of disinterested concern for animal welfare comes from the Life of Saint Malo, who is said to have taken to task a pig-keeper who stoned an 'innocent' sow to death. He was full of pity for the pig and brought it back to life by placing the tip of his pastoral staff in its ear. But it has to be said that some saints, like St-Herbot, who clearly preferred an undemanding life, found the company of animals considerably more congenial than that of humans.

CHAPTER 4
WHERE LEGEND MEETS HISTORY

The turbulent times following the withdrawal of the Romans from north-west Europe have left little direct or contemporary evidence of events in Brittany. Written sources are rare and the archaeological record affords only localised glimpses of armed struggles, although the buried coin hoards of this time show the level of uncertainty and insecurity in the Armorican peninsula. Individual leaders sought control over their own territories and then eyed their neighbours' land acquisitively.

Personalities and incidents enshrined in legends have passed down through the centuries, representing the political struggles of a rapidly evolving society. Thirst for power, the acquisition of wealth and resources by marriage connections, territorial expansionist policies and religious changes can all be discerned within the preserved tales, and surely reflect the historical reality.

Some characters in the most traditional stories can be corroborated by historical evidence, but this does not vouch for the verity of every tale told about them. Conomor is a fine example of this important point. It is characteristic of the times that wonders, magical transformations and miracles stand alongside the grim violence and fierce rivalry of everyday life.

At this time there was no such entity as Brittany. What we see from historical sources and archaeology are the beginnings of political development in the Armorican peninsula. Three main areas were established: Domnonée (north), Cornouaille (south-west) and Bro-Weroc (around Vannes). Léon (Finistère north of the Monts d'Arrée) and Poher (around Carhaix) were smaller spheres of influence. We also see legends reflecting the historical reality of close connections (and parallel stories) between south-west Britain/Wales and the Armorican peninsula.

Nothing was set in stone at this period and the legends reflect the fluctuation of jostling for power, territorial disputes, expansionism, the exploitation of minerals and the inter-marriage of 'royal' families.

The leaders are commonly called kings or counts but their power was rarely undisputed. Such legends became extremely important later in medieval Brittany when both dukes and their rival nobles claimed descent (and therefore superiority over others) from early mythical kings.

Later still it became important for notions of Breton identity to establish a lineage, an 'historical' origin separate and more ancient than that of the Franks. The Trojan descendant Brutus[1] fitted the bill, and this tradition was later augmented by the story of Conan Meriadec. But from the 7th century the Franks too were claiming Trojan origins, indicating the importance and the competitive nature of trying to establish a collective symbolic memory of political worth. Religion was also added to the mix. According to Alain Bouchart in his *Grandes croniques de Bretaigne*, published in 1514, and written with the patronage of Duchesse Anne, Conan Meriadec, first king of Brittany was a Christian king, a hundred years before Clovis (king of the Franks) was baptised.

Conan Meriadec – a foundation legend

This story is an important one for Brittany's past in that it indicates how easily legend can be manipulated into the guise of history. Most historians doubt the very existence of Conan Meriadec, who appears suddenly in the 12th century *History of the Kings of Britain* by Geoffrey of Monmouth.[2]

He is described in legend as the first king of Brittany in the late 4th century, a time long before any idea of the state Brittany existed. But this figure had an important purpose to serve because he indicated a lineage of power in the Armorican peninsula which predated the Franks, and therefore could be used to undermine later French claims on Brittany.

---

[1] He was also Roman through his mother.

[2] Geoffrey himself drew on earlier sources such as the Historia Brittonum, a 9th century text possibly by Nennius but probably of mixed authorship. This is a compilation of information, without distinction of legends and history, from various earlier sources, which no longer exist. He also claimed to have been given a 'very ancient book' probably in Welsh, giving a full history of Great Britain, but there is no trace of such a work.

Geoffrey's political purposes in writing were to restore a sense of resoundingly glorious history to Britain and to establish its identity, after Saxon and Norman conquests – even though this requires a degree of revisionism. Plantagenet, Tudor and even Stewart monarchs would later try to use Geoffrey's work to support their own dynastic claims to power.

And so was the legend of Conan Meriadec used later in Brittany, as a form of legitimisation of political ambition through 'proof' of ancient origins. Geoffrey's claims were eagerly taken up later by Breton noble families keen to trace their lineage back to something more ancient and important than that of the ruling dukes of Brittany of the time (the Montforts), again so as to lay a greater claim to legitimacy of rule. The Rohan family certainly played the Conan Meriadec card for all they were worth, claiming direct descent from Conan's supposed son Ruhan. Les Rieux, another great noble family, also promoted their own similarly distinguished origins.

Breton historians from Arthur de la Borderie in the 19th century to the present day have rejected the Conan Meriadec legend as an invention by Geoffrey. It was not possible that Conan was an independent ruler of a fixed territory at that period, although the Maximus story may certainly contain a true essence: that Rome urged Britons from Great Britain to help defend the borders of Gaul from Saxon incursions, and that these soldiers subsequently settled in the Armorican peninsula.

A summary of Geoffrey of Monmouth's account from *The History of the kings of Britain*:

**t the time of disintegrating Roman occupation of Britain, Octavius had made himself king of a wide area. When he became old and wanted to secure the succession, he consulted his advisors. The only child he had was a daughter, and many suggested that he married her to some powerful Roman noble. Others, however, felt that the king's nephew, Conan Meriadec (Conanus Meridiadocus), would make a good successor.**

Finally Carodocus, the duke of Cornwall, suggested that a Roman senator, Maximus (Maximianus) who had a Roman mother and British father, should be invited to Britain and offered the hand of Octavius' daughter. This proposal angered Conan, who made it clear he would do anything to secure the throne.

But Caradocus sent his son to Rome to contact Maximus, who was very ambitious and in dispute with the two current emperors, believing he was entitled to a third share of the Empire. It was easy for Caradocus' son to play on this, and he urged Maximus to come to Britain, make himself king and then use the extensive wealth of the country to back a campaign against the emperors and take over himself.

Maximus agreed to the plan and marched through France seizing treasure and attracting soldiers along the way. When they landed at Southampton, Octavius was worried about an armed take-over of his kingdom and urged his nephew Conan to go with troops and prevent this. Their arrival surprised Maximus, who had fewer soldiers, and did not want to risk losing a battle. He sent envoys to the British camp, saying he came in peace with messages from the emperors.

At that moment Caradocus arrived with other leaders and they persuaded Conan not to fight. Maximus was then escorted to Octavius in London. The old king heeded his advisors and agreed to marry his daughter to the Roman noble. But Conan was furious and went off to raise an army to oppose Maximus. Various indecisive battles were indeed fought, but in the end they made peace on the advice of their counsellors.

Maximus spent five years in Britain building up his power base and wealth, always with his sights set on returning to Italy and seizing imperial power for himself. Finally he got a fleet and army ready and crossed to Gaul, intending to conquer this land also as he moved south. Conan went with him on campaign. First they fought the

Franks in the Armorican peninsula and achieved a great victory.

Maximus called Conan to him and offered him the kingship of this land in return for his disappointment in not becoming king of Britain. He intended to settle soldiers there rather than letting them return to Britain. "This will be a second Britain," he said, "and we will people it with our own race. The land is productive and the rivers full of fish." Conan accepted willingly and agreed to pay homage henceforth to Maximus.

Further victories followed and the inhabitants were completely cowed by the ferocity of the Britons. Maximus sent for a hundred-thousand ordinary men and women from Britain, to join him across the channel, and distributed them among the tribes in Armorica. Then Conan took over and Maximus went on to conquer more of Gaul and Germany, establishing his capital at Trèves. He managed to kill Gracianus, one of the emperors of Rome and drive the other out. After many further campaigns in Europe, he himself was later killed by friends of Gracianus.

Meanwhile Conan was experiencing much hostility to his in-comers in Armorica, and was forced to fight many battles. He finally decided to send to Britain for women who were to be married to his troops, in this way avoiding any mingling with blood of the Gauls. The current king, Dionotus agreed and gathered eleven thousand nobly born women and sixty thousand from the common people, whether they wanted to go or not. They embarked from London but soon met a storm and many were shipwrecked. Others landed on islands of barbarians and were slaughtered or made slaves.

The soldiers finally took local women for wives, but cut out their tongues so that their children would not learn native speech but follow their fathers' language.[1]

---

[1] This gruesome detail comes from one of the texts of the *Historia Brittonum*. It is a pun on the Welsh name of Brittany, Llydaw, which can mean 'half-mute'.

King Mark/Marc'h

The story of this king illustrates how what may be a kernel of historical truth - King Mark or Marc is thought to have been an early ruler in 5th century Cornwall, Great Britain – can develop into something quite other. It also shows how legends merge and separate over time, leaving a residue of double personages. Here Mark figures in the tale of Tristan and Iseult (see p 188), and also is said to have entertained St-Pol, refusing him a fine bell to take to his new home across the water in Brittany.

It is also possible that he is synonymous with Conomor, sometimes known as Marc Conomor, the great tyrant of Breton legend. A monk of Landévennec named Wrmonoc wrote a *Vita* of St-Pol in which he mentions Mark as also being named Conomor. Some traditions hold Mark as king of Domnonée on both sides of the Channel.

But the name Mark, or 'Marc'h' in Breton (meaning a horse), has also led to alternative traditions of a man with horse's ears.[1] That this may be an ancient Indo-European tale perhaps going back to the domestication of the horse is apparent from the numerous cultures in which such a tale appears, King Midas and the ears of an ass being one well-known example.

Yann ar Floc'h, who published many legends in reviews in the early 20th century, told a version of the King Marc'h story. The south-west tip of Brittany is called Penmarc'h (horse's head) and at Douarnenez there was once an area called Porzmarch or the Court of king Marc'h.

King Marc'h had a wonderful horse named Morvarc'h (horse of the sea), which could speed across water as well as land. It was the most prized possession of the king. One day when out hunting, the king saw and pursued a fabulous deer, but the faster he drove Morvarc'h on, the faster the deer spurred ahead. Finally they came to a sheer drop and the deer went over the cliff and into the waves below. The king immediately drew his bow, firing down at the helpless animal. To his horror, the arrow turned

---

[1] This story of a King Marc also appears in Welsh literature

suddenly and sped back towards him, piercing the heart of his beloved horse Morvarc'h.

In rage he leapt forward with a knife in his hand intending to have his revenge on the deer when suddenly he saw it no longer, but in its place was a beautiful young woman, wearing a crown of seaweed. It was the sea goddess Ahes, once called Dahut and daughter of King Gradlon.[1] She spoke to the startled king: "So you have hounded me when I have done you no harm and in punishment from this moment you will bear the ears of the animal who has carried you to this point." She touched the king's head lightly and then leapt on the back of Morvarc'h, magically restored to life, before the two of them disappeared together into the sea.

From then on King Marc'h stayed in his palace and saw no-one, except a whole string of barbers who never emerged after their visit. Finally only one barber remained in the kingdom, a young man named Yeunig who was in fact the foster brother of the king. He possessed a pair of magic scissors, which could prevent hair from growing any further. The king was delighted with their meeting and agreed to spare Yeunig's life, on condition he kept the king's secret. But Yeunig found the strain of this too much, so he dug a hole in the sand, put his head in and whispered the fatal words: "King Marc'h has horses' ears..." He filled in the hole and went home, but in the night three reeds grew on the spot where he had shared the king's secret.

The next day the king was forced to appear in public at the marriage of his daughter. He wore a hat specially designed to cover up his deformity and took the precaution of setting up a tent to protect himself from the winds.

At the wedding celebrations, musicians prepared to play, but found they needed new strings for their harps. All that could be found were the three fragile reeds from the

---

[1] See page 105.

beach. They began to play and suddenly the wind got up, stirring the reeds which began to sing out 'King Marc'h has the ears of his horse Morvarc'h..."

The king leapt up and left the tent, but a gust of wind at once blew off his hat and his head was revealed to all. He began to run away, but slipped and struck his head on a rock. At that moment a siren appeared on a horse with human ears. "Here is Morvarc'h," she said, "the horse of King Marc'h. His ears are those of the king and the king's ears are those of Morvarc'h."

The party was at an end. Only the king's daughter cared for her father's plight, and the barber Yeunig.

In the evening, all the guests came out to view the rock where King Marc'h had fallen, and they saw, strange to tell, the imprint of King Marc'h's head with its horses' ears on the rock. And so the area changed its name to Penmarc'h or Horse's head.

Here is another version of the story. Off the north coast of Finistère lies the Île Carn. There lived a wealthy lord who owned much land around the area of Ploudalmézeau, although he himself remained in solitary splendour in a large château on the island.[1]

From time to time the lord of Île Carn sent to the mainland for a young man to shave him and cut his hair, but these individuals never returned. Whether they had mysteriously disappeared on the crossing or been detained on the island no-one knew. Attracted by the enigma, a young man named Losthouarn decided to play the role of barber and set off by boat with two friends he could call on in case in trouble.

The lord himself greeted the young man and commanded him imperiously to give him a haircut. He took off the soft hat he was wearing, and his horse's ears

---

[1] In fact there is a large Neolithic cairn on the island, still visible today, which may have given rise to tales of a château.

were revealed. Losthouarn pretended nothing was out of the ordinary and began his work, all the time thinking quickly to himself. He realised that the lord wanted to keep his secret and must have disposed of all the other barbers. Somehow he had to avoid the same fate at any cost. Losthouarn began the shaving process in a normal way, but then suddenly turned the razor and slit the lord's throat. He then left the château calmly and went back home with his friends.

Another versions tell of a barber sworn to secrecy who could hardly bear not to tell anyone so he dug a hole in the ground and whispered "King Marc'h has horses' ears …" and ever afterwards the wind rustling among the plants of the island repeated the words over and over, "King Marc'h has horses' ears …"

Reeds were later cut on the island to make a biniou[1] and when the instrument was played, what sound came out but … "King Marc'h has horses' ears …"

Conomor[2]

Conomor is in many ways the most interesting of all subjects of Breton legend. Popular tradition makes him an archetypal wicked tyrant with a Blue Beard complex thrown in for good measure. He is said to have murdered a succession of wives and to have beheaded his own little son. History gives us a dynamic and ruthlessly ambitious figure, very much a man of his times, seeking territorial expansion and powerful alliances. He has close connections with Cornwall in Britain where an inscription found at Golant reads:

HIC IACIT CUNOMORI FILIUS DRUSTAUS CUM DOMINA OUSTILLA (here lies Tristan, son of Conomor, with his wife Oustilla).

---

[1] A sort of bagpipe.

[2] For a fascinating study of the complex evidence about this extraordinary individual, see *Conomor: entre histoire et légende* by Christiane Kerboul-Vilhon (2004).

This appears to point to a link between Conomor and king Mark of the legend of Trisan and Isolde.[1] Another Cornish connection may possibly be seen in the names of Carhays/Caerhays in Cornwall and Carhaix in Finistère, which was at the heart of Conomor's territory of the Poher region. Other historical links make Conomor the prefect of Childebert I, king of the Franks, who may have used officials in the west to secure his interests in trade and security along the Channel coast.

How is it possible to reconcile the two versions of Conomor? The Dark Ages were not short of ruthless and ambitious men, seeking power and exerting the authority of their powerful personalities over others. These are exactly the circumstances in which exaggerated and condemnatory tales begin to attach like sticky burs. Conomor's appearance in hagiographies of saints like St-Samson and St-Lunaire inevitably present him as the personification of evil over whom the holy men must triumph.

One historical event worth bearing in mind might be the scandalous assassination of young Arthur, Duke of Brittany, in 1203, by his uncle King John of England, this being the time when many stories about earlier centuries in the Armorican peninsula were being written down. This could well have coloured or created the tale of Trémeur, murdered by his father.[2]

The legend given below amalgamates the many stranded story of Conomor Le Maudit (Cursed) and Conomor the Dark Age lord.

onomor was a forceful ruler of the area of the Poher. He probably came from the south-west corner of Britain and first settled in the Armorican peninsula at Carhaix. He later had many bases including Castel Finans in the Forêt de Quénécan near the river Blavet[3], and was backed in his position by Childebert, King of the Franks whose court was

---

[1] See page 188.

[2] The cult of the young murdered Mélar, son of Miliau (see p.102), at Lanmeur was also enhanced by this historical event.

[3] Other places associated with Conomor are the Forêt de Carnoët, Gouesnou, Castel-Beuzit-Lanmeur and Montafilant. Castel Finans would have been a base for controlling the lead-silver mines of the area, and the panning of gold in the Blavet river.

97

in Paris. Conomor had received a prophecy that his son would kill him and he therefore murdered a succession of wives as each became pregnant. Their bodies were buried in the cellar of his castle chapel. His vaunting ambition and greed for power made Conomor keen to expand his territories, and when the king of Domnonée died suddenly, he was quick to marry the widow and gain possession of a vast new area of land. Some whispered that he had had a hand in the king's convenient death.

Conomor also wanted to get rid of Judual, son of his new bride, and a potential rival. The young man's mother recounted a dream to Conomor in which she had seen her son seated in splendour, receiving homage from all the lords of the peninsula. She realised her folly in repeating this when her husband immediately interpreted this as meaning that Judual would be even more powerful than he was, and resolved to kill the young man.

Judual and his mother fled at once, taking refuge in the abbey of St-Lunaire. When Conomor arrived in pursuit, St-Lunaire agreed to a cliff-top meeting at which the king could see Judual. In this way he tricked Conomor, simply pointing out the boat on which the young man could be seen, sailing away to safety. Conomor was so furious at this humiliation that he struck the saint and beat his own horse, which threw him.[1]

Another version says that Conomor himself sent Judual off to the court of his ally Childebert, king of the Franks, and thus had the young man kept in a sort of house-arrest in Paris. Judual's mother conveniently died soon after, leaving her husband free to seek new connections.

After being thwarted in his plans to eliminate Judual, Conomor became openly more and more cruelly tyrannical and many people began to oppose him. He now sought to ally himself with the powerful count of Vannes, Waroc,

[1] In this version – given in a hagiography of the saint and not mentioning any later connection of Conomor with Tréphine - the fall broke his leg badly and Conomor soon died of his injuries, punished for so treating a man of God.

and, now being a widower, he proposed a marriage alliance with Waroc's beloved daughter, Tréphine. Waroc was wary of Conomor's reputation and played for time, sending for Saint Gildas to come and give advice on the situation. One version says that Conomor submitted himself to penitence for all his crimes and convinced Gildas that he was a reformed character. Another story claims that Conomor so terrified the saint with promises of violence and destruction that he thought it prudent to advise Waroc to allow the marriage, promising that he would personally keep an eye on Tréphine. In the end the marriage was to go ahead and a lavish wedding ceremony was held with all manner of feasting and celebration.

For a time all went well between husband and wife, and Conomor began to pressure Waroc to share the control of his wide territories. But things seemed to change when Tréphine told her husband she was pregnant, for he had never forgotten the prophecy that his son would kill him, and so had no intention of allowing any male child to live. His demeanour towards his wife turned menacing and she began to be fearful of the future.

One day she was praying in the castle chapel and noticed the door to the crypt was open. Tréphine went down the steps and saw a row of stone coffins, the end one with no lid being empty. She turned to leave this gloomy place as quickly as possible, but suddenly the lids of the other coffins slid back and out rose the ghosts of Conomor's previous wives. They warned her of her danger, pointing to the awaiting coffin which was destined for her. The terrified girl at once fled from the castle on horseback, through the forest, but Conomor was soon in hot pursuit and he caught up with her where the chapel in her name now stands. Before she could plead with him, Conomor cut off her head and returned without a qualm to Castel Finans.

Meanwhile Waroc had sent Saint Gildas to check up on Tréphine as he was worried for his daughter's welfare. When the saint was turned away from the castle with insults, he feared the worst, and sure enough, found Tréphine's body and severed head in the forest. With a prayer he performed the miracle of restoring her to life and took her back to the protection of her father in Vannes. The unfortunate girl did not live long, however, as she died in giving birth to a son, Trémeur.[1]

Conomor had now gone too far in his misdeeds and arrogant abuses of power. There are various different accounts of his end. In one, St-Gildas calls on him in his castle[2] to take him to task for his crimes, but Conomor refuses to receive him and he is mocked by Conomor's soldiers. Gildas prays to God that an immediate stop should be put to Conomor's perfidy. The walls of the castle tumble and the tyrant lies dead beneath the rubble.

Chapel of Ste-Tréphine, Forêt de Quénécan

The judgement of Conomor (church window at Pédernec)

---

[1] In other versions, Tréphine lives but Conomor catches up with her and his son years later. He stabs Tréhpine to death (although St-Gildas restores her) and beheads the little boy.

[2] Either Castel Cran near Gouarec or Castel Finans on the opposite edge of the Forêt de Quénécan.

In the best known version, he was eventually called to account for his crimes by a group of religious and political leaders. The meeting was held on the summit of Méné Bré, near Guingamp, where the chapel of St-Hervé now stands.[1] The decision was taken that the tyrant should be excommunicated, a severe penalty in those days, but Conomor defied his judges and left the assembly to organise resistance to any attempt to take away his lands. For a long time he lived as an outlaw, protected by bands of his own soldiers.

On one occasion he retuned to the forest of Quénécan and came across some boys playing. He was sure that he discerned his own features in one and concluded that it must be the son Tréphine had borne him. Ever mindful of the prophecy, he did not hesitate to decapitate Trémeur. The child is said to have picked up his own head and walked to his mother's grave.[2]

But Conomor's rule of terror was drawing to an end. Saint-Samson went to Paris to convince Childebert of Conomor's true colours and persuade him to let Judual return. All those who hated the tyrant Conomor flocked to the support of his stepson, a fine young man at the head of an army, and a showdown was inevitable.

St-Trémeur

Conomor was pursued as far as the Monts d'Arrée, where the final battle took place. Judual's army was victorious, but there were huge losses on both sides. The dead were buried on the spot, hence the name of the abbey built later in the valley. It was called Le Relec.[3] Conomor was killed by Judual on the battlefield, a twist on the fulfilment of the original prophecy.

---

[1] See page 44.

[2] Statues often show Trémeur carrying his own head, as on the façade of his church in Carhaix.

[3] From the Latin *reliquies* = remains.

Saint Miliau and Saint Melar (Méloir)

In the legends of these two figures we see the mixture of the real and the miraculous so common in this formative period, with disputed dynastic power and ruthless ambition sitting alongside magical artificial limbs.

Saint Miliau has left his trace in many place-names such as Ploumilliau, Plumeliau and Guimiliau. The church at Plonevez-Porzay is also dedicated to him. What little is known of his story, however, comes from the documentation of his son Melar's life. Some think he is not the same Miliau commemorated in the fabulous Parish Close church of Guimiliau[1], but that there was an immigrant monk of the same name. Regardless of that issue, a richly decorated altarpiece in that famous church shows the story of his death at the hands of his brother, with Miliau holding his own severed head, as his wife stands beside him. In fact the sources do not mention decapitation in the context of Miliau, only his son Melar, a good example of how easily connected legends may merge and mingle.

Information about Saint Melar, child martyr, comes from two *Vitae* from the 11/12th centuries. Together these contain the extraordinary details of the boy's legend, which holds inevitable reminders of another decapitated child of the time, Trémeur.[2] The church at Lanmeur today still contains statues of Saint Melar, one where the saint was interred, in the remarkable ancient crypt[3] with its carved snakes on the pillars perhaps echoing much earlier cults.

---

[1] Not least for reasons of territory, as he was ruler of Cornouaille.

[2] See page 101.

[3] The crypt dating back perhaps to the 8/9th century. Some scholars think the 'snakes' are in fact vegetal decoration.

Saint Miliau was the king of Cornouaille, renowned for his goodness and religious devotion. His wife was a daughter of the count of Bro-Weroc, the region around Vannes, and together they had a little son, Melar.

One day, however, Miliau was brutally assassinated by his brother Rivod who coveted the throne. There was also an attempt at the same time on the life of the seven year old Melar, but this failed when the child made the sign of the cross over the cup of poison he was offered.

Rivod decided instead to mutilate the boy by cutting off his left foot and right hand. In this way he would prevent Melar achieving the two essential attributes of a ruler – riding a horse and wielding a sword. The boy was provided with false appendages, a hand of silver and foot of bronze. But to everyone's astonishment these became fused naturally to his body, working as efficiently as his other limbs. Alarmed by this evidence of yet another miracle concerning Melar, Rivod determined to kill him once and for all, so he could not become a focus for popular support.

The child was put in the care of a couple who had an older son of their own. Rivod decided to bribe the man, Kerialtan, to assassinate Melar. He promised him in return all the land he could see from the top of Mount Frugy in Quimper. Kerialtan's wife appeared to go along with this plan when her husband proposed it, but she sent him back to Rivod to negotiate a better deal. She then herself fled with the child into the kingdom of Dumnonnée, north of the Monts d'Arrée, where the king Conomor, based at Beuzit, offered his protection to Melar. The bonds of family demanded this, as Conomor's wife was in fact the aunt of Melar.

Soon after, Kerialtan and his son Justan turned up in pursuit, only to be greeted with great affection by young Melar, who had no idea of the plot to kill him and regarded them as members of his family. But that very night, Kerialtan beheaded Melar and put the head in a bag for proof to show Rivod. Justan began to descend the outside of the tower, carrying the bag, but fell to his death. His father took up the burden and set off for Quimper to meet Rivod.

It is said that Melar's grisly relic performed a strangely magnanimous miracle on the way by causing a spring of water to appear when Kerialtan could go no further on account of a terrible thirst. Having fulfilled his wicked promise, Kerialtan hoped to profit from his crime, but was suddenly overcome by blindness before he could spy out his new lands, and then struck dead on the spot. The villain Rivod himself died three days later.

Meanwhile Conomor attempted to bury the body of Melar which had been left behind. First he tried in his castle, then in a nearby church and then at Guimaec, but each attempt failed as the body disappeared, as if not content with its resting place. Finally they put it on an ox-cart, letting the beasts wander at will until they stopped at the spot where the body would finally be buried – today the site of the church at Lanmeur.

The separation of head and corpse of Melar was long the subject of dispute between the leaders of Domnonée and Cornouaille. Finally it was agreed to bring each of the two parts of the saint to the border between the territories. When the head miraculously crossed the line and fitted itself to the body, it was taken as sign that the saint wished to remain in Domonnée. An oratory was built on the spot where this took place, but it fell into disuse and ruin after it was claimed that the family who owned the land stole offerings made there by pilgrims.

The Legend of Ys[1] – another foundation legend

This is the Breton Atlantis legend, in that it involves a city engulfed by waves disappearing beneath the sea. This may preserve the memory of an actual historical event, given the precarious nature of the coastal lands exposed to the full might of the Atlantic. But it also has the wider symbolic implication of the destruction of one way of life to be replaced with another. In this sense it can be seen as a crucially important story in the beginnings of Brittany, the final struggle between the 'old ways' and the arrival of Christianity.[2] The tale is most commonly set in the Bay of Douarnenez where the city of Ys was said to have been built by King Gradlon of Quimper, either as his own city in the days before Quimper was built, or as a place of pleasure for his beloved daughter Dahut.

Two versions are given below, one the simplest outline which is a straightforward parable of Good v Evil as seen through the eyes of the Church, and the second a more complex proposition, reflecting contemporary issues and the origins of organised religion in Brittany. Both these stories contain an element of sacrifice, each for a different good.[3]

King Gradlon had one beloved daughter, Dahut, who preferred a dissolute lifestyle to the proprieties of her father's court at Quimper, where she was weary of the grim seriousness of his advisors, St-Corentin and St-Guénolé. Eventually she persuaded her father to build her a fine city in the Bay of Douarnenez, accessible only at low tide but otherwise protected from the waves by strong walls. This was to be a place of her own where she could live a life of indulgence and wantonness, and sure enough, when the

---

[1] Ker Ys means 'the town from below' in Breton. Celtic Britain has two similar legends of sunken cities: Lyonesse in Cornwall and Cantref y Gwaelod in Wales.

[2] Or even specifically the determination of the Catholicism of Rome to get rid of 'Celtic Christianity', an idea woven into a fine tale by contemporary author and *conteur* Loig Pujol in his book *Contes et Légendes du Finistère* (2008).

[3] Many would argue that far from one religion destroying another, the pagan/Christian duality remained and maybe still remains in the present day.

city was ready, she surrounded herself there with like-minded friends, drinking, dancing and offering her sexual favours as she pleased.

St-Guénolé, abbot of Landévennec, repeatedly warned Gradlon about Dahut's wicked behaviour, but could not convince the fond father of the seriousness of the situation. Not only was there licentiousness all day and all night, but it was said that the poor were ejected from Ys with all its wealth. Worse, every night Dahut took a new lover and had him put to death in the morning.[1] Guénolé urged the king to go out to the new city of Ys and witness the depravity for himself so he would be forced to put an end to it once and for all. Such things were an offence to God and could not be allowed to continue. Finally Gradlon gave in and the two men rode out across the sands to Ys.

That same evening, Dahut met a new lover, someone dressed all in red but wearing a mask to conceal his face. She was fascinated and entranced by this man, finally agreeing to grant him anything he asked of her. Even when he demanded the keys of the gate of the city, she did not refuse, but crept into the room where her father slept and stole from the chain around his neck. Soon after, the mysterious stranger opened the gate of Ys and water began to pour in, drowning the city.

Gradlon and Guénolé tried to escape on their horses before the waters spread across the sand, but the king stopped as his daughter called out to him to save her from the waves. He could not resist her plea and hauled her up behind him. They endeavoured to continue but the horses were struggling in the mounting waters. St-Guénolé urged Gradlon to throw his daughter off and leave her to her fate. The king eventually did so, and was able to save himself as Dahut sank below the waves.[2]

---

[1] The Gouffre in the forest at Huelgoat is said to have been one place where the bodies of Dahut's lovers were thrown, and their cries still mingle with the sound of rushing water.

[2] But not without trace - see page 245 for her 'resurrection'. A famous painting of 1884 by Evariste-Vital Luminais in the Musée des Beaux Arts in Quimper graphically shows this scene.

The story can be presented in a very different way:

Gradlon and Dahut were pagans, accustomed to the worship of a pantheon of deities rather than one God. They lived in the city of Ys with its great palace, surrounded by all the trappings of wealth, but tolerant of the ideas and beliefs of all. Dahut became uneasy when her father fell under the Christian influence of Corentin, a hermit on Menez Hom, impressed by his simple faith and piety. Then Guénolé, a monk with followers from across the channel, came to ask for land at Landévennec to build a monastery, and the king agreed.

He began to listen attentively to these two holy men and rely on them for advice. They were practitioners of what has been termed Celtic Christianity,[1] often performing open air services and allowing women an equal role in the sacrament. It was not long before representatives from the Roman Catholic church arrived at Gradlon's court. They disapproved not only of Ys, which had not one single Christian church, but also of the lack of rigour and adherence to practices sanctioned by the Pope in the ways of Guénolé and Corentin. There were also political implications as the Holy Roman Emperor and Pope were now in alliance and would look with hostility on those who tried to remain outside their dictates.

Under pressure of conformity[2] Gradlon agreed to a bishop being chosen for his territory. Despite Dahut's alarm at this concession, he reassured her that he would build a new city (Quimper) for the required cathedral and that her beloved Ys would remain free. But his daughter decided that it was only a matter of time before her precious freedoms were compromised. She resolved to save

---

[1] Some academics doubt that such a distinct form truly existed. See note on page 125 for a useful work on the subject.

[2] This part of the story may well have been created at the time of or after a later historical reality: in 818, Louis Le Pieux, emperor of the Franks, insisted that Landévennec, the abbey founded by St-Guénolé accept the Benedictine rule to come into line with other abbeys in the peninsula.

her city in her own way, and after calling on her pagan deities for aid, she waited for a sign.

When the unknown lover appeared one night, tantalising her with his charm and physical attraction, she hesitated only for a moment before agreeing to steal the keys of the city gates from her father as he slept. She watched calmly as the stranger opened the sluice and the waters rushed in, knowing that her plans were falling into place.

As her father and Guénolé made their escape on horseback, they passed Dahut in the rising waters. Her father could not bear to leave his daughter to drown and pulled at her hand, urging her onto the horse behind him. But it was not part of Dahut's intention to survive in such a way. She knew that she had saved her own people, for the city of Ys would sink to the bottom of the sea and there continue exactly as before, waiting for the day when it would rise again in splendour, undiminished. As for Dahut herself, a greater fate was beckoning. Throwing herself joyfully into the waves she disappeared into the foam, a sea-spirit in the making.

These are the opening verses of a famous *gwerz* about the fall of Ys.[1]

> **What news from Ys,**
> **Where youth is given up to folly,**
> **Where I hear the sound of**
> **Biniou, bombard and harp[2].**
>
> **There is nothing new in Ys**
> **Just the usual frolics,**
> **The same old things in Ys,**
> **As they party every night.**
>
> **Where brambles grow profusely**
> **On the doors of shuttered churches,**
> **And dogs are freely set**
> **On the poor as they weep.**
>
> **Ahés, daughter of Gradlon**
> **Hell fire in her heart**
> **Heads the debauchery**
> **Leading the town to its destruction.**

---

[1] For a recording of this by a skilled conteur, see Yann-Fañch Kemener's album *Enez Eusa* (1995).

[2] The *biniou* (like bagpipes) and *bombard* (a bit like an oboe) are traditional Breton musicial instruments.

CHAPTER 5
LEGENDS IN THE LANDSCAPE

Landscape is intimately connected with the creation and dissemination of legends. Strange or striking natural features attract attention and explanations, whilst atmospheric places like caves and forests give rise to equally characterful tales. Extraordinary structures like the megaliths, so widespread in Brittany, also feature in many stories, deriving from a time long before scientific explanations were possible. How the physical world came to be in the first place is an obvious source of legends, usually involving the antics of giants, from fighting to peeing. The lake of the Arguenon at Jugon is said to have been left after Gargantua relieved himself.

Topography has a great importance in people's lives for fixing them in a geographical context and empowering a sense of identity within the place they live. This was especially so when the world was predominantly rural and many people remained in the place they were born all their lives. Landscape can thus be a comforting and reassuring permanence, despite changes over a long period of time. Such connections can be symbolic, as in many of the saints' Lives, or actual, as the wealth of Breton place-names relating to landscape demonstrates.[1] Hills, fields and trees become signs of identification for individuals and also for communities. The strong Breton sense of place remains in many stories from the oral tradition.

Creation

'Creation' legends include stories of giants, and Gargantua[2] in particular. In Finistère, tradition says he was well-received by the people of Léon after ill-treatment in Cornouaille. He therefore ripped up all the stony surface of Léon, leaving a rich fertile plain, and threw the debris over a wide area to the south-east. Another version to explain the lush land of Léon, one of France's prime vegetable growing

---

[1] For example, Toul Gwin (wine hole) near St-Guénolé recalls an 18th century bounty of a cargo of wine coming ashore after a wreck.

[2] See page 163.

areas, is that the giant ate too much grass up there and eventually was sick over a wide area, thus fertilising the soil!

The giant Hok-Bras

remarkable young man was born between Daoulas and Landerneau. By three years old he was six foot tall and his father took him to Huelgoat to leave in the charge of a relative who was to be his god-mother. There was no need to carry Hok-Bras to the baptismal font! When he sneezed in church, the stained glass windows blew out ...

After this ceremony, he was playing in the woods around the Trou du Diable[1] He began to fill it in with huge rocks that littered the valley. His god-mother, who was actually a very attractive fairy, came to watch him play, but – disaster! – her diamond ring came off her finger and fell down into the chasm. She began to cry, and Hok-Bras could not bear to see such pretty eyes in tears and determined to retrieve the ring.

"If only I was taller!" he said to himself. He climbed down, but already the waters rose up around his neck well before he was near the bottom of the cleft. "You can do it," his god-mother cried, "You can make yourself as tall as you wish!" And lo and behold, the young man wished very hard and felt himself elongating, down and down, his head still above water, his feet stretching to the depths. Finally they reached right down. "I'm standing on a big snake," he called out. "Bring it up," said the fairy, "for it has swallowed my ring."

So Hok-Bras shot up to solid ground again, but now his head was reaching way up into the clouds. "How can I stop growing?" he yelled in despair. "Just say 'Enough'", she called up to him. A great boom like thunder echoed around as he shouted it out. But he did stop growing, and now got down on his knees to embrace his god-mother and restore her ring.

[1] Devil's Hole.

Hok-Bras went back to his father, but he was restless and dissatisfied. Finally he announced that he wanted to be married.

"At your age!" said his father. "I don't think so."

Now it was of course his pretty god-mother that he wanted to marry, but she had told him he had to perform three great exploits first – graciously counting the rescue of the ring as one – and he was not to return to Huelgoat until he had accomplished this.

He pondered and pondered over his mission, idly playing with the rocks all around, piling them up like building blocks until he had created the Monts d'Arrée. And then he stacked up Mont St-Michel[1] so that he could peep across to Huelgoat and try to see the object of his love.

But soon he got a chance to carry out an important task. He was wandering near Landerneau one day when he met a bailiff who, impressed by his great height, challenged him to capture the moon for the reward of ten ecus.[2] He agreed willingly, and the whole town turned out to watch the spectacle as night fell. Hok-Bras said to himself "Up you go!" and his body elongated, towering up into the sky, higher and higher to where the moon lay above the clouds. And then all those assembled saw a strange sight - the moon suddenly appearing, descending through the sky, held firmly in the teeth of the giant, who carefully placed it on the spire of Saint-Houardon's church.

Hok-Bras went home very pleased with his achievement, and suddenly conceived the idea of another great task. He would create a lake in front of his house so that he could have a bathe whenever he felt like it. He set to work, scooping out and shoring up the landscape until finally he had created the Rade de Brest. He plunged happily into the water but unfortunately for him a three-masted ship soon

---

[1] Mont St-Michel-de-Brasparts, one of the highest points of the Monts d'Arrée.

[2] A unit of currency.

came sailing up the new access channel from the Atlantic[1] and before anyone quite knew what had happened, Hok-Bras had swallowed the ship! Oh, what pain it caused in his insides! He staggered out and blundered towards Huelgoat, thinking only of reaching his beloved, but he stumbled over the Monts d'Arrée and fell, crashing to earth and bashing his head on a rock near Saint-Herbot.

He lay lifeless. The fairy came quickly – for the crash had been felt as a tremor in Huelgoat – but there was nothing she could do for poor Hok-Bras, the gentle giant. She sadly retired to the nearby village of Saint-Herbot,[2] where his shadow fell for ever over the torrents of the Chaos.

---

[1] The Goulet.

[2] A giant is carved on one of the choir stalls in the church at St-Herbot.

113

The Chaos of Huelgoat & the Gorges de Corong

The gigantic rocks of the 'Chaos' phenomenon visible in various places in the granite belt of Brittany are so unusual, even today, that they naturally attracted various legendary explanations in the distant past.

The Chaos at Huelgoat was created after a battle between two sets of giants in Plouyé and Berrien, with the lobbed stone missiles falling somewhat short in between. Or was it Gargantua, who cleared all the rocks from Plouarzel, because the inhabitants had welcomed him and offered him a nourishing bowl of buckwheat porridge. And he had to chuck them somewhere ... Or was it because he hated the buckwheat gruel he was given by the poor people of Huelgoat and took his revenge on reaching the Monts d'Arrée by hurling enormous boulders back at them...

Boudédé, cousin of Gargantua is said to have been the first man in Brittany. He stopped near the Forest of Duault to empty his shoe of stones and thus formed the Chaos of the Gorges du Corong.

In Ille-et-Vilaine, the Rochers de Cancale were formed when Gargantua did the same thing.

The Ringing Stones (*Les Pierres Sonnantes*) in the Arguenon estuary were originally the ballast of a fishing boat, vomited up by Gargantua after he swallowed the vessel whole for a tasty snack.[1]

Chaos

---

[1] They are actually a type of stone called amphibole (a hard bisilicate). Their name comes from the fact that if struck with another stone of the same sort they make a metallic ringing sound..

The landscape of Brittany had another 'beginning' or recreation with the arrival of immigrants from Great Britain, especially in the 5th and 6th centuries, the 'Age of Saints'. Most of these new arrivals, including the religious leaders among them, were looking to settle and work the land. Armorica clearly did not have the population pressures and potential land shortages that were already affecting parts of western Britain. The reason that noble land-owners were prepared to grant land to new-comers, especially monks, was to get it cleared and worked, a fundamental of the ethos of monasteries, especially with the later Cistercians for whom manual labour was a form of prayer.

Saint Goulven

The legend of Saint Goulven illustrates not only the economic value of this wave of immigrants to their new land, but also symbolically the fertility and exceptional agricultural possibilities just waiting to be developed in the future Brittany.

couple from Britain were separated from other boats travelling to Brittany and landed alone on the wild shore of north Finistère, in a spot which is today called the Bay of Goulven. The wife was about to give birth and longed for fresh water, so her husband went off in search of a spring. He got lost in the forest and fell to his knees, begging God to help his wife. His prayers were answered at once, although he didn't know it. When he arrived back at the shore the following day, he found his wife and new-born son, Goulven, and a fresh spring which had appeared like a miracle beside them.

Goulven grew up a rather solitary young man who rarely spoke to others, but devoted himself to prayer and the hard work needed to clear and plant the land. He was aided only by a single loyal companion, Maden.

One day, Goulven had the impulse to send Maden to a peasant farmer called Ioncur, who lived in the next valley, asking for a token of friendship – whatever Ioncur had in his hand when Maden spoke. Maden faithfully carried out his errand. For a moment Ioncur was puzzled. Then he bent down and scooped up handfuls of earth, filling Maden's tunic. Maden struggled to return to Goulven. His load seemed heavier and heavier and it was all he could do to put one foot in front of the other. When he reached the hut, Goulven came out to meet him and opened the tunic to find ... three ingots of gold where the earth had been.

With the coming of the Christian church came the symbolism of landscape. Land to be worked and weeds to be cleared were metaphors of conversion and adherence to virtue over sin. The church wanted control over the landscape as well as its people, literally and figuratively.

St Brieuc began to build his monastery on the donated land. He had many trees cut down in the forest, both to clear a space for the building and to provide timber for the construction. Even before it was finished he moved in with all his followers and word sped far and wide that what had been forest but a few days before was now occupied by the monks. Before long not only was the monastery finished, but a whole settlement quickly grew up in the vicinity. (Life of St-Brieuc)

Symbolic acts like placing crosses on menhirs also indicate a significant statement.[1] One of the Lives of Saint Samson relates how, during his time in Great Britain, he used a metal implement to draw a cross on a menhir, having observed pagans worshipping it as an idol.

---

[1] The huge standing-stone Men Marz at Brignogan-Plage (Finistère) and the Menhir de St-Uzec near Pleumeur-Bodou (Côtes d'Armor) are good later examples to be seen today.

Setting a boundary

A story of St-Pol makes the menhir of Men Marz (Miracle stone), one of the tallest in Brittany, a product of Christian endeavour rather than pagan ritual. In so doing he shows the power of Christianity even over that most potent of elements, the sea.

The sea was encroaching onto the land along the north coast of Finistère. St-Pol's own monastery had been threatened and at the behest of his sister he came to the area around what is now Brignogan-Plage to perform a special ceremony. Here he forbade the sea, in the name of the Lord, to come in any further than the limit he would set for it. His sister then threw the long stone which stuck upright in the ground to mark the boundary. And the sea has always obeyed this command ...

Men Marz

Fontaines

Water is the fundamental of life and its value was fully appreciated at a time when supply could not be taken for granted, and hard work was necessary to fetch, carry and preserve stores of this precious resource. Sources were regarded as divine in Celtic religion and perhaps in much earlier times: often menhirs are to be found in the vicinity, deliberately placed in honour of this source of life, and in tribute to the spirits of the element of water. Springs were also associated with healing powers and life-giving properties because of their connection with the divine, in both pre-Christian and later times.

Many stories attribute the creation of natural springs to the action of saints, who struck the ground with a staff to cause water to spring forth from deep in the earth at times of need.[1] But the Christianisation of *fontaines* is often an echo of earlier and very ancient worship of water sources.

Subsequently these *fontaines* were attributed with healing powers associated with the special attributes of their patron saints. Certain rituals were also practised to find out the future, such as if a baby would live to grow up, and also to predict death by dropping an object belonging to a sick person – if it struck the wall, they would die. And for the ultimate - the Fontaine de Juvenence in the Forêt de Brocéliande promised Eternal Youth.

Today these places are stone-clad and many retain the statues of the relevant saint in a small oratory covering the source. Many also have curious traditions.

Fontaine de Ste-Candide, Scaer

At Scaer is a spring said to have had remarkable powers of enhancing human strength. The Fontaine Sainte-Candide had waters of exceptional clarity, as its name suggests. The saint[2] had struck the ground with her staff to produce a spring with healing powers for children. They would be immersed in the water: if they stretched out, it was a sign of long life and the opposite if they recoiled.

Anatole Le Braz was told by an elderly inhabitant in the 19th century that the invigorating power of the water was the reason for the town's prowess in the Breton sport of Lutte.[3] Young men keen to excel in overcoming their rivals and 'become like Hercules' would immerse themselves in the waters up to the neck for hours at a time before a contest. And so they would emerge 'invincible.'[4]

---

[1] See page 194 (St Eflam) and page 65 (St Corentin).

[2] Most likely a personification created from the descriptive name. Latin *candidus* = shining, clear.

[3] *Ar Gouren* (in Breton) is a form of wrestling. A contest is held at Scaer in late August at the time of the Pardon.

[4] The *fontaine* was described by Cambry in 1795 as 60ft long and 7ft deep.

Fontaine à Guillaume

This spring is in Saint-Ouen-la-Roueire (Ille-et-Vilaine), and officially associated with Notre-Dame de Bon-Secours. An indecipherable Latin inscription is on the stones of the little oratory. Tradition has it that this is a secret code for locating a local treasure of great price...if only anyone could work it out.

Fetan en Eutre (Fontaine de Monsieur)

This spring was described by Zacharie Le Rouzic[1] as having attracted some strange stories of mischievous behaviour. A ghost took the form of a dog and played tricks on passers-by. An old woman was thrown into a neighbouring field, but remained unhurt and not a drop of milk was spilt from the jug she was carrying. When two young men tried to grab a large pig drinking at the spring, they kept falling over at each attempt...

Fontaine St-Egarec

At Kerlouan in Finistère, this spring is dedicated to Saint Egarec, a patron of sailors and seaweed gatherers, both vital professions in this coastal region. His specialities of healing were afflictions of the eyes and ears. The method was to dip a silver coin in the water of the spring, then place it on the part of the body needing to be cured. After it was advised to put the coin on the altar in the chapel for the best results...

Fontaine de Barenton

This spring is central to the legend of Merlin and Viviane.[2] It is set in a beautiful grove in the Forêt de Brocéliande. There is a large flat stone at the head which is said to have special powers. If the water is splashed onto it, a storm will immediately break. Many neo-pagan offerings are left on its surface today.

---

[1] 1864-1939. He was the Curator of the Musée de Préhistoire at Carnac for many years.

[2] See page 199.

Woods and Trees

The Fool's Wood

The place-name Fool's Wood (Folgoat/Folgoët) is associated with the same legend in different places, and there has been something of a tussle of debate over centuries as to whether Le Folgoët in Léon with its magnificent church[1] or Folgoat in the woods of Landevénnec (near the famous abbey) with its simple 17th century chapel can truly lay claim to Salaun the simpleton. Atmospherically it feels absolutely right for the setting of the latter, where this tale is easy to visualise.

In the mid-14th century, there was a simpleton named Salaun who lived out of doors, surviving on the fruits of the forest and water from the spring in the glade where he dwelt, sleeping up in the boughs of a spreading tree. He was a well-known figure in the neighbourhood as he walked each day to the village to beg a little bread. He was always gentle and smiling, but the only words he was ever heard to speak in request or thanks were "Ave Maria'.

When Salaun died, he was buried in the beautiful spot where he had lived. Soon after, a wonderful lily was seen growing up from the grave.[2] Even more wonderful was that on the petals of the flower were written the words Ave Maria.

The miracle warranted investigation, and on uncovering the body, it was discovered that the flower was growing from the mouth of Salaun. A simple chapel was built on the spot, and is still there today, restored in the 17th century after suffering damage during the Wars of the League in 1593.

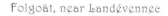

Folgoät, near Landévennec

---

[1] Basilique Notre-Dame du Folgoët. The same story is told to account for the foundation there.

[2] The lily is a flower associated with the Virgin Mary.

Le Chêne à Guillotin

This amazing tree, over 20m high and 1000 years old, certainly deserves its legend from fairly recent times.

In the Forêt de Brocéliande, famous for its Arthurian stories, stands this magnificent oak tree, named after a local priest, Abbé Guillotin. He, like so many Breton priests, was opposed to the Revolution and was forced to flee from his parish in Concoret to escape Republican army soldiers. Passing through the forest with his pursuers close behind, he saw that the base of this huge tree was hollow, and slipped inside to hide. When the soldiers came up soon after they saw an immense spider's web all over the entrance to the fissure and so assumed that no-one could have recently got in. They left without further examination of the tree, and the priest remained hidden for several days before venturing out. Later Abbé Guillotin claimed that Notre-Dame de Paimpont[1] had turned into a busy spider to save him.

Le Chêne Guillotin

---

[1] This representation is a well-known cult figure in the area, with an altar in the nave of the abbey church at Paimpont.

The Apple Tree

In Brittany, the apple (*aval/avalou*) is associated with the legendary Island of Avalon,[1] the place where King Arthur sleeps during the centuries awaiting the moment to return and save the Bretons in a national crisis. The siren Morgane presides over this kingdom of the 'sleeping dead', also thought of as the Isles of the Blessed, a rich and fertile mythical land.

The apple has also a practical significance in Brittany. In Ille-et-Vilaine, apple trees were sprinkled with holy water at Easter, so important a role have they played in Breton agriculture and especially the production of cider.

Saint Magloire and the apple tree

There are various versions of this legend from Dol-de-Bretagne and Léhon.

Saint-Magloire became bishop of Dol-de-Bretagne after Saint-Samson. The apple trees of the marshes in that area were known for their bitter fruit until the day that St-Magloire, being chased by pagans, hid in the hollow trunk of one and relieved his thirst by eating its sole fruit. He found it tasted sweet and ever after the apple trees there were renowned for their delicious taste.

A group of monks looking for somewhere to build a new monastery in the 9th century met Nominoë, the ruler of Brittany, when he was hunting. He promised them land if they could come up with some relics of a Breton saint.[2] One had the idea of stealing some part of Saint Magloire from his burial place on the island of Sark. This they did and came back with their prize. On the way to see Nominoë they stopped to rest and put the saint's relic in an apple

---

[1] In England Glastonbury is the traditional Isle of Avalon. There is an Île Aval in Brittany off the coast of Côtes d'Armor near Île Grande.

[2] Nominoë is a highly significant figure in the history of Brittany. First a local leader appointed by the emperor of the Franks, he began to build the skeleton of a Breton state for the first time and then drove the Franks out.

tree whilst they ate their meal below. Just as they finished eating, all the apples from the tree fell onto their makeshift table. And when the monks tried them hesitantly, knowing how bitter such fruit usually were, the apples were deliciously sweet. This miracle was attributed to the saint and Nominoë granted them land on the spot to build their monastery.[1]

The Golden Pears

There was once a king at Logonna-Daoulas near the Rade de Brest. In the garden of his palace was a miraculous tree that produced three special pears each year. In July they were silver, but in August they turned to gold. The king could not benefit from them, however, because as soon as they took the first golden sheen, they disappeared, one after the other on consecutive nights. Their potential value became increasingly crucial as the king's resources were long spent and he had desperate need of these magical pears to restore his fortunes. His advisors urged him to cut down the pears in July when they were silver, but he adamantly refused. After all, fruit should never be harvested until it is ripe, but, lo and behold, in August the fruits disappeared once again.

The king had three sons who decided to mount a watch the following year and ensure that their father got the benefit of the golden pears. The eldest took the first turn and sat beside the tree, armed and ready to tackle any thief. But no-one came. The same thing happened the second night and he was truly jubilant that it had been so easy to guard the fruit. But the third night, he had a little cider, just to keep warm on his vigil, and fell asleep shortly before midnight. When he woke, one of the fruit had gone.

The brothers argued over what had happened but it was clear there would be no fruit for the eldest this year. The second son took up his place with an axe to watch through

---

[1] The abbey of St-Magloire at Léhon can be visited today, a short walk along the river from Dinan.

the night. For the first two nights all was well, but on the third he was distracted by the movements of shooting stars and then fell asleep. In the morning, another pear had gone.

It was now the turn of the youngest son, who insisted on having his chance like the others. For two nights, no-one came. On the third, he felt himself on the point of sleep, so got up and marched round the tree to keep awake. At midnight he saw a huge shadow come over the land, then a great hand which snatched the last fruit from the tree. At once the young man drew his sword and cut off the hand, which fell to the earth. A terrible cry was heard and the golden pear rolled into the blood. A sudden blast of wind swept through the garden, then all was still.

His father and brothers ran out at the noise. The young man proposed to cut the pear in four and share it between them. But first he wanted to get the huge hand, which was entangled in the tree, the fingers still moving...

Rocks and Caves

Roc'h Trévézel

For a very long time this peak in the Monts d'Arrée was thought to be the highest point in Brittany. Recent accurate measurements give that honour to Roc'h Ruz, a small protrusion near the communications mast, but Roc'h Trévézel remains a spot that provokes the imagination with its craggy silhouette and views north to the Channel and south over the mysterious misty bowl of the Yeun Elez. The following story contains two well-known motifs of legends and fairytales: treasure contained inside a mountain, and rubbing the head of a charm to get a wish.

Roc'h Trévézel

It was said that every 1100 years the rocky face of Roc'h Trévézel opened on the eleventh stroke of midnight and closed again on the twelfth. Inside dwelt a little old wooden saint. Whoever found the saint and rubbed his head would be granted whatever they desired. But the only way to get him out was to use an 11 year old boy to get through the crack in the rock at the appropriate time.

One day a curious old man enlisted the help of such a boy and went to the rock when the 1100 years period was up. Sure enough, the rock opened on the eleventh stroke of midnight and in went the boy. In the first room he saw a pile of delicious-looking apples, but nothing else. He went on into a second room where there was an even greater pile of even more enticing apples. He picked one up and took a bite. Then another. The crunch of the apple obscured the sound of the twelfth stroke. The boy was trapped inside as a great crash indicated the rock had closed up again for another 1100 years.

So as time passed he ate the apples until they were all gone. Beneath the last one the boy saw a worm-eaten old fragment of wood. He picked it up, realising that this must be the old saint. He began to rub the head of the wood.

"What do you want, child?" was the immediate response.

"Old saint", the boy replied, "instead of remaining in this darkness, let's go out and see the sun on Roc'h Trévézel." And so the boy suddenly found himself on the summit of the crest, still holding the old wooden saint in his hand.

His life thenceforth was transformed by the powers of the little statue. As he came to manhood he had a château, a carriage and horses, all the possessions he could desire. He fell in love with the king's daughter and she eagerly consented to be his wife. On their wedding night she was amazed to see that her new husband carefully placed a mouldy old piece of wood on a table in their bedroom. He explained that it was an old Breton saint to whom he owed the greatest deference and devotion.

But the princess wanted to please her husband, and the next day she sold the old wooden saint to a passing rag-and-bone man and bought instead a new brightly painted saint's statue. Her husband was horrified when he found what she had done. He searched everywhere for the rag-and-bone man and then paid a fortune to get back the little old wooden saint. But his relief was short-lived.

"I can help you no more," said the saint. "I am going back to my mountain to wait until the 1100 years are up and another young man comes to take me from my place and receive good fortune from me."

So the unprepossessing morsel of mouldy wood was in fact the treasure of inestimable value that lay beneath the mountain. And only someone who could see the value of simplicity would appreciate its worth...

The blood-red rocks of Bréhat

The count of Goëlo had two sons. They were the black sheep of the family, given to banditry and bad deeds of all kinds to satisfy their greed. They were so bold as to plan an attack on the Abbaye de Beauport, but the abbot closed the gates against them and called on the armed support of the lord of La Roche-Derrien. The brothers went off in a rage, burning and pillaging as they went home. When their father heard of this latest disgrace, he shut his sons up to prevent further incidents, but they escaped and plotted to kill their father. They promised anyone who would follow them a share in the spoils of their father's estate.

The count got wind of the plan and fled to the Abbaye de Beauport, where the abbot hid him away in the underground tunnels below the building, giving him the abbey's treasure to guard. The brothers gained entry to the abbey by one pretending to be a fugitive from their own violence. The gate-keeper opened the door and was killed at once before the whole gang poured in and sacked the place, killing many of the monks. But they could not find their father or the loot.

The wicked brothers finally made a pact with the Devil in the form of a demon named Golo-Robin, who would help them in exchange for their souls. They found themselves transported to the Île de Bréhat where the secret tunnels came out, in close pursuit of their father who was hampered by the bags of gold. They managed to catch up with their victim on the north coast of the island and slaughtered him in cold blood. They then hoisted the body up onto their shoulders to take it to the cliffs where they intended to hurl it into the depths below. But as they approached the edge with their burden, one on each side of a deep crevice, the two brothers suddenly found themselves rooted to the spot as their feet turned to stone. The body remained slung between them forming an arch over the chasm, and its blood drained and spread over all the surrounding rocks, giving them the distinctive red tint that the Pointe du Paon retains to this very day.

Another tragic chasm

The Gouffre (abyss) in the forest at Huelgoat holds a dreadful secret. If you listen very carefully to the noise of waters plunging over the rocks to the depths, you will hear the sighs of dead men, lovers of Dahut,[1] thrown to their doom from the rock above, following a night of passion.

The Dragon's Rocks (Griffones)

At Stangala, near Quimper, these dramatically placed rocks high above the Odet river were said to be the home of a huge dragon.

The monster terrorised the neighbourhood, demanding the monthly tribute of a maiden whom it quickly devoured. No-one dared to come near the beast, for the merest touch of its poisonous breath was enough to kill a man.

One day an impoverished knight learnt that the girl he loved from afar, daughter of the local lord, was the next chosen victim for the dragon. Although he was too poor to be taken seriously as a suitor, he was determined to save her life, and decided to kill the dragon and put an end to its tyranny once and for all. This he succeeded to do after a gruelling combat, and he then cut out the tongue of the great beast. But as he had been within range of the terrible breath, the knight fell seriously ill and lay almost in a coma for weeks.

---

[1] For her story see page 105 and 245.

Meanwhile the villagers discovered the fate of the dragon and the lord offered his daughter in marriage as reward to the hero who had fulfilled this death-defying task. Another knight immediately claimed to have killed the dragon and was feted as a hero in the area. Preparations began for the wedding.

On his sick-bed, the poor knight heard this devastating news and endeavoured to rouse himself. On the day of the marriage, he struggled up and made his way laboriously to the church. Here he claimed the great victory for himself, and when ridiculed, threw down the dragon's tongue in proof. The lies of the other were exposed and the poor knight married his lady on that very day.

Today the rocks of the dragon's lair are called Griffones, and gargoyles in the shape of dragons and griffons can be seen on the nearby chapel.

The Devil's Works

Many landscape features are associated with legends concerning the devil and bear his name to this day. Two famous examples of distinctive rocky outcrops are Les Roches du Diable (Devil's Rocks) near Le Faouët above the Ellé river and Le Château du Diable (Devil's Castle) on the Pink Granite coast between Perros-Guirec and Ploumanac'h.

Les Roches du Diable (Devil's Rocks)

Near Le Faouët the beautiful Ellé river runs through a granite gorge. It was here that St-Guénolé sought to establish a hermitage, amongst the wild scenery of a boulder-laden hillside. He found natural placements of stones to act as his table, chair and bowl. It was a perfect setting for a life of contemplation and prayer – except that the Devil claimed it as his own. An almighty battle ensued, but the saint was victorious and banished his foe to the opposite bank of the river.

Later St-Guénolé decided he needed a bridge for evangelising a wider area. He made a pact with the Devil to build it in exchange for the soul of the first to cross. The saint made sure this was a squirrel, thus infuriating the Devil who flung himself down into the river, creating the gorge you see today...

The Devil's Grotto

In the granite chaos of Huelgoat lies the La Grotte du Diable, a mysterious subterranean cave above rushing waters. Descend on a metal ladder to get the full experience if you dare![1]

The Devil's Cauldron

One night in the commune of Plouhinec the devil mingled with a crowd of young people dancing in the open air. At midnight he opened up a great cleft in the earth and they all fell down into the flames of hell.

The Devil gets everywhere

At Argol, God agreed to give the Devil all the land between the Tas de Pois and Menez Hom if he could roll a huge stone from Hirgarz to the Bay of Douarnenez. But the devil got exhausted and was forced to abandon the stone at Menez Caon.

At Dingé in Ille-et-Vilaine lies the rock the Devil intended to take to Mont-St-Michel in his struggle with Saint-Michel. It bears the marks of his claws, his buttocks and belt.

At Kerhiec near Guern, the Menhir du Diable bears the Devil's claw marks. He rammed it into the ground in a rage after being cheated in a bargain with the local squire.

---

[1] See a later legend associated with this place on page 285.

Megaliths

Brittany has the greatest concentration of megaliths – monuments from the Neolithic period (c5000-2000BC) – in Europe. These consist of burial sites (cairns, dolmens, tumuli) and standing-stones or menhirs.[1] The latter may stand alone, marking a special spot, or be arranged in alignments with others. At Carnac thousands of stones range across the landscape and a similarly vast configuration once stood at the south-west tip of Brittany around Penmarc'h.

With the advances of science and archaeological techniques we know today a great deal about the burial sites and developing styles and techniques of construction, even though a major question that remains unanswered and probably unanswerable is exactly why the menhirs were erected. The purposes and significance may have varied – boundary markers, territorial statements, ceremonial usage, shipping marks are all possibilities, without even setting foot on the road of astrology.

It is the size and unknown significance that lends mystery to these structures, as well as their often atmospheric relationship to the landscape in which they stand. Given these factors it is hardly surprising that earlier societies interpreted their presence in ways that often involved magical powers and fabulous tales. They appeared to the medieval mind to be the work of giants, or even parts of their body, like the Doigt de Gargantua.[2]

In the 19th century, before contemporary dating techniques could rule out the idea, many believed the megaliths were products of Celtic society, and hence had close connections with Druids. This easily led to stories of human sacrifice on certain stones and claims that some dolmens were actually priests' houses. This period saw a revival of Druidism and names reflecting this often appear in the landscape from that time. The Bois de Kerohou near Mael-Pestivien contains some evocative granite rocks, one called the Chaire des Druides, said to have been used for Druid sacrifice as the marks of a body can still

---

[1] Breton speakers oftenp refer the word *peulven* meaning 'upright stone' rather than *menhir* (long stone), a term invented in the 18th century.

[2] Gargantua's finger is the name of a menhir near Forte La Latte on the Côtes d'Armor coast.

be seen.[1] This title did not figure on the land registry document of 1828. The Hotié de Viviane above the forest of Brocéliande is said to be the secret refuge of the fairy of that name. She would certainly have enjoyed a fabulous view there, but it was (at least originally!) a Neolithic burial place.

Menhirs (and even some dolmens) were often thought to mark spots where buried treasure lay, a belief that led to the destruction of many of these monuments in the scramble to lay hands on the gold. This has given rise to many stories about the stones moving on the eleventh stroke of midnight and returning on the twelfth, providing the narrowest of windows for treasure-seekers! This tale is told of the largest of them all.

Menhir de Kerloas

The tallest upright standing stone (10m) in France is located near St-Renan, north-west of Brest. It was once even taller, but a lightning strike took off the top. It has the common fertility associations encouraged by the shape of many large standing-stones, although here the tradition has a nice twist. Newlyweds came to rub their bellies against the stone, the man in the hope of fathering male children, the woman with the promise of ruling her household.

The legend of Le Bossu (hunchback), as the menhir is known, is that a buried treasure was thought to be concealed beneath it. This could only be seen on Christmas night when the menhir went off to drink at the shore on the first stroke of midnight, but returned before the last peal of the bell, crushing anyone foolish enough to be scrabbling around for gold and riches.

---

[1] The 'victim' must have been extremely tall! Human hands in more recent times seem to have contributed to the shaping, but this is a highly atmospheric site, naturally the source of legends.

Roche aux Fées

This magnificent dolmen at Essé in Ille-et-Vilaine is perhaps the most impressive in Brittany with measurements of 19.5m long, 4.7m wide and 4.1m high. The lintel stone alone weighs about 20 tons. Not surprisingly it has attracted many legends and hence the traditional name 'Fairies' Rock.'

This tale – La Fée des Houx[1] – connected to the Roche aux Fées was recorded by Adolphe Orain in *Contes du Pays Gallo*.

It is said that fairies built this monument to honour their dead. They carried the huge stones under their arms and on their heads for a long way – if a single one fell to the ground, the Devil ensured they had to leave it and go back and get another. This explains the many large stones littered in the surrounding countryside.

An elderly couple lived near the dolmen in a small house with a tall holly tree outside. One night they sat by the hearth exhausted. Jérôme was a woodsman and he was complaining of the weariness in his joints after a day of cutting down trees. His wife Gertrude said he needn't think he was the only one suffering as she had been digging up potatoes and was just as tired as he was. It wasn't right that they should be toiling like this day after day at their age, she reflected miserably.

"Aye, it all goes back to the first woman, Eve," said Jérome.

"You're right," his wife replied. "If it hadn't been for her insatiable curiosity we'd all be living in Paradise."

"Too true, alas," he replied with a sigh.

At that moment they heard a peculiar noise outside, some disturbance that shook all the leaves of the holly tree. They looked out and saw to their amazement that a small, pretty fairy had come down from the tree and was approaching them. She was wearing a garland of holly

---

[1] The holly fairy.

Roche aux Fées

leaves and had little red berries as earrings and a necklace of seeds – she was the Fairy of the Holly Tree.

She spoke to them kindly.

"I heard your worries and I've come to help you. Here is a store of gold coins that will take care of all your needs and never run out. You need never work again! All I require in return is that you help me bury this covered pot in the Roche aux Fées and that you never seek to know what it contains. And you must never breathe a word to another soul about it." Her tone turned solemn. "Be warned! If ever you seek to see inside the pot, all your good fortune will vanish at once and your happiness will be lost."

The old people, amazed at their luck, swore an oath immediately and helped the fairy to carry out her task of burying the pot inside the monument. Then she returned to her tree and they were able to start enjoying their new-found wealth, in a state of great happiness.

The first few days passed in a daze of eating and drinking, and buying useful things for their house. They sat at table for whole days feasting their friends and neighbours. But as the weeks went by, they began to tire of this idle existence, having been used all their lives to the structure of toil and production. Boredom soon set in.

Every day they walked past the Roche aux Fées, and Gertrude never failed to speculate about what might be in that covered pot they had buried. She was sure that it must contain a great secret as the fairy had made such a to-do about leaving it alone. Jérome bid her be silent, knowing that such ideas could only lead to trouble, but his wife turned the same questions over and over in her mind, night and day, believing that an enormous treasure must be in the pot.

"Just think what we could do!" she said to her husband. "With a real treasure we could buy grand houses and lands, which is hardly to be thought of with only a few gold coins! All they're good for is to die of boredom."

She kept up a veritable barrage of complaints like this, all with the object of provoking Jérome to some action, but without success. She even pretended to wake in the night hearing noises coming from the Roche aux Fées, terrible sounds that clearly portended ill for them. Perhaps they'd be accused of a terrible crime, or perhaps they'd be damned for agreeing to such a pact with the fairy!

Finally she herself rose one night, got dressed and went out of the house and across to the Roche aux Fées. She fell on her knees and began scratching away the earth where the pot was buried. Her husband had followed her, but he made no attempt to intervene. Gertrude eagerly pulled out the pot, took off the cover and turned it upside down. They both let out a cry of surprise. For what fell from the pot was not the treasure they had expected, but ashes and bones.

The unfortunate pair both began to cry when they realised their gold coins had already disappeared from the purse in Gertrude's pocket. She scooped the contents of the pot back in, put the cover on and then buried it again in the same place. Then they went back home and she sat in the corner by the hearth sobbing tears of frustration. While they were both still steeped in gloom, the fairy of the holly tree appeared in the doorway.

"And so," she said, "have you both kept your promises?"

"Yes," replied Gertrude at once. "Go and look and you'll see the pot is still in its place." She thought perhaps she could deceive the fairy in this way.

"It's a lie!" said the fairy. "You failed to overcome your curiosity, and so through your own fault you are poor again like before. Do you remember the conversation you were having when I first appeared? Does it become you now, Gertrude, to lay such blame on Eve?"

Legends of standing-stones being petrified human beings are numerous all over Brittany. At Carnac, the legend of St Cornely[1] explains the alignments as Roman soldiers turned to stone by the saint after he faced his pursuers and made the sign of the cross. Three stones at the magnificent Neolithic site of St-Just in Ille-et-Vilaine, Les demoiselles de Cajoux, are said to be young girls who dared to dance on the moor instead of attending a church service and paid a terrible price. Worse, one had a baby...[2] Not far away at Langon[3] a large group of stones has the same name, Les Demoiselles, and the same explicatory story.

One of the most famous legends of this type concerns An Eured Ven (The Stone Wedding Party) in the Monts d'Arrée. This long wavy line of standing-stones running across the moor below Mont St-Michel-de-Brasparts is in legend the petrified remains of a group of revellers returning from celebrating a wedding. They roused the wrath of a priest by not getting out of his way or showing him any respect, hence his curse and their permanent resting place where they stood. The following modern legend adds a new twist to an old tale.

---

[1] See page 84.

[2] There is a small fourth stone lying nearby.

[3] Where the oldest chapel in Brittany, with parts dating back to the Roman occupation, can be found.

An Eured Ven (The Stone Wedding Party)

Everyone knows our story, or the crux of the matter, how we were turned from laughing revellers to lumps of solid stone. How we now sit motionless on the heath, frozen in our folly, evidence of man's power to impose his will on nature. But that is only half the tale...

It was an unforgettable evening, aftermath of a wedding party, a crowd of cheery souls making their way back from Brennilis. We diverted from the route to revive our festivities on the lonely moor, singing and dancing merrily, young men and girls, reluctant to return to sober hearths. We weren't so much drunk as merry, pleased with ourselves, with life and our lot on a fair May evening after a day of celebration.

There was a lot of banter, especially when Lanig tripped headlong into the heather, and when Lom pulled Maï behind a gorse bush for a kiss. It was at that moment someone saw a figure up ahead and called to us to hush our noise. We took no notice, laughing at our own antics, pushing and shoving each other playfully.

The priest was not without a measure of communion wine himself, it seemed to us as he drew near. His path weaved more than the bracken warranted and what sounded like a muffled oath reached us through the gloaming as he missed his step. He was carrying the sacrament, doubtless called reluctantly from his warm fire and full tankard by some old one's final plight.

But when he saw us in our frolics, it was all pride and superiority, the act all the more forceful for its pretence. He ordered us rudely out of his path, and when Lom pointed out the way was wide enough for a herd of cattle let alone free men, he stabbed a finger in the lad's face and told him to get off the moors and away to his bed where God-fearing folk should be. Maï giggled at that point and a few ribald remarks were passed, but we did break ranks to let him through, the sacrament wobbling dangerously as he tried to maintain a dignified gait. All might have been well, had Lom not called after him for a blessing.

The priest turned, face livid, quivering with barely-suppressed indignation. "A blessing you want, is it?" He spat the words into the soft evening air. "Have this from me instead. A curse in God's name to keep you here forever, witness that the mockery of sinners will never triumph over all that's holy." We laughed good-humouredly and waved him on his way, continuing gradually on our journey, straggling across the heath.

After a few moments, a faint cry came from behind where Lom and Maï had lingered but oddly we saw no sign of them. Then Lanig seemed to be missing and then, then suddenly all of us were gone - slowing, stopping, stiffening - until only a line of stones remained where we had stood.

Everyone knows our story, but that was not the beginning at all, and to this day no-one knows the earlier part, the start of it all. For we were not so much men turned to stones, but stones turned to men and then back again, strange as it is to relate.

We were formed from the original rise of Arrée, millions of years in the making, gradually evolving into individuals – you could say the same of men, I suppose, but they had neither our tenacity nor inner strength. It was that strength that caused all the trouble in the end. We made a united stand against Lagad Fall, the wicked wizard bent on destroying this land to find the secret of metal. Below the height of Tuchenn Gador where he had built his lair, we stood shoulder to shoulder, impenetrable and impervious to his magic charms. His frustration at our obstinacy knew no bounds but he did not have the means to destroy us, essence of the earth that we were. Alas he had acquired other powers, of ancient craft and cunning. He knew that in the world of stone there is nothing worse than lively movement. So one day he unleashed a fearful storm over the Arrée and vowed the foulest retribution for our resistance to his domination. He cast a spell and – shocking to relate - transformed us into men. Men destined to remain so in perpetuity and work this stubborn land, in memory of our own obstruction. So in fact on that fatal night of the Wedding Party, we only took back our essential nature and that old priest unknowingly did us an immeasurable favour.

And to this day no-one knows that part of our story.[1]

An Eured Ven
The Stone Wedding Party

[1] Story reprinted from *The Shape of Mist: Tales of the Monts d'Arrée* by Wendy Mewes (2011).

Religious foundations

Abbaye de Bon Repos

One day a nobleman, Alain de Rohan, was hunting in the forest of Quénécan. He finally sank down exhausted in a beautiful spot and had a miraculous dream in which the Virgin Mary appeared and told him to endow an abbey where he had lain. He did so, and this was the origin of the Abbaye de Bon Repos (the Abbey of Good Repose), which lies on the Blavet river near Gouarec.[1]

Chapelle Ste-Barbe, Le Faouët

Jehan de Toulbouden was out on a hunting expedition, separated from his men as he chased a hind through the forest. A terrific storm broke out suddenly and he was forced to seek shelter under an over-hanging rock. All around him lightning flashed and torrential rain caused the rivers to overflow. The power of nature was forcing stones from their places to tumble down the steep hillside and Jehan de Toulbouden was terrified that he would be crushed beneath such a rock-fall. He prayed silently to Ste-Barbe, patroness of those endangered by storms. He promised that he would build a chapel in her honour on the very spot where he knelt in prayer on a narrow ledge of rock, if only she would save him from death. He felt the rock trembling all around him, but no disaster unfolded and he emerged unscathed from the grip of the storm.

He did not forget his pledge and soon after began to erect the chapel promised to Ste-Barbe on the top of the hill where he had so nearly come to grief. But a strange thing happened - each night the work achieved during the day was destroyed by an unseen hand. Recognising the intervention of a higher power, Jehan de Toulbouden

---

[1] This Cistercian foundation was founded in 1184 by decree of Alain de Rohan. What remains can be visited today.

decided he must keep to the letter of his promise and began again, constructing the chapel on the narrow and precarious ledge of rock where he had made his plea for divine protection.

This time all went well, despite the difficulties of the site and the lack of any access road. It was said that each night a pair of fine red oxen brought all the materials necessary for the following day's work. The Chapelle de Ste-Barbe was completed within twenty-five years – quite a feat for the period – and it is one of the most remarkably sited in Brittany, accessible only by a steep stone staircase or a pilgrims' path winding up from the valley below.[1]

Chapelle Ste Barbe, Le Faouët

---

[1] The chapel, in Flamboyant-Gothic style, dates back to 1489. The odd location means there is no room for a nave, but only choir and transept. Some interesting votive offerings to Ste-Barbe, who is also the patron saint of fireman, can be seen inside. Her legend of martyrdom comes from Turkey, where her father beheaded her and was then himself killed by a bolt of lightning.

CHAPTER 6
STORIES OF THE SEA & SHORE

The sea is perhaps the strongest essence of Brittany, important throughout Breton history for trade, fishing and the seaweed industry. The extensive, heavily indented coastline has also brought more than a fair share of maritime raiders, notably Vikings and the English navy, leaving traces of many coastal defence systems from the Iron Age to WWII. The most famous of the Breton sea legends, that of the lost city of Ys, has been told elsewhere,[1] reinforcing the idea that the edge of anywhere is a precarious place.

Added to these practical issues is the semi-mysticism of the sea, born of its deadly power and caprices, its female nature linked to the lure of the moon. This is a realm of sirens and sea spirits who can act for good or ill. It is also the scene of Celtic Paradise, the setting of adventure and danger, tragedy and loss. For coastal communities there is a last symbolic journey across the water after death: on Christmas night the Baie des Trépassés[2] echoes with the cries of souls in agony stuck on the boat and unable to pass over.

---

[1] See page 105.

[2] Bay of the Departed.

Smugglers' tales abound too and there is still the visual evidence of the look-out buildings for spotting incursion or contraband along the Customs' Officers Path, which was the origin of the *sentier côtier* or GR34 coastal footpath. The notorious smuggler 'Cruel Coppinger' who lived in Cornwall is said to have had an estate in Roscoff,

from which smuggling activities were masterminded.[1] Grim stories of wreckers luring ships to destruction on the rocks or lying in wait for natural disasters to bring lost cargoes ashore still cause furious arguments today, but they are of course by no means peculiar to Brittany, although the subject was often romanticised in 19th century art. Similar allegations have always been strong in Cornwall, where a recent serious study failed to find convincing evidence to support popular myths.[2] In Brittany it was said that wreckers tied lamps to cows' horns and then led them on the coastal path to draw ships in towards the light, or that locals lay in wait for ships in trouble in bad weather. The *Gwerz Penmarc'h* describes the bell-towers of Penmarc'h being lit on a stormy night, drawing ships en route from Bordeaux onto the rocks, leaving many women of Audierne as widows:

> *A curse on you folk of Penmarc'h,*
> *For lighting your steeples at night!*

It is more likely that tall stories grew from isolated incidents and soon became judgemental generalisations, another possible development of legends. The geography of dramatic rocky coastline

---

[1] A ballad by the Rev.R.S.Hawker is the source of this legend. Coppinger was probably Irish, but some sources say Danish. There was an 18th century English wine-merchant named Coppinger in Roscoff, but his story may well have been confused with that of another man of the same name. The legendary figure certainly had a reputation for terrible cruelty and was said to be a practised wrecker.

[2] *Cornish Wrecking 1700-1860: Reality and Popular Myth*, Cathryn Pearce (2010).

and severe Atlantic weather fronts contribute to an atmosphere made for such stories. In reality there were comprehensive and complex laws concerning the rights of salvage[1] on the seashore from medieval times, and also many well-documented accounts of islanders and coastal-dwellers acting heroically to save lives at risk of their own in a crisis. Queen Victoria gave the inhabitants of the island of Molène a water cistern in thanks for their efforts when the *Castle Drummond* went down nearby in 1896 with terrible loss of life.

The Blessed Isles

Far out in the western sea, of no precise location, are the Blessed Isles, a paradise awaiting souls after death. Pierre Jakez Hélias has a memorable description:

> **he Irish call them *Tir na n'Og* and the Bretons *Bro ar Re Yaouank*, which is to say the Land of Youth, because time has no meaning for the lucky ones who dwell there. One island or perhaps more, no one can say, but a floating land certainly whether one or several, attached to no continent, never feeling the same wave twice, pausing only an instant beneath each star. This place is much further away than one could possibly say, as far as the furthest nautical mile imaginable, and yet - a single tide will be enough to reach it if the right hour is come.**
>
> **One cannot die when the tide is rising to the full, for it is then that people on the point of death feel a sudden improvement before the end. Their last breath goes out when the sea rests at its high point and it is the ebb tide that launches the soul into the heavy spume of the retreating wave, murmuring as it sweeps the sand with the echo of regrets for earthly life.**

[1] In Brittany *'le droit de bris'* was part of ducal (later the French state) rights which could be sold to local lords or even monasteries. There's a big difference between locals luring ships onto rocks and locals trying to pick up what they could from a wreck to deny officialdom the spoils. A basic argument against the wreckers' tales is that something lit up is to be avoided when at sea.

The Bag Noz (Night boat)

The sea plays a large part in the legendary world of death in Brittany as one would expect from its importance in daily life. The *Bag Noz* was the vessel that carried souls who had passed away. On the west coast, the Baie des Trépassés near the Pointe du Raz has long been associated with dead souls.[1] The boatman is said to be Ankou, or sometimes the first or last dead soul of the year.[2] The dead are carried in a boat from here to the Île de Sein (Enez Sun) and then beyond to a final resting place, but those who have drowned or not been buried with proper ritual are destined to drift on the sea in a state of lamentation. It is said that their sighs can be heard in the Raz de Sein. Many sailors claim to have seen the night boat, and resisted the urge to follow it, making the sign of the cross for self-protection, as the sight of the boat is a harbinger of death.

This eerie sight might appear on the wild and unpredictable waters between the Pointe du Raz and the Île de Sein, a notoriously difficult strait for navigation. It was said that the helmsman of the boat was the last person to be drowned in the area. A woman working in a party of seaweed gatherers at the Pointe de Kilaourou saw the phantom boat and recognised her husband, who had been lost at sea. She called out his name, but the boat went silently on its way, leaving no trace in the water of its passage.

Sailors returning from their fishing-grounds have seen the boat and sometimes tried to go to its aid, believing it to be in danger, but the mysterious vessel simply disappears or seems in an instant to jump a great distance towards the horizon. One night a pilot boat from the Île de Sein came very close to the phantom boat. The skipper could see a single figure aboard, at the helm. He called out, offering help, but there was no reply. At a single movement of the rudder, the boat disappeared...

[1] This may stem from a confusion between Anaon (departed soul) and An Aon (the river), the latter a reference to the waterway emptying into the bay.

[2] Around the Gulf of Morbihan the *Bag Noz* is described as manned by devils, fierce dogs and the souls of criminals.

In coastal communities, death by drowning has always been a deep-felt fear. The lack of a body to bury added to the grief, because without the proper rituals of mass and burial, the dead were condemned as lost souls. At Plogoff near the Pointe du Raz tradition said a candle should be placed on a circle of rye bread and sent out to sea. The bread will return to land in the spot where the corpse can be found. The Baie des Trépassés and the caves at Morgat were the places where tides often carried the bodies.

Yann an Aod - be very afraid...

A traditional figure of fear, used as a warning to children not to linger outside at night! His name means John of the Shore, and he is particularly associated with Pays Bigouden and the Odet river around the Moulin de Rossulien, south of Quimper.

It is in the changing light of dusk that the tall, sombre figure of Yann an Aod wanders the shore. He calls out to anyone he sees, imitating a normal cry of peasants returning to their homes after a hard day's work in the fields. But if anyone dares to respond and approach, he seizes on his victim and drowns or strangles him.

Once a young man had the temerity to call back, feeling that Yann an Aod was far away, but suddenly found himself face to face with him. He ran away at top speed to his house and plunged through the door, only to feel an enormous kick up the backside as he fell indoors. The young man escaped with his life, but for two months after, he suffered from terrible sickness.

Another version describes how if anyone replies, Yann an Aod in the blink of an eye halves the distance between them. He calls again and if there is a second echo, again the space separating him from his potential victim is halved. At the third response, he is right up close...

Sirens

Mari Morgan are female spirits, 'born of the sea,' often living in caves along the shore. They may be malevolent, calling seductively to lure sailors and fishermen to their deaths, but they have other powers. The most famous of them all, Dahut,[1] can calm a stormy wind if so she wills.

Sirens are traditionally women, although in Brittany the island of Ouessant has another legend telling of the Morganed and Morganezed, male and female members[2] of a siren people who have an underwater kingdom, and also play on the shore and comb their long blond hair.

The following tale was told to Luzel in 1873 by Marie Tual, an inhabitant of the island of Ouessant.

Once upon a time on the island of Ouessant, there was a beautiful young girl named Mona Kerbili. Her father Fanch was a fisherman and her mother Jeanne grew vegetables and grain on their small patch of land or spun flax in their thatched cottage. Mona's beauty was noted by all, and some said she must be the daughter of a Morgan, although her mother vehemently denied it. In fact even the Morganed were amazed at her stunning appearance for they saw her as she went to the beach every day with friends to collect shell-fish and crabs among the rocks.

Often their girlish talk turned to young men, but Mona was full of disdain for the rough sons of the soil who had only a life of hardship as fishermen ahead of them.

"I am too beautiful for that kind of life," she said. "I want to marry a prince, or the son of a great nobleman – or even a Morgan!"

At that moment, an old Morgan who had overheard all this leapt from behind a rock and carried the girl off, down under the sea to a great palace, for he was indeed the king of the Morganed. He was determined to have Mona for

---

[1] See page 108.

[2] Singular Morgan and Morganez.

147

himself, but his handsome young son fell in love with the girl on sight and begged to be allowed to marry her.

The King refused. "No son of mine will marry a daughter of the soil," he said. "In that case," his son replied, "I won't marry at all." His father flew into a rage at this and immediately arranged a marriage between his son and a Morganez, daughter of one of his advisors. The wedding was to take place at once, and preparations were made to leave for the church.[1]

The king told Mona she must remain in the kitchens and prepare a wedding feast. If she failed in this task, she would be put to death. All she was given were empty saucepans and a few old shells. She wept bitterly, in utter despair at the hopelessness of her situation. But on the way to the church, the prince stopped and said he had forgotten the ring. His father tried to go with him, but the young man rushed off and reached the palace where he found Mona still crying.

"Don't worry," he said. "I will help you." He called out to the fireplace and at once a blaze sprang up, then he touched the handles of the saucepans and commanded each to produce a different dish. In this way, Mona would have nothing to do but serve up the feast.

The prince rejoined the wedding party and was married to the Morganez. They returned to the palace and the King was astonished to find the banquet Mona had produced. He knew that only through magic could she have succeeded in the task.

After the lavish meal followed by music and dancing, the newly-weds were to retire for the night. The King told Mona to go with them and to hold a lighted candle in their bed-chamber. He had decided that when it was burnt right down, she would die. He stationed himself in the adjoining room, and called out every so often "Is the candle still

---

[1] The story-teller added that they even had churches in this underwater kingdom and bishops, although they were not Christians.

burning?" His son would reply "Yes", because he knew his father's plan, but he could see that eventually Mona would no longer have a candle to hold. He waited until it was nearly finished and then said to his bride, who knew nothing of the king's intention, that she should hold the candle for a moment. She obeyed him, and at that very moment the King called out "Is the candle still burning?" "No," said the prince. The King rushed into the darkened room and cut off the head of the girl holding the candle stub. Then he left.

The next morning, the prince said to his father that he would like to marry. "But you got married only yesterday," he said, puzzled. "True, but I am already a widow." "What? Have you killed your wife?" asked the astonished king. "No, father, but you have. You burst into my chamber last night and cut off her head."

The king rushed up to the bedroom and saw the evidence of what he had done. He knew that he was beaten, and allowed the marriage of his son to Mona to take place. The young husband adored his wife and there was love and harmony between them, but after some time Mona began to long to see her family again and thought constantly of the little cottage where she had grown up. She confided in her husband and reluctantly he agreed that she should visit the island. He made a crystal bridge appear to carry them over the sea and they set off, with the old king following behind. As they neared the shore, the prince caused the bridge to disappear, throwing his father into the waves.

He told Mona that he would wait for her on the shore. She must return before midnight and must not, on any account, embrace anyone on the island or she would be cut off from her beloved husband. She agreed and set off joyfully for the family home. Here she found her parents at a simple meal. At first they did not recognise her, so grand and rich did she appear, but when they did, all were overwhelmed with tears and laughter and hugged each other happily. The moment Mona touched her parents, she lost all memory of what had happened to her with the Morganed and her marriage. She went back to her old life, sleeping in the tiny cot bed and tending the vegetable plot for her mother. Time passed and she thought of nothing but the life she was leading now. Many tried to woo her but she had no interest in getting wed and was content to remain with her parents.

But sometimes at night when the wind howled around the rafters, she seemed to hear cries outside the cottage. She imagined they were the restless spirits of unburied shipwreck victims and prayed with all her heart for them to find peace. One night, however, a single voice became clear to her and she heard the words of her Morgan husband, bemoaning her loss and begging her to return. At once she remembered all that had happened and her great love for the prince. She went out to him and they returned to their underwater kingdom. Nothing was ever heard of Mona again on the island.

Ouessant

Also from Ouessant...

One day two little girls were looking for pretty shells on the beach when they saw a Morganez laying out treasures on a sheet in the sunshine. The girls went closer out of curiosity and came right up without being seen. When the Morganez saw that they were just sweet, harmless children, she smiled kindly and gave each of them a treasure. But she warned them that they were not to look at what she had folded in their aprons until they reached home.

They set off at a run, but one of the girls could not wait to see her prize and opened her apron. All she found was a handful of horse-dung. The other, however, went straight back to her parents without peeping and together they marvelled at the wonderful treasure. It made them rich, and they and their descendants lived well on the proceeds in a beautiful house on the island, all thanks to a spirit of the sea.

The following story is told by Pierre Jakez Hélias:

Once upon a time the Île aux Moines and the Île d'Arz in the Gulf of Morbihan were not separate islands, but joined by a causeway. There was nevertheless a great difference between the economic status of the two. Large ships from the Île-aux-Moines sailed far and wide bringing commercial prosperity to the island, but the inhabitants of the Île d'Arz remained poor fishermen. For this reason there was consternation when a young nobleman from the Île-aux-Moines fell deeply in love with the daughter of a family on the neighbouring island. Apart from her great beauty, this girl had the voice of an angel, so remarkable that when she sang all stopped what they were doing to listen, enchanted by the sweet sound. But the young man's parents determined that he would never marry beneath them, and asked the monks to shut him up in the island's monastery to break up the young lovers. Even then the

151

power of love seemed to triumph as every day the girl made her way across the causeway and sang outside the walls of his prison, keeping alive their hopes of mutual devotion. The monks stopped mid-service to listen to the miraculous voice echoing around the monastery. The prior regarded this as proof of the Devil's hand and he determined to put a stop to it once and for all. Next day, the causeway between the islands had disappeared and the girl could no longer express her longings to her lost love. Mad with despair, she threw herself into the sea. But her magical voice was not entirely lost, for she became a siren of sea, offering up a song of grief which can still be heard even today...

Emile Souvestre preserved many Breton tales and songs in his work *Les derniers Bretons* and *Le foyer breton*, published in the mid-19th century. Although in the context of a lake rather than the sea, this is his version of a siren in the making.

princess was demanded in marriage by a powerful lord but she did not want to marry him. Thinking to impose an impossible condition she said, "I will be yours when your boating lake flows into the Lac du Duc." He determined to make her keep her promise, and had a great canal constructed between the two stretches of water so that his lake did indeed flow into that of the duke.

He then invited the princess to a celebration at his castle and took her in a boat on his lake before sailing along the canal to the other to show her that he had fulfilled her conditions and now expected to marry her. Distraught, because in fact her heart was engaged elsewhere, she threw herself overboard, sinking to the depths of the Lac du Duc, which became her home. Later on she was sometimes seen early on summer mornings, sitting on a rock, combing her long hair of green seaweed.

One day a soldier saw her there and was captivated, creeping up unseen to get close to the object of his desire. But the Morganez grasped him firmly in her arms and dragged him down, down, down to the bottom of the lake.

In his work 'Littérature orale de la Haute-Bretagne' (1881), Paul Sébillot describes the houles, the name given to marine grottoes and caves in Ille-et-Vilaine and the non-Breton speaking parts of Côtes du Nord.[1]

Some of the *houles* are flooded at high tide, others remain free of the sea. There are many such places at Cancale, Saint-Briac, Saint-Jacut, Saint-Cast and Cap Fréhel, where there are at least a dozen.

The imagination of the inhabitants of these coasts has peopled these caves with fantastic and mysterious creatures. This is the home of fairies, who live with their husbands and children, coming out as night falls to stroll on the cliffs or on the water. According to several of my story-telling sources, their grandparents knew these beings well enough, but today they have disappeared, quitting our shores at the time of the French Revolution.

Every *houle* I know has a legend, often several ... and it seems to me they are most curious and striking of all the tales told in Pays Gallo.[2]

Sébillot also wrote of the *lutin*[3] Nicole who was notorious around St-Malo and in the Bay of St-Brieuc in the early 19th century.

It was impossible for fishermen to carry out their work without being impeded. Nicole shot through the nets or tangled them, or some times he pulled them so forcefully that the ties came loose and fishermen had to fasten them

---

[1] This was the name of the department of Côtes d'Armor up until the 1990s.

[2] The east of Brittany where Gallo rather than Breton was spoken.

[3] See page 170.

to the benches of the boat, waiting for Nicole's next caprice as his mischievous humour would surely target another object. He often jumped into the middle of all the little fish caught in the nets and made holes in the mesh so they could escape. It also amused him to lift the anchors of the oyster-boats while the sailors were trawling along the oyster banks in their light skiffs: then they only just had time to rush back and make the drifting boat secure. Often too Nicole took the dragnet and tangled it in the other nets.

He also enjoyed changing the position of vessels, twisting up the cables, or even taking the shape of a porpoise to frolic about among the fleet of boats.

Many fishermen claim to have seen Nicole. A captain at St-Briac avowed that he could tie such knots as only an experienced sailor would know, and that he thought it fun to swap anchors, giving a sailing ship the grappling irons of a fishing-boat and vice versa. A certain Rose Piron told the story that Nicole first appeared on Ascension Day when fishermen of Saint-Cast went to sea despite the will of the priest. The fish were rising up to the sea surface and spitting "mouthfuls of fire".

He played many jokes on the fishermen and each time he arrived and managed to confound them, you could hear him guffawing by the boat. One day he made the oars of a fishing boat fall in the water and then led the craft far out to sea where there was no controlling it. When the fisherman saw himself so far out, he said "Nicole, it was you who threw my oars out and led me here. Now you must take me back to port." Nicole was in a good humour that day, and he brought the boat back safely into harbour.

But what happened to Nicole? Did he take ship for Newfoundland one day with the cod fishermen and never return, or did a sprinkling of holy water put an end to his tricks when he was about to displace a ship during its blessing...

Perhaps the most famous port in Brittany, St-Malo has an extraordinary heritage of explorers and corsairs as well as maritime commerce and fishing. It is a town inextricably linked with the sea. The English navy regarded it as a 'wasps' nest' of danger and in 1693 sent a boat packed with explosives, the *Infernal Machine*, on the tide against the city walls. It blew up short and failed to harm its target.

Cat's Gold

Many fairies dwelt on the beaches and in the waves around St-Malo. A group of them liked to dance on the sands at night. One evening they were accosted by a bunch of young men who were a lot the worse for drink after a night on the town. They wanted to join the dance, but the fairies soon realised that the youths had neither the stamina nor the skill to be worthwhile partners and in annoyance they tapped them with their magic wands and turned them into six black tom-cats and six white she-cats.

The poor animals ran about crying their distress until the fairies relented a little and set them a task in order to gain their freedom. They were to make a golden robe and a silver dress for each fairy from the mica sand[1] on the beach. The other condition was that they could only work during the twelve strokes of midnight...

A long time later the garments were complete and the fairies kept their word, turning the cats back into young men. 'Cat's silver' is now the name of the grey mica on the beach and when the light reflects a golden sheen, it becomes 'Cat's gold' in memory of the robes made for the Ladies of the Sea.

Two helpful saints...

St-Lunaire arrived from Ireland on the north coast of Brittany in his little boat. He was well pleased with the spot where he landed but after a few days the mist came

[1] Mica is a group of sheet silicate minerals, commonly found in granite and gneiss which are both widespread in Brittany. In sand form, it shimmers.

in from the sea, so thickly that he couldn't see his hand in front of his face. He finally got in such a rage of frustration that he drew his sword and began to hack at the mist as if it was his opponent in a duel. When the mist cleared, the saint was able to make his way over the rocks of Décollé, where his footprints can still be seen.

From this story, St-Lunaire has become the patron saint of the mist for sailors, who invoke him when their vision is impaired.

Saint Clement set out to walk across the bay between Saint-Servan and Saint-Malo, wearing his customary anchor round his neck[1]. When the tide rushed in, the anchor weighed him down so he was not able to move quickly enough to escape. He sank beneath the waves and was drowned.

A year later a women out on the flats searching for shell-fish at an exceptionally low tide saw a body on the sand. She recognised it as that of the saint himself. She was carrying her little son, and put the child down as she knelt in prayer by St-Clement's corpse. So fervently and at such length did she pray that not only did the tide began to trickle in around her knees before she realised her danger, but she forgot her son in her sudden rush to safety, leaving him to the mercy of the waves.

A year later at the time of the same very low tide she went back to the spot where she had found the saint's body. Lying in its place was that of her son. When she went up, she saw in wonder that the boy woke from sleep, rubbed his eyes and called for his mother – a miracle for which she ever after thanked St-Clement.

---

[1] Clement was said to have been martyred by the Roman emperor Trajan, being thrown into the sea with an anchor round his neck. Hence he is a patron saint of mariners.

Gwin Zegal

This unusual little port on the Côte de Goëlo consists of tree trunks placed in the sea for moorings. It was only established in 1854, but its striking appearance, especially at low tide when the gaunt trunks are fully exposed, gave rise to the legend that robbers were tied there to drown when the sea rushed in.

Danger from the sea

This gloomy story reflects a serious historical reality, when coastal dwellers were often in danger not only of being attacked, but even snatched from their homes for evermore.

One day a Saxon[1] ship put in to the estuary of the Dourduff for a short stop, and they seized a young maid who was walking by the shore at that fatal moment. Her name was Marivonig and she came from Plougasnou. A prisoner on the boat, she gazed across the water at her receding homeland.

---

[1] Saxon = English (Saoz in Breton).

"Goodbye, my dear father" she said to herself. "You will never receive a suitor for me over your threshold, nor a fiancé with a ring. Goodbye my dear mother, your daughter can no longer finish her tasks with you, now she must serve a foreign captain and his hundred and one sailors."

The red-haired captain commanded Marivonig to come into his bed-chamber on the ship, but she asked for a little time to take the air on deck and he agreed, telling her only not to be too long. At once, the girl threw herself overboard, calling on her protectress, the Virgin Mary.

Marivonig fell like a stone to the bottom of the ocean, but there a tiny fish took pity on her and swum beneath her, miraculously supporting the maid on his back up to the surface again. Once there, the fish gave her a little push and the wind took her at once back to her father's courtyard. He watched in silence as she made three circuits of the house, and then on completion of the last one, she fell dead...

Below is an extract from a ballad published by Luzel. Its subject perhaps dates right back to events of the 9th century and Viking raids in the Trégor.[1] The title *Bleizi Mor* or Sea Wolves refers to the savage invaders.

> *Ships of wolves of the sea have come*
> *To bring warfare upon your home;*
> *They have taken old Yaudet town*
> *And the church there they have burnt down...*
>
> *Nobody will stay any more,*
> *For fear of them, next to the shore.*
> *Fields, houses, cattle and men*
> *Are ransacked again and again.*[2]

---

[1] Remains of a Viking camp can still be seen at Péran, near St-Brieuc.

[2] Translated by Christian Souchon, who has kindly given permission for his work to appear here. His website pages on the Barzaz Breiz (http://chrsouchon.free.fr/barzaze.htm) provide a very useful resource in Breton/French/English.

The Black Rocks of Penmarc'h

This story is the basis of Chaucer's Franklin's Tale[1], which mentions the 'blakkes rokkes' of Penmarc'h in the opening lines. Visiting *Les Rochers* at nearby St-Guénolé today gives an idea of the dangerous reality of this shore.

Arveragus of Kerrud was very happily married to his wife Dorrigen. They lived by the sea in Penmarc'h, the south-west tip of Brittany. In the age of medieval chivalry, it was necessary for a knight to win fame and prowess through deeds of arms in tournaments and jousting. Arveragus decided to go to Great Britain to participate in these competitions to make his name.

His departure left Dorrigen in misery. She feared for his safety, not only in the combats he would face, but also on the dangerous journey back to her. Every day she walked by the sea, thinking of her beloved husband, and looking with despair at the black rocks barring the way into the harbour. Her thoughts became more and more obsessive as she feared for Arveragus' safe return. What a terrible irony if he triumphed against his peers only to return to a fatal accident so near to home!

Dorrigen's friends tried to distract her from these morbid thoughts with songs and dancing amongst flowers in the meadows. But her heart was too heavy and she always wandered away, bent on her own fixation about her husband's return.

A certain young man called Aurelius, a fine singer, had long been attracted to Dorrigen. Secretly he composed songs in her honour and for a time kept his feelings to himself, but one day they burst out and he begged her to have mercy on him in his passion. Dorrigen was horrified at first at his boldness, but as he continued to importune her, she responded in what was intended as a form of mockery.

---

[1] From the famous collection of Cantebury Tales, published in the 14th century.

"Very well," she said at last. "I will agree to become your lover when you make all those black rocks so hazardous to sailors disappear. You have no hope of favour from me until this is done."

Aurelius made a passionate appeal to the goddess of the Moon to aid him in his task and send a tide high enough to enable safe sailing over the rocks for the next two years. But there was no response.

Arveragus returned home safely soon after this event, and Dorrigen rejoiced to have her beloved husband back in her arms. How sweet was their reunion! How happily their life together continued!

But Aurelius did not desist from his desires, now that Dorrigen's promise had been given. He began to consult books of magic for supernatural ways to win his lady. His brother heard of a sorcerer near Orleans who could create the greatest illusions in the world, and they had him brought to Penmarc'h to see if he could magic away the fearsome black rocks. And it so happened that he could. The sorcerer clapped his hands and the sea at once appeared calm and smooth, with no trace of the sharply crested dark rocks of Dorrigen's nightmares.

Aurelius in triumph demanded that Dorrigen keep her promise. The poor woman was broken by her grief and the result of her folly. She was forced to confess what she had promised to her husband. For Arveragus, fine knight that he was, it was a matter of honour. His wife must go to the house of Aurelius and obey all the wishes of this man as she had promised she would if the rocks disappeared.

With a broken heart Dorrigen made her way to the house of Aurelius. But when he saw her grief and heard of the magnanimity of her husband, he could not go through with his claim, and released the lady from her promise, escorting her back to her rightful home. And there she and her husband lived happily for the rest of their lives. As for the rocks – of course, they reappeared, and are there still to this very day.

Black Rocks, Penmarc'h

CHAPTER 7
STRANGE CREATURES GREAT AND SMALL

One of the most enduring (and, some would say, endearing) symbols of Brittany is the korrigan, the little gnome that figures so largely in the legends of Basse Bretagne. But there are plenty of other 'little people' in the oral tradition of the region as a whole, and each may have their own distinctive characteristics and practices. At the other end of the scale are the giants, with their often especially obnoxious habits, commonly held in European tales to have been the earliest inhabitants of many areas, before civilisation took hold.

A 'David and Goliath' story

There is a tradition of enmity between these creatures great and small. The following tale from the Crozon peninsula provides one example of this rift. There are some remarkable rock formations around the Pointe de Dinan with its dramatic arch linking the mainland to the natural outcrop called the 'Château de Dinan' for its citadel-like shape.

Deep in the mists of time, there was a great falling out between the giants and the little people. A group of the latter lived in a huge cave under the arch of the Château de Dinan near Camaret.

Château de Dinan

They passed their time with music and dancing, catching fish and collecting seaweed, which they dried on the rock and then smoked. It would have been a good and happy life, were it not for the giants who lived above in the château.

These giants were cruel creatures, wreckers who liked to feast on human flesh. They passed their time hurling great rocks as far as they could for sport, shaking the very foundations of the rock, that is to say the grotto that housed their small neighbours.

The little people were anxious to find a way of living in greater harmony with their crude neighbours and tried to be friendly, but the giants, who were not very bright, misunderstood their overtures and made an attack on them during the night. The little people, however, had built a great fire for smoking the seaweed in their cave, and once the giants rushed in they blocked the entrance and left them to suffocate to death.

Then the corpses of the giants turned to great slabs of rock, and so the victors danced a celebratory dance on the new floor, over the dead bodies of their enemies...

Giants

Almost every department in France has its Gargantua stories, but Brittany's powerful oral traditions have preserved the greatest number by far, with hardly a district escaping these tall tales. Many legends here relate to this giant, immortalised by the poems of Rabelais,[1] but deriving from much earlier legends. The giant motif is pretty universal in world folklore, used often as an explanation of landscape features.[2] Before the Age of Enlightenment and scientific analysis, it is not surprising that 'inexplicable' phenomenon like the megaliths, whose true purpose was not apparent, were thought of as

---

[1] Rabelais (c1485-1553) was a doctor as well as the author of satirical works, such as Gargantua. Published in 1534, this novel was controversial for its graphic scatology.

[2] See Chapter 5.

being works of an age when giants walked the earth. There are also echoes of tales from other cultures – classical mythology has many stories of Giants eating children and fighting Olympian gods.

Giants by their physical nature are representatives of great bodily powers, rarely matched by their intellects, although low cunning is often present. The one-eyed Cyclops of Homer's Odyssey is a familiar example, although modern works like the Harry Potter series still make use of the type. The crude, raw strength of giants is often expressed in cannibalism and remarkable feats of lifting and throwing. Generally they represent a primitive age before a sense of community developed and society established rules and modes of behaviour.

Gargantua in Haute-Bretagne

The locations tie this tale to eastern Brittany, but the story-line is well-known in many other traditions.

One day Gargantua saw a tiny boat emerging from a creek in the Rance. Bending down he saw it contained a water fairy, and he instantly fell in love with her. At first she fled in fright at the sound of his booming voice, but finally he won her over with his devotion. He was keen to marry her, but the water nymph's relatives made it a condition that there should be no children of the match. Gargantua agreed to honour this promise. Unfortunately they forgot to invite an evil spirit to their wedding, and in revenge he made the fairy fall pregnant to the giant. When she told Gargantua, he said they must not break the terms of the marriage, and that he would eat any babies on birth.

The fairy wanted to prevent this and confided her dilemma to the midwife. This woman told her not to worry: she would present Gargantua with a baby goat, tightly wrapped in swaddling clothes, and the real baby would be taken down into the underwater world of the water spirits to be brought up safely. The plan went smoothly, but it had to be repeated as more pregnancies followed. Gargantua

unknowingly devoured a piglet, a puppy, a lamb, a heifer and a foal, believing them to be his own children.

But with the seventh child, Gargantua happened to be present at the birth and the midwife had to think quickly. She wrapped an enormous rock in baby clothes and presented it to the giant. Unfortunately, this was to prove his undoing. First he broke off a tooth biting on the rock and stuck this in the ground.[1] Next he had such a stomach-ache that he went to St-Malo and drank all the water in the Channel, swallowing an English fleet that was passing.[2] They hadn't a clue where they were and fired canons which caused him further pain. Finally he consulted a doctor who told him to go to India. There Gargantua vomited up the fleet, but then fell dead. The Himalayas were created as his tomb.

Sailors troubled by mist on the Côte d'Emeraude give warning that they will call on the giant for help if it doesn't disperse…

Returning from Jersey to Plévenon, Gargantua swallowed all the sea mist. It remained trapped in his stomach for three days and three nights before he finally vomited it all up. The giant warned the mist that if he ever saw it again he would keep it in his paunch forever. The mist was so frightened that it was not seen again until long after Gargantua's death.

And from Basse Bretagne

Another anachronism typical of these stories from oral tradition.

Gargantua was so huge that the bell-tower of Pleyben church, one of the finest in the area, did not even come up to the giant's bottom. But the pinnacle did give his thigh a nasty scratch: "Well, I'll be damned," he said, "the ferns round here are tall."

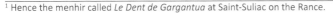

[1] Hence the menhir called *Le Dent de Gargantua* at Saint-Suliac on the Rance.

[2] An amusing anachronistic reference to St-Malo's later tussles and trade-wars with British corsairs and fleets in the 16-18th centuries.

The Giant Goulaffre

This horrible, convoluted tale related by Barbe Tassel at Plouaret in 1869 depicts the giant as a primitive, savage monster beyond the pale of society, who must be destroyed.

There was once a poor widow named Godic, who lived in a hut with her little son Allanic. Every day she went out begging all around the countryside, calling at houses and manors asking for food, and with a handful of barley here and a buckwheat crêpe there she managed to bring up a strong and healthy boy. When he was about fourteen, neighbours began to say to Godic that it was time the young man went out to work and supported her after all she had done for him. Allanic was not averse to this and announced that he would set off for France to seek his fortune and be able to care for his mother as she deserved. She did not want him to go but knew it was inevitable.

Allanic set off with a bundle of food – a rye loaf and six crêpes – tied to his staff. After a few hours on the road, he stopped to rest and have a bite to eat beside the clear water of a *fontaine*. Here he met another traveller, who introduced himself as Fistilou, a dancer. "And I'm a musician," responded Allanic. "But where is your instrument?" asked his new acquaintance.

Allanic jumped over the bank into a field of rye, selected a straw and soon fashioned a little whistle. He began to play a lively melody and Fistilou danced, throwing his hat into the air and shouting "*Iou, hou*", in the way of dancers from Cornouaille. The pair were well pleased with each other and went on to the nearest town. There they performed in the street, Allanic playing his whistle whilst Fistilou danced. To their amazement they got an enthusiastic reception from the people, who showered them with coins.

This prompted the ambitious Fistilou to think that if they had a proper instrument, they'd soon be rich, so the money was spent on a violin and Allanic tried to get the hang of it before the next town. But here they were not only badly received but abused with insults and even had stones thrown in their direction. So they went on, disappointed, and Allanic soon made himself another straw whistle.

In the evening they reached a château with towering walls. The entrance door-knocker was so high they couldn't reach and Fistilou had to stand on Allanic's shoulders. The door opened and they stepped into a garden where two very large young girls were strolling. The two young men began to play and dance and the girls rushed over to watch them, excited by this distraction in their monotonous lives, for these were the daughters of the giant Goulaffre and they were always kept inside the walls. When their giantess mother came out to call them to dinner they begged that the young men should be allowed to stay, but fearing her husband's reaction, she hid them in an old sideboard when he came in to eat.

The first thing the giant said when he entered was "I smell Christian, and I will eat him!" His wife explained who the young men were and asked that they should be spared for the amusement of their daughters. Goulaffre let them sit at the table and offered them each a foot of the roast Christian he was eating. After the terrifying meal, Allanic and Fistilou were shown upstairs by their hostess with the girls to a large chamber. She gave them red hats to put on, whilst the girls had white hats. Soon the young giantesses were snoring away, but the two men lay awake wondering how to escape and suspicious of what might befall them during the night. Finally they had the idea of swapping hats with the girls in case of any foul play, and kept to their beds, facing the wall.

Soon after they heard the giant lumbering up the stairs. He entered the chamber carrying a huge knife. Seeing the two red hats he pounced on his own daughters, cut off their heads and took the bodies down to the kitchens ready to be cooked the next day. Meanwhile Allanic and Fistilou used their sheets as a rope, descended from the tower and ran away as fast as they could.

In the morning, Goulaffre discovered his terrible mistake and was full of grief and rage. He put on his seven league boots and determined to catch the two young men. When he passed above them, they hid under one of the granite boulders strewn across the landscape. Later they came across the giant sleeping in a valley. Fistilou proposed that they should steal his magic boots and use them to travel a great distance and be safe from the giant's revenge. This they did, despite a hairy moment when the giant appeared to wake.

Allanic carried Fistilou on his back and with the help of the boots they were in Paris in a few moments. Here they entered the service of the king, where Fistilou was prone to boast of their adventures and Allanic impressed the young princes by appearing to be a much better hunter than they were, by virtue of secretly using the special boots to cover a vast area in a short time. When the king heard of their exploits, he summoned Allanic and questioned him about the giant.

"For you see," he said, "Goulaffre once stole two precious things from me. If only I could get back that half-moon that lit up the palace! Then I should be truly happy." His voice changed to an order. "You must get it for me!" "But, sir," said Allanic, "it is certain death for me!" "If you don't," was the response, "I will have you put to death anyway."

So Allanic went and managed to steal the half-moon from the highest tower, as roofers had left their ladders in place. But Goulaffre saw him go and knew who had robbed him. Soon the king called on Allanic again and demanded – on pain of death - that he retrieve a golden cage Goulaffre had once taken. Again Allanic had no choice, but he demanded special cutting tools to be made, because he knew the cage hung over the giant's own bed. This time the giant woke up as the last chain was cut and he seized Allanic and vowed to eat him. But Allanic spoke up sharply and said that the giant knew nothing about cooking. Human flesh tasted best when put in a sack and beaten to a pulp with a tree-trunk before being put in a casserole pot. So Goulaffre tied him in a sack and went to uproot a tree. Allanic called out to the giantess, who was unaware of his identity, and claimed to be a poor man with starving children. She let him out and he tied her in the bag, so Goulaffre savagely killed his own wife by mistake.

Allanic returned with the cage, but the king was still not satisfied. It was not long before he demanded that Allanic bring him the giant himself. The resourceful young man made a plan and the king provided him with a vast golden carriage that could not be unlocked from the inside. He then drove off and at last came near the château where he met the sad giant pacing back and forth swearing oaths of vengeance on Allanic. In disguise, Allanic hailed him and asked what the matter was. When Goulaffre told him and said he would devote himself to finding this villain, Allanic said "That's easy, I know him. Get in and I'll take you." Once in, Goulaffre could not get out. They went all the way to Paris and stopped in the palace courtyard. But the fearful noise and roars of the giant inside terrified everyone and no-one would open the carriage door. Finally Allanic suggested that he drive the carriage to an open space and surround it with bonfires so the giant would perish in the flames.

This was done and at last the king was happy. And so was Allanic who married the princess. And so was Fistilou, who Allanic made general of the army.

But no-one relates if Allanic remembered his poor old mother back in Brittany and made her happy too.

Little people

Stories of the 'Little People' abound in cultures all over the world, and there are many different manifestations of these characters in Breton life and legend, with different names according to the location or to the teller of the tale. It is impossible to assert an exact description for each one or to make a clear distinction between nains (dwarves/gnomes) and *korrigans*, *korrigans* and *lutins* or *lutins* and *folliked*.

The terms '*nains*' (dwarves) and '*lutins*' (imps/elves) are both sometimes used collectively to cover all the subdivisions and overlaps of *korrigans* (*nozegans* in the area around Vannes), *poulpiquets*, *poulpicans*, *follets*, *folliked*, *bugel-noz*, *korils*, *boudiks*, etc. in a full list of small creatures which inhabit the shadowy 'other world' of the Breton landscape.

Descriptions from those who claim to have seen them or who have been told in stories passed down through families reflect this variety. Often the expression 'little black men' is used, with the addition of long hair and large hats which conceal their faces. Nozegans may be green or yellow, or around Lorient white and dressed in a cabbage leaf, according to one account. Others wear short trousers and a loose shirt, whilst at Port-Louis the males wore a flat hat with a ribbon which trailed down their backs, whilst the females sported little purple bonnets.

They are largely nocturnal beings, and they love to sing and dance in the round[1] in a lonely spot, or sit around the hearth in a house when the humans have retired to bed in the case of more domestic little people. Their relationship with humans may be positive and close or potentially dangerous, as the stories below illustrate. Certainly it is not a good idea to fall foul of these tiny but very powerful creatures.

---

[1] Their dance lasts all night and is far too strenuous for any human to endure. The methods of extricating oneself unharmed from the circle are precarious, like taking off your clogs and placing them exactly where you will land at the end of the first round, or planting a staff in the ground and holding onto it at the same moment of the dance. Some unfortunate souls were literally danced to death.

Les Nains (goblins/dwarves)

La Villemarqué records this typical story of man's greed for goblin gold. Because of the dwarf or korrigan connection with underground they are known to have a great fondness for precious metals, and stores of this wealth in their possession. Here the *nains* seem indistinguishable from *korrigans*, singing their favourite song.[1]

Tall Paskou, a tailor, became a thief one Friday evening.

He could no longer make trousers, as all the men had left for war against the army of the king of France.

So he took his spade to search for gold in the goblins' cave. When he uncovered the treasure he bundled it up and rushed home.

But soon the goblins came searching...

Close the door, lock it carefully – here come the goblins of the night!

Monday, Tuesday, Wednesday... and Thursday... and Friday...

Look, they are entering the courtyard; those who dance until no breath remains.

Monday, Tuesday, Wednesday... and Thursday... and Friday...

Here they are climbing on your roof; look they are making a hole in it.

You are lost, my poor friend! Throw out the treasure quickly!

Poor Paskou, you are dead! Sprinkle the holy water!

Hide under the sheet – don't make a single movement!

---

[1] See page 173.

Aaaaah! I hear them laughing; you'll be lucky to escape.

Lord God! There's one,
his head poking through the hole;

His eyes gleam like embers;
he's sliding down the pillar.

Lord God! One, two, three of them!
Look how they dance on the threshing floor![1]

They join together in their fury.
Virgin Saint! I am being strangled!

Monday, Tuesday, Wednesday...
and Thursday... and Friday...

Two, three, four, five and six! –
Monday, Tuesday, Wednesday!

Tailor, dear little tailor, we hear you snoring there!

Tailor, dear little tailor, show us the tip of your nose.

Come and dance with us, we'll show you the steps:

Tailor, dear tailor! Monday, Tuesday, Wednesday.

Tailor, you are a rascal. Monday, Tuesday, Wednesday.

Come and steal from us again,
come on, naughty little tailor.

We'll teach you a dance that will break your back.

Goblin gold is worthless to man.

Korrigans

In western Brittany, the *korrigan* has become a symbol of the Celtic nature of Brittany. This image is used everywhere – in advertising, in the decoration and naming of bars and restaurants and popping up relentlessly as a motif in tourist information. Their quirky ugly

---

[1] This was a common practical purpose of Breton dancing.

appearance is naturally an irresistible subject for endless artwork of varying degrees of taste and quality.

But there is much more to the *korrigans* than an amusing gimmick. They admirably represent the Breton lack of conformity, the unruly element lurking beneath the surface, full of mischievousness and humour. They are not to be crossed or disrespected, as some of the stories below illustrate.

Korrigans also provide a link between the world of men and the other shadowy world that exists when men's backs are turned. They live underground or inside dolmens, having a close connection with the element of earth and the long-during character of stone. At Brennilis, they inhabit the dolmen Ty ar Boudiked – House of the Little People (*boudiked* being a local name for *korrigans*). The *landes* or moors of the Monts d'Arrée are one of their favourite haunts. The dangers of travel at night in such places in olden days emerge clearly from these tales.

The Two Hunchbacks

There are differing versions, featuring differing days of the week, of this famous story, which neatly illustrates the volatile and mischievous nature of the *korrigans*. In Haute-Bretagne the same tale is told but with wizards – who also dance in the round – instead of *korrigans* in 'Les Sorciers de Knéa'.

The korrigans loved to chant a little song. It went "*lundi, mardi, mercredi, jeudi, lundi, mardi, mercredi, jeudi*[1]... repeated over and over. They used to dance and sing this song at night on the moors.

In a nearby village lived two hunchbacks: Guillaume was kind and helpful to others, whilst Jean was a miserable so-and-so. One day Guillaume had worked late cutting wood for an old lady and he took a shortcut back across the moors. He heard music and saw the korrigans singing and dancing in a circle. They saw him too and before he knew what had happened, he was surrounded. The dance recommenced and continued for what seemed like ages,

[1] Monday, Tuesday, Wednesday, Thursday...

but he waited patiently until there was a pause. Then Guillaume said politely. "I like your song, but it could be longer." An elderly *korrigan* said, "We do not usually listen to humans, but you may speak." So the hunchback sang in his croaky baritone:

> *"lundi, mardi,*
> *mercredi, jeudi,*
> *vendredi, samedi."*

The korrigans were thrilled and sang their new song with great pleasure. Then they offered their benefactor a reward. "We can give you anything you want," they said.

"All I want is to be rid of this dreary hump," the hunchback said ruefully.

"But are you sure? We have masses of gold," they cried.

"No, thank you. I have enough for my needs," said Guillaume, "but life would be so much sweeter without this great burden." So the *korrigans* pulled off the offending hump and Guillaume felt himself spinning through the air and falling to the ground.

When he opened his eyes he was alone. He stood up gingerly and then realised that his hump was indeed gone and he stood tall and straight for the first time.

He proudly returned to the village and told his story. Everyone was pleased for him and shared his great happiness, except for the other hunchback, Jean. He thought to himself what a fool Guillaume was to have left the gold behind, and decided to go and try his own luck the next night.

He found the spot and saw the korrigans in their circle. Without waiting for an invitation he walked into the centre. He heard the words of their endless song – "*lundi, mardi, mercredi, jeudi, vendredi, samedi*" - and laughed to himself that stupid old Guillaume had not finished the week for them.

Impatiently he interrupted the dance.

"I know the end of your song..." he began, "that other idiot didn't tell it properly." There was a sudden silence. Jean blundered on: "I can improve it for you."

The elderly korrigan spoke sternly. "We do not usually listen to humans. If ..." But Jean did not wait to hear the rest. He sang "*lundi, mardi, mercredi, jeudi, vendredi, samedi, et dimanche.*" A hostile silence fell. The korrigans did not like the sound of that harsh ending 'che' at all.

In his folly, Jean was adamant: "I finished your song, you must give me my reward."

After a moment the eldest korrigan spoke. "And what do you want in return?" "What a question:" said Jean. "I want what that fool of a Guillaume didn't take!" "Very well, it is agreed," was the quick response. Jean felt himself spinning through the air. When he opened his eyes the korrigans were still there regarding him unpleasantly. He tried to get up but fell down again because of the new weight on his back.

"You did not keep your word," he howled.

"On the contrary," said the korrigan leader. "We have given you what you asked for. What the other left behind was his hump."

A dangerous journey...

In a deep valley separating two hamlets, a river ran through marshy bog. To go from one place to the other it was necessary to make a steep descent and then cross the ford, which consisted of large stepping-stones with an equal distance between them. Nothing pleased the korrigans who lived here more than a bit of sport with humans and they kept a sharp look-out for passers-by foolish enough to travel in the darkness. If a traveller approached, he would be challenged to answer three questions before he could cross the ford. With each wrong answer, one stepping-stone would disappear. If three were lost, there was an impossible gap for the unlucky man to leap without anything but the strength of his own legs to prevent him from falling prey to the slimy creatures of the bog. So their nightly dance in the round took on a special form if anyone was unlucky enough to find themselves unwittingly in the centre of the circle. This happened one night to a man named Tarz.

Tarz the potter lived in one of the two hamlets above the valley, constantly henpecked by his wife, who chided him daily for laziness whilst she tried to provide them with a meagre living. Tarz certainly preferred hunting to potting and he often spent long days in the valley, keeping well away from home. He didn't catch much, but one day he rescued a turtle from being savaged by a hungry fox which had pawed at the shell and turned over his hapless prey. Tarz took the turtle home until it had recovered and then returned it to the riverside, ignoring the scorn he earned from his wife for this good deed.

Some time later Tarz had been sent off to the village on the other side of the valley to barter some rough pots for things they needed. He took his time, chatting away with anyone who would spare a moment for gossip. As he left the village he passed a house a little away from the others and saw an attractive woman in the doorway. She beckoned him in and Tarz was delighted to discover not only more women inside but a good strong honeyed liqueur freely dispensed. He soon lost all sense of what was happening and next thing he knew, suddenly found himself on the edge of the steep drop into the valley, minus the basket of goods he had been carrying. A sharp push sent him tumbling down, down, down the steep hillside and then – oblivion.

When he came round it was night, although the moon provided a steady light for him to make his sorry way to the ford. He got there slowly, gingerly putting one foot in front of the other and wincing at the pain of his bruises.

All his effort was concentrated on getting home and he did not notice, until it was too late, that he was caught in the middle of a circle of korrigans!

Their leader was sitting on a huge stone, and as Tarz blinked in horror, he began to call out the rhythm of the dance - 'kou-ic...kou-ac, kou-ic...kou-ac'[1]: On 'kou' alternate korrigans took a step forward and then a step backward on 'ic', whilst the others went back on 'kou' and forward on 'ac'. The whole manoeuvre produced a remarkable wave-like movement that mesmerised Tarz and made him sway drunkenly from side to side on the spot. He could do nothing but gaze in awe and not a little fear while the dance continued. But when it stopped, all attention was on him.

"To cross the ford, you must answer our questions," said the chief korrigan.

Tarz gulped. His head ached and his vision was none too clear, but he struggled to stay upright and face his ordeal.

"The first question is: what is the difference between a bard and a chicken?"[2]

Tarz pondered desperately over this riddle, while the dance completed another round. But he had no answer when they stopped. Before his eyes, one stepping-stone immediately disappeared from the crossing.

"The second question is: what can pass through thorns without a scratch?"[3]

The dancers ebbed and flowed around him in another circuit as Tarz floundered in his dull brain for a response. But again he had nothing, and another stone vanished.

The leader was ready with the third question. A frisson of anticipation went round the circle. "What is worth a fortune and of no value to man?"[4] Tarz was silent as the

---

[1] To the inexperienced ear, these calls would seem remarkably like that of tree-frogs... As in Aristophanes' play *The Frogs*, performed in Athens in 405BC, where the frogs form the chorus and sing 'brekekekex koax koax'.

[2] Answer: the bard earns his keep by his mouth, the chicken by its bum.

[3] Answer: sunshine.   [4] Answer: goblin gold.

dance wove around him for the last time before his inevitable doom. The round finished and all was still. He could not get out a single word, and moments later the last stone was gone.

Tarz was led to the spot from which he had to make the impossible leap. Fear made him ready to try rather than await a worse fate, although he knew full well the task was impossible. But just as he was about to launch himself into the air .... from the marshy depths appeared the head of the turtle he had once rescued. It had come to save him in his hour of need! And as he watched, other turtles broke the surface of the water, enough to fill the yawning gap completely and allow Tarz safe passage and freedom.

The korrigans loudly grumbled their dissatisfaction as he crossed, thanked his friend the turtle profusely and carried on home - where for once, his wife seemed not displeased to see him.

Lutins[1]

The following 'evidence' from the late 19th century gives an idea of the more domestic role envisaged for some little people. It is said that the *lutins* attached to particular premises were often motivated by their love of horses and their desire to look after animals on a farm. They might also help out around the house and generally bring good fortune to their chosen human family.

After staying in Paimpol in August 1873, Luzel met a postman named Tanguy who was able to tell him about local tales of little people on the island of Bréhat. This is his description of '*lutins du foyer*' or house elves.

'They tend to stay up in attics and stable lofts during the day, then come down at night to take care of the animals, horses above all, changing their bedding, filling up the hayracks and making up for any negligence by the servants. A good *lutin* is a

---

[1] For a less than helpful *lutin*, see the story of Nicole, *lutin de la mer*, page 153. Françoise Morvan's study *Vie et Moeurs des Lutins Bretons* (1998) is an entertaining and erudite look at this vast subject.

blessing on a farm, and the animals thus cared for are always sleek and fertile. Sometimes the *lutin* will go into the house and do some housework while the young serving-maid is asleep, sweeping the floors, doing the washing-up and bringing in fresh water... but there are no more *lutins* on the island now, because they are great horse-lovers and we have only two left. They don't like donkeys. We still have *folliked* but not as many as before, for the same reasons.

He goes on to describe how the *folliked* help in the house at night in much the same way as the *lutins*.

'In recompense for their efforts, the servants leave a well-buttered buckwheat crêpe and some sweet milk by the stove and the *folliked* sit in a circle round the hearth when their toil is over, eating and drinking and warming themselves. But at the first cock-crow, they disappear under the furniture or into holes in the walls, like mice.'

He then recounts the following tale told to him by his father:

A rich man named Iann Kertanhouarn lived on the island of Bréhat with his wife. Despite being the best off of all the inhabitants, they gave little away and thought only of increasing their own wealth. They had no servants because a group of *folliked* lived in the house and did all the work. For this they got no gratitude or reward, except the crumbs that fell from the table and vegetable peelings. They stayed out of loyalty to the house, because the parents of Kertanhouarn had been good and generous to them. They only managed to survive by waiting for the odd time when the mean couple forgot to remove the bread or crêpes from the table after dining. If the house was empty they might also manage to extract some cabbage or a bit of bacon from the cooking-pot on the fire.

This was sometimes possible because Kertenhouarn tended all his fields scattered round the island on his own to avoid paying out any money, and sometimes his wife had to help. But she would return to the house every so often to see to the fire and stir the pot, and it was sometimes obvious that some vegetables or bacon were missing. Her husband accused her of eating extra when he was out, and when she protested, asked who else was in the house but her? She said it might be the cat, and so the cat was never left alone at the house again. But the mystery of the missing food continued.

Kertanhouarn decided to supervise the preparation of meals himself, but still when he came to serve it up, there was clearly less than at the beginning. The whole affair both intrigued him and made him bad-tempered.

One day he said to his wife that there must be *folliked* in the house eating the food, and that one of them must stay outside and peer in to see what happened on their absence. So his wife was sent off to the fields to lift potatoes and he remained to spy on the house. Sure enough, he saw the *folliked* taking cabbage and bacon from the pot, and burst in with a big stick to have his revenge – but the *folliked* all vanished, up the chimney or through the open door.

After that, husband and wife discussed how they could get rid of the little thieves, and they decided to adopt a plan which they'd heard had been successful elsewhere. The *folliked* were accustomed to sit around the fire late at night with their leader on a round stone, common in all the houses on the island, which could serve as a stool, in the corner of the hearth. So before going to bed one night, Kertanhouarn heated this stone in the fire before replacing it and getting into his box-bed and pretending to sleep. From there he could observe what happened. When the leader of the *folliked* sat down he let out a terrible cry of pain and fled with all his companions in a great hullabaloo which left all the crockery in the house broken. From that time on *folliked* were rarely seen on the island.

As to Kertanhouarn and his wife, they had nothing but bad luck from that day forward. Robbers broke in and stole all their money. Some say it was *folliked* who made off with all that gold and silver. In the end the couple died paupers, having been the richest on the island.

Luzel then asked Tanguy about the little people stealing babies and substituting their own.

'Yes, so they say. If anyone was foolish enough to leave a baby in the cradle unattended in the house, the *folliked* stole the pink fresh-faced babies of humans and left their own tiny ugly black offspring in their place. Imagine the horror of the mother or nurse returning to find these hideous little monsters, wayward as the devil, whinging interminably and drawing blood when sucking the breast. They would viciously scratch anyone trying to soothe them to sleep with caresses. But there was a way to get your own child back. Instead of feeding the interloper, beat it three times a day with branches of broom. The real mother will hear its cries and on the third day return the stolen child and take her own away.'

Le Lutin de Bruz[1]

Adolphe Orain recorded this tale from Haute-Bretagne.

Father Richard from Cicé was well-known in the area as he travelled about fetching grain for processing, taking it to the mill and later returning the sacks of prepared flour. So he journeyed all over the place, stopping at every village and he had a great capacity for chatter and gossip. His arrival was eagerly awaited by those anxious for news from round about. Often he did not get on the road back to Cicé until nightfall.

On such a late journey one clear moonlit night, he was passing along the bank of a meadow when he saw a gnome-like creature with a great beard which tumbled down over

---
[1] Near Rennes.

his stomach, and a mass of hair falling right down his back. That was the only covering he had. He was just knee-high and appeared to be very old and grinning, his large mouth open wide.

When the traveller approached, the gnome called out: "Father Richard, you've certainly drunk your fill today, but your horse hasn't been well-fed – he's hardly moving."

"You couldn't keep up with him, you little squirt," came the brusque reply.

"I bet I could," said the gnome. "The first to reach the lake over yonder can chuck the other in."

"Agreed," said Richard, spurring on his horse.

But when he arrived at the lake, the gnome was waiting for him. Without letting him get off his horse, the gnome grabbed his foot and threw Father Richard with incredible force into the water.

Soaked to the skin, he cried out angrily, "Let me get my revenge!"

"Agreed", said the gnome. "First to the marsh of Apigné."

Richard forced his horse forward with all his might, but nevertheless, again found the dwarf waiting. And this time he was dragged back and forth in the muddy marsh until no-one could have recognised him!

He finally got home, soaked, battered and sick, taking to his bed for eight days with high fever. He never again told the tale without shivering at the memory of his encounter with Petit Jean, the *lutin* de Bruz.

Stories of *lutins* are often far from the world of fantasy, being integral in normal everyday life. The little people may be involved in many ordinary occupations and not only domestic or farm-related ones. The linen industry was once a main-stay of the economy, especially in Léon and parts of the Trégor.[1] Mining was also important, with the lead-silver mines at Poullaouen/Locmaria-Berrien

---

[1] Much of the Breton cloth trade was with England. The *Route des toiles* links many relevant places in Brittany – www.linchanvrebretagne.org

being the largest in France at one time. In such a dangerous environment, the help of a 'little miner *lutin*' was invaluable.

A thorn in the side...

One day a weaver went to a farm to prepare the raw material for his work. He ate there with the family and was asked to tell a story after the meal. The one he chose happened to involve great ill-treatment of *lutins*. During his tale, the wax candle in the hearth went out three times. The *lutins* were sending him a sign, but he failed to heed it.

When he left with the combed flax fibres piled on his back, he felt a sudden increase in the weight, as if someone had jumped on his shoulders. He was very scared by this, and arrived at his house in a state of fear and trembling. He threw down the packet of flax on the table and saw it was full of thorns.

The next morning when he went to weave his thread, he couldn't find the end. It was all tangled up. Sadly he returned to the farm and related his misfortune to the farmer, who didn't believe him. But from the old house came the sound of a *lutin* laughing loudly. The weaver finally understood what had happened to him, but there was nothing he could do about it.

A helping hand...[1]

The *lutin* of the mines is a friend to miners and tries not only to help them but also to save them from danger. If someone sits down to eat his bit of bread in a dangerous place, the lutin sends a shower of dust like a hail-storm down on his head, with progressively bigger missiles until he clears out of that spot.

When rock-falls threaten, the *lutin* sees all in advance and gives the alarm, striking blows on the threatened areas

---

[1] This account recorded by Adolphe Orain came from a miner at the lead-silver mine of Pont-Péan not far from Rennes. It ceased production early in the 20th century.

so the miners can escape. Some miners even testify that they were called by their names in warning at moments of potential catastrophe. The *lutins'* warnings were so often followed by disaster that their powers seemed supernatural indeed.

At crucial times, like handling the pumps or descending in the cage to the lower levels or in any other especially fraught circumstances, suddenly from the darkness sometimes came strange commands which warned of an approaching danger. When the danger was past, it was found that no human gave those orders. It could have been none other than the little miner *lutin*.

Sometimes shafts were given up on as having yielded all their mineral worth, and abandoned after the studies of engineers and mine directors declared those places useless for future work. Then from the dark, silent depths will sometimes come the sound of pick-axe blows falling steadily. Investigation proves that recent work has been done and – sure enough – a workable seam has re-appeared.

CHAPTER 8
ARTHURIAN CONNECTIONS

The world of Arthurian legend - and scholarship - is a crowded and often confusing one. There is a wide gulf between a potential historical figure of the late 5th/early 6th century who rallied defence against the Anglo-Saxon invaders of England[1] and the familiar king of the Round Table knights of legend. Two principal strands of development come from Great Britain (via the Welsh tradition and Geoffrey of Monmouth) and France, the latter possibly drawn from early Breton sources that have not survived.

In about 1160 Marie de France, the first female *conteuse* known, wrote lays which she said came from old Breton tales and whilst they are not directly about the Arthurian knights, they make reference to the Round Table and presume that the audience would be familiar with this world.

It is argued by some that the wave of immigrations to Brittany in the Dark Ages may have brought Arthurian stories from insular Britain to the Armorican peninsula. His brief appearance in one version of St-Patern's life has already been mentioned.[2] Another possibility is that Bretons who went to England with William the Conqueror in 1066, many of whom were rewarded with lands there, may have returned to Brittany with new stories later given a Breton setting. Or the reverse might be true and they took them across the water in the first place...

Geoffrey of Monmouth, writing a chronicle in the early 12th century places Arthur in the line of kings of Britain. He ascribes continental conquests to him which would explain Arthur's presence at times in the Armorican peninsula. Geoffrey drew on earlier sources like the Historia Brittonum, from about 830, which is the first text to present Arthur as an historical figure, a leader in battle. Merlin also

---

[1] Evidence for his existence is scant and, many claim, dubious.

[2] See page 67. In this episode Arthur displays distinctly un-heroic tendencies.

appears in Geoffrey's text but as a pre-Arthurian figure, although his mysterious prophecies refer to the triumph of the later king.

It was Chrétien de Troyes, however, writing later in the same century, who really put the Arthurian saga on the map in France. He developed the romance tradition, giving substance to familiar ideas of courtly love and heroic ideals found in these stories. Writing at the same time as Marie de France, he introduced Lancelot du Lac and also the whole tale of the Holy Grail quest. The patroness for whom he produced his poems was the Countess de Champagne, a region at that time in the possession of the House of Blois, which had close Breton connections. The supposition is that Chrétien de Troyes also had Breton sources for his work. Stories were spread widely by minstrels and troubadours of noble houses who travelled with their masters and entertained their guests.

Whatever the origins and diffusion of the Arthurian tales, it is undeniable that they have taken their hold on Brittany itself, although in the final analysis this is mostly manifested in a topographical context. Certain places and objects in the landscape are associated with certain characters like Merlin or Arthur, but whether there is any real reason behind these connections, other than a tradition exploited by tourism, is often dubious.

Arthur's Grotto, Huelgoat forest

The atmosphere and romantic landscape of forests lend themselves to becoming worthy settings for legendary tales in the popular imagination. Arthur's grotto and Arthur's camp in the forest of Huelgoat are good examples of this phenomenon. There may be no specific reason to associate them with King Arthur, but the setting looks the part.[1] Old postcards of the Brasparts area in the Monts d'Arrée show a series of stepped jagged rocks with the title

---

[1] The camp was actually an Iron Age fort, established long before Arthur's time, and possibly used by the Celtic Osismes tribe in defence against the Romans.

Château de Comper

L'escalier d'Artus.[1] Such a dramatic landscape warrants association with a famous figure.

Things get more complex with the fabled forest of Brocéliande of the Arthurian legends. In Brittany this location has been claimed by the Forêt de Paimpont in Ille-et-Vilaine to the west of Rennes. A vast development of tourism and commerce is built on a rather flimsy pretext, although this beautiful forest is undeniably a suitable physical context for the tales it is said to enshrine.

Brittany retains traditions connected to the story of Arthur, but the stories surrounding Merlin and Lancelot figure more strongly. Prosper Merimée, writing in the mid 19th century said "the Breton peasants seem to me to know more of Caesar than of Arthur, their compatriot and the hero of stories it is said arose in their country."

In fact the Arthurian connection in Brittany is often an association with places in the landscape rather than the source of numerous extended stories. The Château de Comper today houses the *Centre de l'imaginaire Arthurien*,[2] a centre of Arthurian study and related exhibitions which combine such elements of history as exist with the powerful sweep of the imagination associated with the medieval tradition of Arthur and his knights.

---

[1] Arthur's steps.

[2] www.centre-arthurien-broceliande.com

Tristan and Iseult (Isolde)

The famous story of illicit love between Tristan and Iseult (or Isolde) is sometimes linked to Arthurian material: Tristan is often said to be one of the Knights of King Arthur, and in Welsh versions of the tale, King Mark seeks help from Arthur to gain redress from Tristan for stealing his wife. The story may also have influenced the later adulterous tale of Lancelot and Arthur's wife. The story has innumerable versions.[1]

The Brittany connection comes with Tristan's exile and marriage with the second Iseult, always given the epithet 'Of the White Hands' to distinguish her from Iseult the Fair, Tristan's true love. Places associated with this legend are the romantic ruined castle of Trémazan on the Finistère coast, and the Île Tristan at Douarnenez,[2] where the lovers' deaths are said to have occurred.

Tristan was the nephew of King Mark of Cornwall. He was sent to Ireland to fetch Iseult the Fair, the extraordinarily beautiful bride destined for his uncle. On the journey back, both he and Iseult drank a potion, intended by the bride's mother to stimulate her daughter's love for King Mark. As a result Tristan and Iseult fell deeply in love.

Iseult went through with her marriage to King Mark, but was also the lover of Tristan. This adulterous affair was soon suspected and eventually the king had proof of their guilt. The pair were condemned to death, Tristan by hanging and Iseult to be burned at the stake, but Tristan escaped from his prison and rescued his lover. They fled and managed to live secretly in the forest for some years. King Mark finally caught up with them but pardoned them both. His anger had died down and he was again moved by love for both his wife and nephew. He took Iseult back on condition the affair was ended and Tristan would go abroad.

---

[1] Wagner's opera Tristan und Isolde is the most famous dramatic telling of the story.

[2] This may be a corruption of the earlier Tutuarn, linked to the saint Tudy and have nothing to do with Tristan at all.

The heart-broken Tristan crossed the channel to Brittany. Here he helped the duke, Hoël, in many campaigns and became close friends with his son Kahedin. This young man one day heard Tristan singing longingly of Iseult and got the wrong end of the stick, as this was also his sister's name, although she became known as Iseult of the White Hands. When the duke heard this he was happy and asked Tristan if he would like to marry his daughter. Tristan realised the mistake but decided to go ahead as he had given up all hope of seeing his own Iseult again and he found Iseult of the White Hands beautiful and charming. But he was not able to consummate the marriage, so deeply was his heart still tied to his former love. His new wife had no idea why he seemed to reject her love.

Tristan was given lands by the duke, but warned not to antagonise his neighbour, a brutal giant named Beliagog. Eventually the two did come into conflict and fought a terrible duel. Tristan finally cut off the giant's foot. When Beliagog begged for mercy, Tristan granted it on condition that he created an effigy of Iseult, his old love. This turned out to be so life-like that Tristan spent all his time in the giant's cave gazing longingly at it. Iseult of the White Hands eventually confessed to her brother that she was still a virgin and Kahedin confronted Tristan. He took him to the cave and Kahedin was overwhelmed by the beauty of the statue. Tristan resolved that the two of them should go to Cornwall and see Iseult the Fair again.

This they did and the two doomed lovers resumed their affair, whilst Kahedin became enamoured of her maid Branwen before they returned to Brittany. But they did not remain there for long, for both wanted only to be back with their desired partners. Their next visit to Cornwall, however, provoked tragedy, as Tristan received a terrible wound in his thigh from a poisoned lance whilst attempting a chivalrous deed.[1] He managed to get back to

---

[1] In another version it is King Mark himself who stabs Tristan.

Brittany but he knew that only Iseult the Fair could save him from death.

He sent Kahedin with a message and the ring she had once given him, begging her to come to him. If his mission was successful, Kahedin was to hoist white sails[1] so Tristan would know that Iseult still loved him and would soon be at his side. But his wife, Iseult of the White Hands, had discovered her husband's secret obsession and had long been jealous of her rival.

So when the white-sailed ship from Cornwall finally hove into view and the dying Tristan asked her to tell him the colour of the sails, she lied and said they were black. In his despair at believing that Iseult the Fair had finally deserted him, Tristan gave up his fight for life and perished. When the ship docked and Iseult rushed to her lover's side, she found them already mourning for Tristan. Her own heart broke and she died as she embraced her true love.

King Mark in his double grief had the bodies of his wife and nephew returned to Cornwall, where they were buried.

Île Tristan, Douarnenez

---

[1] An echo of the Theseus legend of ancient Greece, where white sails would signify Theseus' triumph over the Minotaur. He forgot to hoist them, and his aged father threw himself off the cliff, believing Theseus to be dead.

King Arthur

A connection may be made between Arthur and Brittany in various ways. In some views, he was king of Britain and Brittany too, so naturally made appearances in the Armorican peninsula. Some sources, like Geoffrey of Monmouth, have him fighting extensively in Gaul and seeking support from Breton lords. In the Trégor there is a tradition that the Château de Kerduel in the commune of Pleumeur-Bodou was Arthur's residence in Brittany. This explains (or derives from) the stories linking him with the northern coastline.

Another tale has him brought to Brittany when fatally wounded in battle by his half-brother Mordred, and laid to rest in Avalon, where he 'sleeps' until a great crisis will call him forth again. The Breton word for apples is *avalou* and the Île d'Aval near Île Grande is one of the proposed candidates for the sacred isle.[1]

King Arthur also makes a surprise appearance as a stand-in for Conomor in one story of the Breton Ste-Tréphine[2]. This legend used in popular theatrical tradition in the Trégor region of Brittany was published by folklorist François Luzel in the 19th century. The concept stems from medieval Mystery Plays once common all over France, but surviving in Brittany by virtue of the power of oral traditions and an initial acceptance by the church. The play, running over two days, describes how Tréphine married Arthur and was then the subject of machinations by her evil brother who wanted to seize power for himself. He kidnaps Tréphine and hides the son she bears, then accusing her of murder before Arthur. Tréphine manages to escape and hide for years but is later reconciled with her husband. The calumnies persist, however, and she is accused of adultery, with witnesses bribed to condemn her. At her execution, her long-lost son Trémeur appears and so she is saved. Trémeur kills his wicked uncle in a duel, and Tréphine and Arthur are finally reunited. There are clear echoes of the Arthur and Guinevere story here.

---

[1] Off the coast of Côtes-Armor at Pleumeur-Bodou, this island also has a connection with King Marc'h of the horses' ears, see page 93.

[2] See page 99.

Arthur and the Giant of Mont-St-Michel

Geoffrey of Monmouth has this tale.

Hoël, an early king in Armorica, was one of Arthur's staunchest allies, and provided soldiers for his wars. Hoël's niece Helen[1] was seized by a ferocious giant who had set up camp on the barren rocky heights of what today is the architectural marvel of Mont-St-Michel, and was terrorising the area so that all the inhabitants had run away.

Arthur vowed to help his friend, despite a dream the night before his arrival that a dragon had defeated a bear[2] in a fierce fight. With his companions Kay and Belvedere, Arthur scanned the peaks on the island, and saw a fire burning in the distance. But before he could reach that spot, he came upon a woman weeping by a new grave. This turned out to be the mother of Helen, grieving her daughter who had spurned the giant's advances and been killed. Arthur determined to avenge Helen and went on to tackle the giant in his lair. He found the monster outside his cave, cooking over an open fire.

Tombelaine and Mont St-Michel

---

[1] Possibly the mother of Lancelot and widow of King Ban, who is also associated with the area around Combourg and Dol-de-Bretagne.

[2] The name 'Arthur' means 'bear'.

A desperate struggle ensued as Arthur sought to evade the giant's clutch that would surely squeeze him to death and yet to inflict wounds on his opponent. He managed to slash the giant between the eyes, so blood trickled down and obscured his vision, but still the thrashings of a huge wooden club threatened to pound Arthur to death. They fought on until Arthur managed to pierce the giant's skull and finally topple him to the ground.

Arthur's followers cut off the head to prove to everyone that the giant was no more, but Hoël was full of grief at the loss of his niece and had a tomb built for her on the spot where she died. It therefore took the name Tombelaine (tomb of Helen) and is today a separate islet in the Bay of Mont-St-Michel.

Arthur and St Efflam

Efflam was an Irish prince who arrived on the northern coast of Armorica in the 6th century. He settled as a hermit where his chapel now stands on the bay near Plestin-les-Grèves. His own story is a strange one: he is said to have reluctantly married Enora in Ireland, but then refused to break his vows of chastity to consummate the marriage. He ran away instead and his journey brought him to Brittany. In other versions of the story, Enora came with him through loyalty, but they remained chaste, living in separate huts, each devoted to the service of God.

St-Efflam is perhaps best known for his meeting with King Arthur.

One day King Arthur was in hot pursuit of a ferocious dragon, a beast the size of a bull with red eyes and green scales, sometimes described as having a human head, the body of a serpent and the tail of a sea monster. The chase was a long one, following the northern coast of Armorica until the dragon finally went to ground in a cave near the Grand Rocher, which dominates the bay to this day.

Arthur sank down exhausted near the hermitage of Saint Efflam. He was sorely in need of water to revive his strength and called imperiously on the holy man to provide for his needs. St-Efflam struck the rock with his staff to perform a miracle and provide fresh spring water for the king.

He then watched as Arthur tried to lure the dragon out and then to overpower it on each sortie, but all his efforts were without success, and it seemed that even such great physical prowess as the king possessed was unlikely to prevail against a monster like this dragon.

Finally the saint suggested to the king that the power of faith might be more efficacious than brute force. Arthur was unimpressed by this argument, but St-Efflam stepped forward fearlessly to the mouth of the dragon's lair with nothing but his holy cross for protection. He then called the dragon out and, to King Arthur's astonishment, ordered the beast to submit to the power of Christianity and hurl itself off the cliff into the waters below. The dragon did so and vanished forever.

Arthur and the siren

Morgane La Fée[1] lived on the Île Talbert, separated from the mainland by a narrow stretch of water. King Arthur had been hunting in the region around his castle at Kerduel and came to rest on the shore when he saw the siren sitting on the rocks of her home, combing her long hair. He fell in love at first sight. But the sea separated them and Arthur had to return to his castle without reaching his lady. He concealed his feelings from the queen and his court, but he longed to see Morgan again. She too was full of love for the king and had the idea of filling the skirts of her long dress with pebbles and wading into the

---

[1] In early tales, Morgane is a sorceress, one of nine sisters prophetesses on the Island of Avalon where the dying Arthur is taken. Later traditions make her Arthur's half-sister and an enemy of the king. Her name also suggests connections with sirens, see page 147.

sea, throwing the pebbles ahead of her as she went so that they turned to rocks and formed a causeway. So the Sillon of Talbert[1] was created to bring the lovers together, but the siren left a little gap between its end and her island, so she would receive no unwanted visitors ...

These two tales from Ille-et-Vilaine show Arthur in his common guise as an indefatigable hunter: The phenomenon of a battle or ride appearing to take place in the sky, is common in European legend. In Brittany it can take the form of Arthur's celestial hunt.

rthur was known to be a great hunter, never happier than on the chase. One day when he was participating in the rituals of Easter service he heard his pack of hounds baying outside, and rushed out of the church to lead them in pursuit of a hare. Through the forest they raced until suddenly they burst out of the trees onto a precipice. Arthur tried to pull up but some irresistible force seemed to draw him, his hounds and the hare over the edge. They hurtled into the void. In punishment for the abuse of his Christian duties, Arthur was condemned to chase his elusive prey through the heavens until Judgement Day.

La Chassartue (Arthur's Hunt)[2]

peasant working in the fields in late evening was startled to hear a gathering noise in the skies above, like the barking of a pack of hounds. The sound grew louder as it got closer and suddenly the clouds parted to reveal the brilliantly lit clamour of a mounted hunting party dashing across the heavens, led by King Arthur. As the man watched, Arthur seemed to take on the form of a hunting-dog himself, merging with the baying hounds in close pursuit of his prey. Moments later the vision

---

[1] A geological wonder created by tides and winds, this spit of pebbles reaches out for 3km into the sea near Pleubian.

[2] This is also a topic for song: there's a 19th century ballad *La chasse du roi Arthur* by Siméon Pécontal.

disappeared from sight, silence fell once more, and the peasant made his way home under an empty sky.

Some claim that on winter nights in the forests around Kerduel, Arthur is still pursuing the hunt, sounding his horn to drive the hounds. *Man Arzur oc'h ober e dro!* - It's Arthur making his rounds![1] the saying goes.

La Villemarqué records a song he heard from an 'old Chouan' of Leuhan, often sung as the anti-Republican armies marched. It reflects the many legends of sleeping heroes who will rise at a time of national crisis.[2]

Arthur could not fail to be of interest to Bretons as a representative of struggle against incoming oppressors. His fight against the Anglo-Saxon invaders of Britain attracted a symbolic value, especially to the Bretons who had undergone their own long fight against the Franks and French.

The knights are on the top of the mountain!

The knights pass by, mounted on grey warhorses
which snort from the cold!

In ranks six by six, in ranks three by three;
a thousand lances gleaming in the sunshine.

The ranks go two by two, following the flags
which blow in the wind of Death,

Nine times the length of a sling-shot
from their head to their tail.

It is the army of Arthur, I know.
Arthur marches at the front on top of the mountain.

And if it is Arthur, quick to our bows
and our living arrows!

---

[1] This tradition is recorded by Daniel Giraudon in his excellent book *Traditions populaires de Bretagne – du soleil aux étoiles.*

[2] Such a story is told of Arthur and his knights at Glastonbury Tor in England.

Brocéliande

The famous Arthurian forest of Brocéliande is today identified with the Forêt de Paimpont in Ille-et-Vilaine, creating a tourist mecca in an outstandingly beautiful area. It is possible that a medieval lord brought back Arthurian tales to Brittany and began to identify his own land with the mythical forest of Brocéliande, but it was in the 19th century when tourism began to open up that the identification seems to have become established.

There is, however, much dispute over the 'true' location of the forest of the Arthurian tales. Many interpret the imprecise existing references to mean an area near Dol-de-Bretagne, on the grounds that the legendary forest is supposed to be near the sea and situated in the Marches of Brittany, a sort of buffer zone established by the Franks between the Armorican peninsula and the rest of France. Mont Dol is often said to be the Mont Douloureux of the Graal legends. It certainly looks the part, rising abruptly from the flat marshlands opposite Mont-St-Michel.

Romantics may not care much about the niceties, and the Forêt de Paimpont is a superb environment for imaginative tales, but there are further prosaic impediments to the unsullied Arthurian dream. A notice at the entrance to the Valley of No Return states clearly that in the 19th century another valley was designated with this title, but when a factory was built there it seemed expedient to change to the current location of the Vallée de Gurwant. Tourism marketing is, after all, no more of an exact science than legends. But who could complain, when this valley offers such atmospheric gifts, like the crystalline lake called Miroir aux Fées (Fairies' Mirror) and the rocky outcrop where Morgane watched over the trapped lovers.

Miroir aux Fées

197

Morgane La Fée and the Val sans Retour (Valley of No Return)

Morgane was the half-sister of Arthur, and a formidable sorceress. When she discovered her lover Guyomarc'h with another woman in the forest, she took her revenge by laying an enchantment on the lonely valley. Guyomarc'h himself she bound in a prison of air to remain fixed in the spot for evermore. She then widened the scope of her fury and decreed that any false lover who passed through this territory would be trapped here forever by the power of her spells. High above this secret valley are the rocks where she sat to observe the helpless victims of this curse. First attracted to the spot by the songs of fairies on the lake below, the hapless men then remained without any sense of time in Morgane's world of magic, kept in by impenetrable walls of air.

The other knights came in search of their lost companions' plight and tried to come to their aid against the fierce guards outside the valley, but finally it was Lancelot - whose heart was totally devoted to one woman, Arthur's wife Queen Guinevere - who was able to overcome the giants and dragons that guarded the place, and when he approached the walls of air, they fell before his loyal heart. So the magical bounds were released and the trapped knights freed from their captivity.

Merlin

Merlin is a complex and intriguing figure, a magician with powers over nature, a schemer, a sage and an advisor. His dual aspect is symbolised by the legend that he was born of a virgin and the devil. His role in the Arthurian story is concerned with Arthur's birth, the trial of the sword in the stone and the establishment of the Round Table, none of which has particular connections to Brittany.

But tales of Merlin probably pre-date the Arthurian cycle - he may be the prophetic figure Myrrdin of Welsh oral tradition – although Geoffrey of Monmouth created much of the well-known persona. In Brittany, his character taps into the strong Druidic traditions of Celtic culture.[1]

Falling for Viviane...

Merlin first met and fell in love with the fairy Viviane at the Fontaine de Barenton, a romantic spot in the Forêt de Brocéliande.[2]

He had come to Brittany to seek support for Arthur's struggle against invaders among the nobles here and was travelling back through the forest when he had his moment of fatal attraction. The young woman by the spring beguiled him at once and he willingly became her teacher when she sought to understand the art of magic. She was an apt pupil, and Merlin recognised from the start the dangers Viviane posed for

Fontaine de Barenton

---

[1] A detailed picture of his chameleon-like character is presented at the Château de Comper's exhibition centre.

[2] This is a beautiful 1km walk from the hamlet of Folle Pensée (Mad Thoughts). A stone by the head of the spring is called Merlin's Step. Splashing the water on this rock is said to cause a storm to blow up, and the Black Knight will appear to challenge the intruder (see page 202).

him as he fell more and more into her power through his deep love.

He returned to Britain for a while but was then drawn back to the leafy grove around the spring and the embraces of Viviane. One day she asked him if there was a way to bind a man forever. Knowing the consequences of his reply he still admitted that it was possible with the right formula to construct a tower of glass from which the poor individual would never escape. While he slept, Viviane bound him in nine circles of air and then kept him captive in the forest forever. Unfortunately this also deprived Viviane of his company as he remained in a permanent state of suspended animation.[1]

Merlin's tomb

Lancelot

Marie de France mentions a knight called Lanval who is loved by the wife of Arthur, but he already has a beloved, a fairy in the island of Avalon.

In Brittany the lake at the Château de Comper is said to be where Lancelot grew up beneath the waters with his foster-mother, the Lady of the Lake, otherwise known as the fairy Viviane. She lived there in a crystal palace built for her by Merlin.

[1] Visitors to the Forêt de Paimpont today can see what is fancifully called Merlin's tomb. It is probably in fact the remains of a Neolithic dolmen or burial place, and lacks the presence one would expect for such a legendary spot. It is rather confusingly nowhere near the Fontaine de Barenton, but on the way to the spring of Eternal Youth. Another tradition has Merlin's place of incarceration as a cave at Mont-Dol.

Lancelot was the son of King Ban and Queen Helen, who held lands in the Marches of Brittany.[1] They were forced to flee from their home when he was just a baby, by the aggression of one Claudas, and made for the château at Combourg where they had relatives. They stopped by a lake to rest and Ban climbed a hill to look back, only to see his own castle in flames. The terrible sight stopped his heart and he fell dead from his horse. His wife rushed to his side, leaving the baby by the water. Here he was snatched by the fairy Viviane and taken to her palace beneath the waters to be brought up as her son. From this came his epithet, Lancelot du Lac. Viviane later educated the boy and prepared him to be a great knight, sending him to the court of King Arthur at Camelot. But although Lancelot became the greatest of the Knights of the Round Table by his prowess, he fell in love with Arthur's wife Guinevere and thus brought ruin on them all.

Château de Joyeuse Garde

One of Lancelot's exploits in Brittany was said to be set in La Forest-Landerneau[2] where the ruins of the Château de Joyeuse Garde still stand.

The castle was known as Douloureuse Garde because it was a place of terrible violence and misery, held by 20 knights for their wicked master[3] who terrorised the area. One of Lancelot's earliest tasks as a knight was to liberate the inhabitants from this terror and he managed to defeat all the knights, who attacked him simultaneously, by means of magic shields given him by the Lady of the Lake. He then destroyed the tyrant and kept the castle for himself, despite the unnerving discovery of a tomb there with his name already on it.

[1] The ruined Château de Coëtquen has been proposed as a location.

[2] Other claimants for the location of this castle are Elven in Morbihan or Bamburgh and Alnwick castles in Northumbria, England.

[3] Or a vicious monster in other versions.

From then on the castle was called the Château de Joyeuse Garde, although there was more unhappiness years later when Lancelot saved Guinevere from death for her adultery and brought her here. Arthur then besieged the castle, but finally made peace with both his wife and her lover. Lancelot's body was brought back to this place when he died.

Yvain and the Black Knight

This 12th century romance by Chrétien de Troyes describes the adventures of Yvain, one of Arthur's knights.[1]

A mysterious Black Knight guards passage through the grove of the Fontaine de Barenton in the fabled forest of Brocéliande. If water is splashed onto the magic rock beside the spring, a storm is caused, and at the first clap of thunder, the dark guardian appears on his dark steed.

The knight Yvain sought to avenge his cousin who had been defeated by the Black Knight, so he came to seek him out in the forest of Brocéliande. He found the place and flicked water onto the rock. Sure enough, at a clap of thunder, the Black Knight appeared and they fell to battle. Yvain had the upper hand and pursued the Black Knight all the way back to his castle, where he died.

At the sight of the grieving widow of the Black Knight, Yvain fell madly in love and, through the intervention of her maid, managed to persuade Laudine to marry him. She later agreed that he should go off with Gawain on a quest of chivalry, on condition he returned within a year. Yvain forgot his promise, and Laudine refused ever to see him again. Almost mad with grief at his own folly, the knight decided to persuade his wife to relent at all costs and performed various acts of heroism, including killing a giant, with the help of a lion which had saved him from a

---

[1] Probably derived from Owein, a 6th century historical figure from the Borders.

snake. The lion became his loyal companion and he is therefore sometimes given the epithet Yvain of the Lion.

Eventually Yvain saved his wife's maid from death by burning at the stake and in gratitude she persuaded her mistress to relent, so Yvain (and the lion) were at last welcomed back.

St-Ké/St-Quay and Sir Kay

This 5th century figure from Britain, called Ké or Quay (or even Kénan in a biography by Albert Le Grande) is sometimes said to be the Sir Kay of Arthurian legend. The Arthurian connection is rather nebulous, and hardly fits the courtly Sir Kay.

Ké arrived on the north coast of Léon near Roscoff in 472 with his companions Kérien and Péran, and founded a monastery at Cléder. He also created a miraculous healing spring by the beach that is now named after him, La Gréve de St-Ké.[1] But he was soon called back to Britain to intercede in a rift between King Arthur and his wife Guinevere. Failing in this mission, Ké set off again for the Armorican peninsula and landed this time at what is now called (after him) Saint-Quay-Portrieux on the Côte de Goëlo. Here he was set upon by local women and beaten with branches of gorse before being left for dead. The Virgin Mary created a spring beside him to heal his wounds, and this *fontaine* can still be seen there today. St-Ké then returned to Cléder where he died and was buried.

---

[1] Some say Cléder was actually founded by St-Clether, one of Ké's followers. A Pardon in honour of St-Ké with a Breton mass is held each year in Cléder on the first Sunday in July.

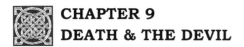

CHAPTER 9
DEATH & THE DEVIL

Death and the devil are not inextricably connected in Breton legend, but there is considerable interaction between the two, particularly in the context of Christianity, which wages a war against evil, and the fate of humans in life and after death. The seminal work on legends and traditions about Death in Breton oral culture is *La Légende de la Mort* by Anatole Le Braz, a collection of tales published in 1893, personally collected from Breton speakers in Basse-Bretagne.

Death

Pre-Christian or Celtic notions of death and what happens afterwards are naturally at variance with Christian views and not easy to define, as documentation of beliefs is lacking from that time. Archaeology and the oral tradition can give a picture but it may not be consistent. Was the afterlife one of pleasure and eternal youth? Did one life simply follow another? Was there an idea of reincarnation or the transmigration of souls, as when Julius Caesar wrote of the Druids passing on to another world? All of these concepts are possible. The physical nature of the Underworld and its location are equally elusive. There seems to be a tradition of crossing the water to an island or the Isles of the Blessed, always situated in the west, the direction of the setting sun. Tales in Brittany tell of souls travelling from the Baie des Trépassés near the Pointe du Raz towards the Île de Sein, although this is particularly associated with those drowned at sea.

Various entrances to the underworld appear in legends, particularly that of the Yeun Elez, the eerie marshy bowl at the heart of the Monts d'Arrée. That the Breton Hell is a cold, dismal place is graphically evoked by an inscription in Breton from the ossuary at the unusual parish close of La Martyre in Finistère. It reads "Death, Judgement and cold hell – man must tremble when he thinks on these. Foolish he who ignores it, knowing he must die." The Celtic legend of sleeping heroes, who rest under a hill after death awaiting a call to return to the world as saviours certainly conjures up a chilly atmosphere, but this is not a place of punishment. The early Christian texts of St Patrick's Purgatory and the Apocalypse of Paul both contain a similar sense with the idea of suffering cold as a punishment after death or crossing a river of ice. Hell later becomes a furnace with the idea of gruesome punishments for sin supervised by demons and the Devil himself, whose element is fire.

It is certainly true that Death looms large in legend in Brittany, and the stories depict a fascination with the transition between this world and the next. The intense religiosity of the Heaven and Hell preachers like Père Maunoir in the 17th century also contributed to an emphasis on Death and the Devil, especially among the poor and superstitious. This is not to say that an innate gloominess prevails, but rather a respect for death and an acceptance of its essential part in the nature of human life. Catholicism laid much emphasis on promises of a radiant afterlife if the precepts of the Church were strictly followed.

The Dance of Death

Only a few versions of the medieval Dance of Death or Danse macabre remain in the whole of France, and two of these are in Brittany.[1] These graphic wall-paintings are an allegory not a legend, but the verses displayed underneath the frieze[2] at the Chapelle de Kermaria-an-Isquit near Plouha are exchanges between the skeletal figure of Death and the personages from all walks of life whom he calls to join the Dance.[3] The dancers hold hands, skeletons and life-like figures alternating. The dance reminds everyone, male and female, high and low, that they will eventually be called to participate in the '*danse*

---

[1] These allegorical paintings exist all over Europe.

[2] Today the verses are almost illegible but they were recorded in full in the 19th century when the frieze was rediscovered. It dates back to the late 15th century but was covered over in the 18th century.

[3] Another frieze on the same theme can be seen at the magnificent church at Kernascleden in Morbihan.

macabre' by the great equaliser, Death. One example will give the flavour of the exchanges.

Death addresses the Cardinal

Kindly approach, Cardinal,
Though you appear amazed,
Let us follow all the others.
Put aside your astonishment,
You've always loved parades,
Honour and the grand lifestyle.
Come then, join the dance:
In the high life, one loses spirit.

The Cardinal responds

I've good reason to be amazed
When I receive such an overture.
Death came as an assailant
And now invites me on a jaunt.
To my distress, I must leave behind
My mitre and ermine cape,
Because now it's all over:
All joy finishes in sadness.

Danse macabre - Chapelle de Kermaria-an-Isquit

Ankou – the Grim Reaper

In Breton legend, Ankou is the Grim Reaper, agent of an abstract Death, or *'ouvrier de la mort'*. Concerning his origins, Jean-François Olier[1] has a legend telling of Ankou's emergence from Roc'h Toul[2] in prehistoric times, which imagines death inextricably linked with early human life around 10,000BC.

Ankou's origin

The leader of a group of early settlers living in the cave of Roc'h Toul emerged after sensing a preternatural stillness settle outside. Through the canopy of trees he could see that the sky in the distance glowed red. Alarmed, but curious, he climbed up above the roof of the cave to a viewpoint. There he became rooted to the spot as he saw the world in what seemed to be a turmoil of fire. All the sky was in agitation, and as he watched a glowing cloud silently moved towards him, driving large-winged birds and animals in its path, burning up any too slow to flee to safety. The trees too were engulfed, leaving only fossilised remains in their place.

Suddenly he felt himself immersed in this same terrible cloud and endured a moment of fiery heat before it passed as suddenly as it had come, and all returned to normal. He went back down to the cave to tell his companions, but to his great surprise they screamed and ran away, hiding from him behind rocks at a distance. Truly puzzled, he went down to the nearby river to look at his reflection and saw that he had been transformed into a skeleton, with a bright light shining inside his skull.

Realising that everyone on earth would be afraid of him now, he gazed up at a pale star in the sky and wished that

---

[1] *Légendes du pays des enclos.*

[2] An atmospheric cave site dating back at least to the Mesolithic period, which has yielded many flint tools as evidence of human occupation. It is situated at Luzec, near St-Thégonnec, and now contains a protected bat colony.

he was there – and magically his wish became true in an instant. In this way he took himself beyond the world of human life and gained the power of appearing at once in another location.

So for many thousands of years he travelled the universe, searching for a home, but no-one would receive him kindly. Finally he heard a mysterious call, telling him to return to where he started. Back on earth he was entrusted by the Master of the Universe with the task of leading souls to the next world when they had departed from the body.

Ankou's iconography in religious sculpture, particularly on ossuary buildings in the precincts of the parish closes, where the bones of the dead were kept, shows a skeletal figure, armed with a scythe or arrow and often accompanied by a slogan such as *'Je vous tue tous'* (I kill you all). A fine example of this can be seen at La Roche Maurice near Landerneau.

When personified in legend, Ankou is described as a tall, thin man sometimes with long white hair, in dark clothes of an ancient style and with a large black felt hat low on his brow. This is to conceal his eyes shining like red fire below the brim. His skull head can turn through 360° degrees, so that he never misses anything or anyone – a fact that gives him a reputation of fairness, as everyone must die eventually. He also carries a scythe, symbolic of his role of pruning souls from the body. In some stories he is a figure of terror, whilst in others he holds normal conversations with the living.

Ankou travels at night in a creaking cart drawn by white horses, one fat, one thin, collecting the souls whose time has come and escorting them to another world. In this sense he is a sort of psychopomp,[1] one who leads the dead to their resting place. Two men may accompany the cart, one to lead the horses and the other to open gates or doors of houses to gather in the souls reaped by Ankou. Once Ankou has a soul in his sights, there's no escape, as some of the legends below illustrate.

---

[1] This is one role of Hermes in Greek mythology and Gwyn ap Nudd in Welsh tradition.

Ankou - Tales of Death's henchman

No escape

As told to Anatole Le Braz in 1890 by a woman from Bégard.

young man from Tézélan had just taken his horses to leave in the meadow overnight. The moon was high and full as he walked home, whistling, through the countryside. Suddenly he heard the unmistakable creaking approach of a cart and knew at once that this must be the famous vehicle of Ankou. He wanted to see it for himself, but without being seen, so he got off the track and hid himself in a thicket of hazel.

What he saw was a cart drawn by white horses, with two men in black with broad felt hats walking, one in front and one behind. To the young man's horror the cart stopped level with his hiding-place, after a sharp crack in the axle was heard. Ankou, who was driving the cart, ordered one of his men to cut a new piece for the cart from the hazel thicket. The young man was now terrified of discovery and punishment, but nothing happened. The cart was repaired and Ankou's entourage proceeded on its way. So he returned home, safe and sound and able to tell his story. But by morning, he had succumbed to a terrible fever, and he died the same day.

Ankou not all bad?

here was once a wealthy peasant farmer named Laou ar Braz who lived near Pleyber-Christ. Each year he slaughtered his best pig on a Saturday, and after mass the following day, he mounted the steps of the *calvaire* in the churchyard and invited everyone to a slap-up dinner at his place on the Tuesday. "There's plenty of room," he said. "If the house is full, there's a barn and if that's full, there's the great outdoors to fill! Everyone must come," he added, surveying the great throng surrounding him. "Don't forget

– on Tuesday." The crowd echoed his words – "On Tuesday!" As they began to disperse among the graves, Laou heard a frail little voice. "Am I invited too?" He waved his arms expansively – "Of course, everyone is welcome to attend."

There was great eagerness and anticipation of the feast, and the country roads to Laou's farm were packed with carts and pedestrians making their way. Soon they were all happily seated at long tables in the barn in front of a loaded plate. But one guest turned up late. He had a most miserable appearance, dressed in his tattered rags.

Laou saw that a place was made for him, and the wretched man sat with lowered head among the festivities. He did not respond to any of the overtures made by his neighbours, and nobody seemed to know who he was, although he reminded some of the older folk of a vague acquaintance, now dead.

After a copious meal, and equally copious amounts of cider, a good deal of gossip and pipe-smoking, the crowd began to drift away. Laou stood outside the barn and shook each one by the hand, accepting their thanks, pleased with their pleasure. "It's been a good day," he thought to himself. "And I'm sure the ditches along the country roads will be running with piss like a stream before they get home!"

He felt a great satisfaction with all that had happened. As he turned back to the barn, he noticed that one guest remained. The old man in rags still sat at the table. "No hurry," said Laou cheerfully. "You take your time. Last in should be last out, it's only fair. But your plate and glass are empty."

The man got up slowly and raised his head to meet the astonished gaze of Laou. It was the face of death. His rags fell scattered to the ground, in the form of strips of rotting flesh. The stench and a pang of fear gripped Laou's throat.

"Who are you and what do you want of me?" he managed to ask the skeletal figure before him.

A bony hand was placed on Laou's shoulder. "Thank you," he said. "When I asked you at the cemetery if I was invited, you included me without hesitation. It's a bit late to wonder who I am now. My name is Ankou. And as you were kind enough to invite me just as you did to the others, I in my turn will give you proof of my goodwill. Let me tell you that you have eight days to put your affairs in order. I will be back at the end of that time to collect you, whether you are ready or not. So, until next Tuesday. The feast I offer you may not be up to the standard of yours, but the company will be much more numerous."

With these words, Ankou disappeared.

Laou ar Braz spent the next week ordering his affairs and distributing his possessions between his children. On the Monday he took communion in Pleyber-Christ. On the Tuesday evening, he died. His generosity in life had enabled him to have a good death.

A poor reward

Manch ar Floc'h the blacksmith of Ploumilliau had always a great deal of work to get through. On Christmas Eve he told his wife that he could not accompany her to church as he had promised to complete a job for the following morning. Once he had done it, he assured her, he would go straight to bed. As she departed for the service she warned him to listen out for the chime of Elevation,[1] because no good Christian should continue to work after that time.

He set to work assiduously in his forge as the evening crept on. Somehow, perhaps in the striking of his hammer on the anvil, he failed to hear the bell toll. He was still engrossed in his task when suddenly the door swung open

---

[1] The Elevation of the Host became part of the ritual of mass in the late medieval period. A bell was rung as the priest lifted the Host.

and he found himself greeted by a tall man dressed in clothes of a long-gone style. "I saw your light," the figure said, "and I have need of your services." "I'm sorry," said Fanch, but I haven't yet finished this wheel and I must not be still working at the bell of Elevation." "Well, I must tell you that it has already struck, maybe quarter of an hour ago," said the stranger. "No!" said the blacksmith in agitation, dropping his hammer at once. "It's true," was the reply. "But I'm not asking you to do anything major. A single rivet needs tightening." With that he produced a large scythe from behind his back. Fanch had only been able to see the handle and assumed it was a walking staff. "If it's nothing more than that," he said, "there's no problem."

Now he took the implement and laid it on the anvil. Then he looked closely at it, and exclaimed "But the handle is fixed on back to front! What idiot put this together!" "Never mind that," said the stranger sternly. "Not all scythes are the same. Just do what I ask." "As you like," said the blacksmith, who was forming a not very good impression of his client. He swiftly rectified the loose nail and handed back the scythe. "Now I must pay you," said the stranger. "Oh, there's no need just for that," replied Fanch. "But yes," was the reply. "All labour is worthy of reward. And here is yours. I will not offer money, Fanch ar Floc'h, but what is better than silver or gold – a good warning. Go off to bed, think of the end of your life and when your wife comes home, send her at once for a priest. The work you have done for me is the last you will ever do. Kenavo."[1] With that, he disappeared.

Fanch ar Floc'h felt his legs giving way beneath him. He struggled to reach his bed-chamber, where his wife found him in the throes of death. "Go and fetch me a priest at once," he gasped. The next morning, he died at cockcrow.

---

[1] 'Goodbye' in Breton.

Ankou's godson

This story was recorded by François Cadic (1864-1929), a priest from Brittany who became a spiritual advisor for Bretons in Paris. He was also a notable folklorist, specialising in the oral tradition of his native Morbihan.

There was once a poor carpenter living in a village in Morbihan. Although he worked as hard as he could, he could never manage to support his very large family adequately. Fortune may have withheld financial blessings, but he was truly rich in progeny. There were already twelve children, housed with difficulty in every nook and cranny of the house and even in straw in the stable and hay in the barn. Imagine the carpenter's dismay when a thirteenth baby arrived! What could he do to ensure the welfare of this new addition to the family? His only hope was to find a godparent who might give the child a helping hand in what would otherwise be a life of unrelenting misery. But he had already asked all his neighbours to stand for the other children and had now run out of options.

One night he wandered along a narrow sunken way, his heart sorely disturbed by his problem, ideas bred of hopelessness crushing his spirit. In the darkness he suddenly heard a creaking cart approaching, and as it came close, saw a strange apparition. For it was Ankou himself, making his tour of the country hamlets, scythe over his shoulder, fleshless bones scarcely concealed by a grim shroud.

The carpenter was terrified, but Ankou spoke to reassure him.

"Don't you worry, my good man! Your final hour has not yet struck. I wish you nothing but well, for it is not right that misfortune falls always on the same shoulders. I know your difficulty. You are seeking a good and just godparent. Here I am, and I doubt you could find a better candidate. Do you accept me in the role?"

213

"I do so willingly," replied the carpenter. "People say you take some souls too early and others too late, but all must face their time. You deal honestly and fairly in the eyes of the world. This is exactly the sort of godparent I was hoping for!"

The very next day, the baptism of the thirteenth child took place. No expense was spared: the church was richly decorated and a veritable feast was laid out on tables in the village square so all the inhabitants could eat and drink their fill.

Ankou said not a word during the celebration, but at the end he turned to the carpenter. "Through this baptism I have all rights over your son. I want him to become a doctor. You must bring him to me when he is seven and I will instruct him in such a way that no medical man in the world will rival him." With that, his skull-like head gave a grin and he mounted his cart, drawn by a horse of the apocalypse, and disappeared over the horizon.

Seven years passed as the carpenter struggled to provide for his family. He then kept his word to Ankou and handed over his youngest son.

"Have no fear," said Ankou. "You will have reason to be proud of this boy. No illness will be able to resist his knowledge."

The carpenter went home and Ankou conducted the boy into his mysterious kingdom. His education began with learning his letters and then good manners. By the age of eighteen he was a model young man, but no mention had yet been made of medicine.

"Don't worry about it," Ankou told his charge. "Medical knowledge is of little importance. I've more power in the tip of my little finger than that of the finest doctor in the world. I will teach you a simple method which will give you the advantage over the tortuous practices of those from medical school."

At the age of twenty, the carpenter's son finally learnt this secret. "It is very simple," Ankou said. "I myself will be your guide. When you are called on to treat a patient, I will let you know if there is any chance of recovery. If you see me at the foot of the bed, that's a good sign and the patient will be cured. If you see me by the head of the bed, there is nothing for it: they are lost to life. So come now, take account of what I've taught and I promise you that soon you will be the richest doctor in the land. But don't forget that I demand complete obedience from you. The slightest deviation from my wishes will be fatal for you."

Ankou's words were true. No doctor was more successful than the carpenter's son. He was never wrong in his opinion, stating at once if the patient would live or die. Soon everyone wanted his services and he was entrusted with all manner of extraordinary cases. In a few months he was rich, whilst his fellow-doctors lost money hand over fist. The public hoo-ha brought news of his achievements even to the royal court. And just at that time the princess had contracted a mysterious disease and her life was gradually slipping away. In vain had the court doctors tried their remedies and cures, and the princess reached her final hours.

The king, who adored his daughter, was beside himself. He commanded the famous newcomer to attend the princess. There was no response and the king was forced to seek out the young man himself. "Cure my daughter," he begged, throwing himself to the ground in supplication. "Cure her and I will give you half my kingdom!"

But when the young man reached the bedroom of the princess he saw at once to his great disappointment that Ankou was standing by her head, sickle already raised and about to take the girl's soul. "It's too late," he said sadly to the attendants. "She has only a matter of hours to live."

"Cure her, cure her," sobbed the king, "and I will give you her hand in marriage and make you my heir."

The young man was moved by the father's grief and the weight of sadness in the room. He was also stirred by the glittering prospects held out before him. A glance at Ankou showed his patron's triumphant smile and raised arm. "I'm going to play a dangerous game," thought the carpenter's son, "but I cannot resist the king's grief and my own ambition." Moving swiftly, he pressed hard on the end of the bed, causing it to turn on its axis, with the result that Ankou stood not at the princess' head but by her feet. In this way she would avoid death. Ankou left the room, but not before turning his scythe towards his godson with a furious and menacing look. It was clear that he was already thinking of vengeance.

After only a few days the princess was fully restored to health, and the court was soon occupied in preparing joyously for a grand wedding. But the young man was not so happy, full of foreboding about what punishment he would receive from Ankou. After the marriage ceremony, there was a great banquet in the palace. But behind the celebrating guests, Ankou waited impatiently for his moment of vengeance.

The young couple retired at midnight. The princess was already in bed and her new husband about to join her when suddenly at the head of the bed he saw Ankou, infernal joy suffusing his face, eye sockets glowing with fire. The carpenter's son rushed forward to try to protect his wife, but it was too late. The scythe did its work and the unfortunate girl passed from life instantly.

Her executioner sneered: "See, godson, how your patron can act quickly when it suits him. There's no cheating death you know. Sooner or later, it gets even. I have the power over your wife, even though you tried to usurp it. But that is not enough. Now you too must pay the penalty for what you did. The same tomb awaits you and your bride for your wedding night. Follow me."

The young man did not dare disobey. It was a long route through the night to a gloomy château surrounded by a triple wall. From within came cries of lamentation. The doors opened and they went forward into a huge room glittering with candles, some almost burnt down, others barely lit.

"Look," said Ankou. "These candles represent the lives of men on earth. Once burnt down their lives are over and I can take them. The one in that corner is that of your wife, already extinguished. You tried to revive her and prevent me having my rights. She will never live again. Turn this way now and look at that candle. It is your own." The candle went out before the young man's eyes. "Alas," he said. "I can see my time has come."

"It is come," agreed Ankou and raised his scythe once again. The young man struggled for a moment, thrashing his arms and legs, and then was gone. The next day the young couple were buried together under the cold earth, as Ankou had promised.

One can never try to get the better of death. It always has the last word in human history.

Death is no joke

There was once a girl of remarkably good looks and equally high spirits. Her name was Liza Roztrenn and she was regarded as the biggest catch in the area around Le Faouët. She became engaged to a young man from Plourivo, Loll ar Briz, who came to visit her every Sunday. He was quite a serious character who was devoted to his beloved – she on the other hand was inclined to play mischievous tricks on him. Love appeared to have rendered him rather gullible, and Liza and her maid Annie delighted in plotting together to tease poor Loll.

When he arrived to see his lady love each Sunday morning, Annie would present him with more and more fanciful excuses to explain Liza's absence. Her mistress meanwhile was hiding around the place, in the hayloft or behind a pile of straw in the courtyard. Then as soon as the disappointed young man turned sadly back towards his home, Liza would pop out and surprise him, to the great mirth of the two girls. Even Loll would laugh at himself, whilst reproving his fiancée for wasting their time together when he was good enough to come all the way to whisper sweet nothings to her.

But Liza was incorrigible. One Saturday night she said to Annie: "What can we think up to fool Loll ar Briz tomorrow morning?" "I don't know," replied the maid, "but it must be something new, for I fear he has got used to our usual tricks." "I agree," replied Liza, "and I've come up with a really original plan. I think it's time to test if he really loves me as much as he claims. When he comes tomorrow and asks for me, you must look very sad and say that I have gone to my Maker and he will never see me again in this world."

"You are going to play dead, mistress?"

"Exactly."

Annie looked thoughtful.

"You don't think this might be asking for trouble?"

"Nonsense. It's just a joke. I want to see if he's heartbroken at the thought of losing me forever."

And so they passed much of the night plotting their deception. The next morning the two young women went off to early mass, and soon after their return all the other occupants of the house left in their turn for the next service. In this way Liza ensured that there was no-one else in when Loll arrived and had time for her final preparations. She lay on the long kitchen table, her head on a loaf of bread wrapped in a tablecloth. Over her body, Annie placed a sheet and then sat herself on a bench beside the supposed corpse.

Loll duly arrived at the open door and called to the servant: "Good day, Annie. Where is your mistress?"

In tears, Annie mumbled that it was an evil day of unimaginable sadness.

"But what has happened that you should talk this way," asked Loll ar Briz.

"My mistress can never become your wife!"

"What! You mean that she has changed her mind about me or found a new admirer since last Sunday?"

Annie replied solemnly: "Liza Roztrenn will not be your wife, nor the wife of any man. She is now before God!"

"Dead! Liza! Be careful now, Annie. There are some things it does not do to joke about."

"But look at the table! Lift the sheet and see what is underneath!"

The young man turned pale, which amused Annie no end though she took trouble to conceal it. He went to the table, lifted the sheet and recoiled in horror.

"Alas! It is only too true!"

"But Loll," said Annie, trying to keep a straight face, "haven't you heard that lovers can resuscitate their dead sweethearts by falling to their knees and giving her a kiss? Perhaps you should try that remedy..."

"You wretch! You dare still to go on fooling about!"

"Go on, try I tell you, and don't get angry. Come on, I'll help you."

She got up, but no sooner had she reached the table than she fell flat on her back.

Liza Rostrenn was indeed the colour of death and her eyes were sightless.

"It's not possible!" cried out poor Annie. "Loll ar Briz, help me, we must sit her up. I swear to you she is alive, she cannot be dead!"

But she was. Liza Roztrenn was dead. The efforts of Loll ar Briz and the maid Annie did nothing more than shake a corpse. The next day she was buried in the cemetery at Le Faouët. Her fiancé grieved for a long time. The little maid went mad.

So Death is no laughing matter.

The Door of Death

Plague and pestilence were a very real threat at times in Breton history from the 14th–18th centuries. Whole villages could be wiped out by virulent infections.

One morning the occupants of a farm found an old woman whom they took for a witch asleep in their barn. They threw her out unceremoniously and she turned on them, spewing curses. "I am the Plague!" she said. "And I won't forget you..."

She went on her way and came to a stream which she could not cross, as plague can only cross water by human means. Eventually a man driving a cart turned up and she asked him to take her across. He was a bit surprised as it was just a little brook, but he agreed and picked her up. To his amazement she weighed virtually nothing.

"Thank you," she said. "I am the Plague, but I will spare you because you helped me willingly. Now I can carry out my work in this area. Meet me next Sunday by the main entrance to the church. We will stand one on each side of the door and no-one will be able to see us. Watch carefully during the procession, for each person I touch with my stick will die."

But the man went straight to the priest and told him everything. The priest decided that to thwart the plague the procession would no longer use the main entry.[1]

Death and beyond

After death souls may be on the path to Heaven or Hell. This description from *La Légende de la Mort* reflects a common and stereotypical allusion to the reputation of Bretons as over-fond of alcohol.

Even along the route to Hell a soul is subject to temptation. There are ninety-nine inns on the way, each with charming staff ready to offer a wide variety of drinks, and in increasingly large measure as the soul advances as he must from one to the other. He who reaches the end without being drunk is allowed to turn back and freely retrace his route, but woe betide the man who has succumbed to this severe trial. In the last inn he will be forced to drink a mixture of snake and toad blood, which will secure him as the Devil's own, destined to eternal torments.

---

[1] This story may have originated as an explanation of why the entrance gate to a church enclosure was used not by the living but only for the dead in funeral processions. It is called Porz ar Maro, the Door of Death.

Five men in a boat

Two sailors from Quimper were out in the Odet estuary in their boat one evening when they heard a cry carrying across the water. They looked at each other uneasily. "It sounds like the call of that malevolent Yann an Aod," said one.[1] "But look," said the other, "there's a boat up ahead." Sure enough a strange light had settled on a vessel not very far away. It was a white boat, rowed by four men with one sitting at the helm. The oarsmen were rowing frantically, but the boat remained stationary. "These are not good sailors," said one of the men. "We must go out and try to help them. The water is low, we can leave our boat and wade towards them." This they did. As they got closer, the oars went faster and faster but the boat did not move. Then suddenly the light faded and all was in confusion, darkness and water. When they could see again the two sailors saw only four candles burning where the rowers had been, and the helmsman in the water with just his head and shoulders visible. Scared by this weird phenomenon, one of the sailors called out: "Are you of God or the Devil?" "Do not fear," the helmsman replied. "We are five suffering souls. For a hundred years we have waited for a man of goodwill to help us on our way." Much moved by their plight, the sailor asked "How can we help you?" "Ask the rector at Plomelin to say five funeral masses for us for five consecutive days, and see that thirty people are in attendance at each."

[1] For Yann an Aod, see page 146.

"God bless you," said the sailors and made the sign of the cross. "You can trust us."

They went to the rector and themselves paid for the series of masses, and organised all their own families and relatives to attend each one. When the rituals were over, the two men decided to take their boat out again to the same spot. Again they saw the strange light and again the five souls in their white boat, but this time their faces were full of happiness and they all turned to bow in the direction of the two sailors, calling out "Thank you, thank you, thank you!"

Allowing the dead to rest in peace is a recurrent theme – they may need the help or the understanding of the living to achieve this.

Giving the dead a helping hand

A lady of Landeleau died before she could carry out her vow of completing the Troménie, or pilgrims' tour of the local chapels. Fearful of Purgatory because of the broken promise, her ghost then appeared to one of her friends and begged her to carry out the ritual on her behalf. There was one major stipulation – it must be performed in silence, in conformity with the tradition. "But how is it possible?" asked her friend anxiously. "The chapels will all be closed and I must surely ask for the keys, thus breaking my silence!" The dead woman reassured her that there would be no obstacle if she only did what she was asked. The friend set out apprehensively, but to her astonishment the door of the first chapel was open – and the next, and the next... candles burned steadily within each one, and she was able to carry out the duties of her pilgrimage. When she returned home, the dead woman appeared again, but this time she was dressed in white and thanking her friend as the Gates of Paradise opened before her...

The young woman of Coray who cried too much

young woman of Coray had lost her beloved mother. Each day she wept copiously for the dead woman and nothing anyone said or did put an end to her passionate laments. Above all she longed to see her mother again and often yelled like a mad woman over and over again "I want to see my mother! I want to see my mother!"

Her neighbours finally went to the rector and begged him to help the afflicted girl in some way. He came to see her and gradually managed to calm the flow of tears a little. When she confirmed that what she wanted every minute of the day was to see her mother again, he told her that this wish would be granted if she came to the church for confession that evening. That she did willingly, and after receiving absolution, she obeyed the priest's instruction to wait where she was in prayer and then to throw back the curtain of the confessional when the first stroke of midnight sounded.

What a strange sight met her eyes! A line of deceased souls seemed to almost float noiselessly along the nave towards the choir. One figure at the back was struggling with a bucket full of black water. The girl recognised her mother, but was stunned by the expression of wrath on the dead woman's face. She returned home and renewed her tearful laments with increased vigour. Early in the morning she went to question the rector about the possible cause of her mother's dire expression. "Go back again tonight and do as you did before," he said. "Perhaps you will find out what you want to know."

The young woman waited in the confessional until midnight and threw back the curtain. Again the dead souls processed before her, although her mother was no longer the last in line. This time, however, she was bent over under the weight of two buckets and once more bore an expression of anger on her face.

Unable to bear it any longer, the young woman burst out: "Mother, mother! Why are you so unhappy!"

Her mother rushed at her and grabbed her by the apron so violently that it tore.

"Why am I unhappy?" she shouted. "When will you stop crying over me? Don't you see that you have made me into a porter, at my advanced age? Those two buckets are full of your tears, and if you don't stop this nonsense at once I'll be condemned to carry them until Judgement Day! Is there any need to cry a great river? Don't you realise that such behaviour troubles dead souls who should be in paradise, or delays their joy if they are not yet saved? If they are damned, the tears of grief fall on them as a rain of fire, redoubling their torment and their regrets."

The next day, the young woman reported all this to the rector.

"Have you cried since then?" he asked gently.

"Certainly not", she replied, "nor will I again."

He told her to go back to the church that night. To her joy she saw her mother at the front of the line, radiant with celestial happiness – and no buckets.

The Devil

The Devil has almost a dual personality in Breton legend. The pre-Christian Paol Goz (Old Paul, like the Anglo-Saxon Old Nick, or Old Guillaume in Haute-Bretagne) is often treated with familiarity and even a jocular tone. In Basse-Bretagne he may be called *Ar potr rouz*, the Red Man. This devil presents a more congenial figure than that pursued so hotly by the church. Priests used harsher terminology with names like 'the cruel prince' or 'terrible monster' for the grim evil that must be feared and driven out at all costs.

Once Satan, the Church's creation, enters the fray, a polarity develops between good and evil in many stories and the Devil is himself demonised. Missionaries like Vincent Ferrier in the 15th century and Père Maunoir in the 17th saw evil everywhere – thus raising the profile of the Devil - and preached vehemently against the insidious dangers of associating with the devil or failing to comply with the Church's precepts. Fire and brimstone became the theme of thunderous sermons, and rituals of exorcism were increasingly common.

The 'Christian' Devil is a foil for saints and archangels. To some extent it represents the church's fear of the 'old gods' and pagan powers such as nature and weather gods. The Devil is a symbol of all the Church perceived as being against it, but often he is presented as not very bright, frequently tricked by priests or even mere mortals. These stories are obviously designed to please their audiences! Temptation is a well-known symbolic role for the Devil from biblical times onward, and a standard scene for the sculpted Breton *calvaires* is the temptation of Jesus in the desert by the Devil.

Plougonven Devil

The 'Contract with the Devil' is a common theme of Breton legend, with humans making a pact in order to get what they want and then either outwitting the evil one or having to pay a terrible price. A common devilish trick was to agree to give a man anything in return for whatever his wife was carrying. Rather than the simple pot or bag of flour her husband imagined when he agreed, the woman turned out to be pregnant, so the child was forfeit to the Devil. A priest could 'smell' if someone possessed a magic book called an Agrippa[1] because this indicated that they were in league with the Devil. Similarly, the Devil could 'smell out' a Christian in his vicinity.

In stories and iconography the Devil takes many forms. He is usually dressed in black or red: in Haute Bretagne they say 'in the manner of a gentleman'. At Plougonven the Devil tempting Christ on the *calvaire* is presented in dress like the local priest at the time the portrait was sculpted! He travels on horseback or on the wind and enters houses down the chimney. He may have horns or blazing red eyes, but he is also renowned for changing shape, so may take the form of a young man. He can conceal his claws under leather gloves, but what always give him away are his cloven hooves. Scenes on some *calvaires* show Jesus tempted by the Devil dressed as a monk, those tell-tale feet poking out from under his long habit.

All over Brittany tales record that the Devil takes on animal form or has wolves and black cats to do his bidding. Emile Souvestre[2] mentions a chant to ward off wolves:

> *"Go away in the name of God if you are Satan*
> *Go away in the name of St-Hervé if you are a true wolf"*

The association of the Devil with domesticated animals like horses or with bulls may be an echo of Celtic polytheism.[3] In the 18th century, Jacques Cambry in his travels around Finistère records that a spate of drownings in the river Odet are attributed by the superstitious to the Devil in the form of a black dog, pushing people in.

The Devil presides over Hell, and he is master of the element of Fire. *Calvaires* often display the entrance to Hell as a huge gaping

---

[1] Named after the German occultist Cornelius Agrippa (1486-1535).

[2] Author of various works on Brittany and the Bretons. He was born in Morlaix in 1806 and died in 1854.

[3] Like the cattle cult of Saint Cornely, see page 84.

mouth with the Devil's helpers pushing the damned through and down into the horrendous torment and torture awaiting sinners. Graphic details are shown on the frieze at Kernascleden with boiling cauldrons and stabbings with pitchforks. The *taolennou*[1] used in Basse Bretagne in the 17th century by missionaries like Michel Le Nobletz and his successor Père Maunoir also depict terrifying monsters and the savage punishments in store for those who stray from the path of virtue.

Many legends concerning the Devil in Brittany are related to geographical features in the landscape.[2] At Pluzunet a rock retains the hoof prints of the Devil's horse as he rode away after failing to make St-Idunet act in a way offensive to God...

The Devil and the Archangel Michel[3]

There are many different versions of this legend.

ach claimed the right to Mont-St-Michel just off the coast of Brittany, and a competition began to see who could build first on the island. The Devil began collecting material and carried two huge stones near enough to see how St-Michel was faring. When the Devil saw that the abbey was almost complete, he dumped one rock and hurled the other in a rage towards the island. This landed short and today is called the Menhir of Champ Dolent. On Mont Dol you can still see the Devil's claw marks and the seat from which he observed St-Michel's progress.

They fought a great battle in the air with the devil in the form of a huge dragon.[4] But finally St-Michel hurled the Devil back to Mont Dol and there opened up a chasm in the earth and threw him down.

---

[1] Painted skins illustrating heaven and hell used by preachers in Basse Bretagne to put the fear of God into their often illiterate flocks and encourage adherence to the rules of the church.

[2] See Chapter 5, page 129-130.

[3] The common representation of St-Michel in Breton (and other) churches with his foot on the devil/dragon symbolises their essential conflict.

[4] This may be symbolic of earlier pagan gods in this area.

The Devil began building on the island now called Mont-St-Michel. Overnight St-Michel constructed a magnificent palace of crystal on the mainland at nearby Mont Dol. He offered to exchange with the Devil who agreed as he had never seen anything like the glittering masterpiece of the Archangel. So St-Michel took up his place on the island and heard the Devil's roars of rage when he discovered that the wonderful palace was not made of crystal after all but of ice which was slowly melting in the heat of the day. This conflict led to their savage battle in the air, which left the Archangel victorious and the devil cast down into the earth.

St-Michel

The Devil – a master-builder

Many stories record the Devil's role in construction work, when he uses his powers to complete a building or structure overnight.

The spire of Tréguier cathedral

In the late 14th century the bishop of Tréguier ran out of funds for his project of completing a fine steeple for the cathedral. After all the wars, plagues and famines of the age, few people had money to spare for donations, and he had exhausted all ideas of how to raise the funds.

One night a stranger appeared and offered to provide the necessary help. He promised that the spire would be magnificent and the envy of all other churches. "But what do you want in return for this generous offer?" demanded the bishop. Then he saw the stranger in his true guise of the Devil. "All I ask is that you let me take all the souls who die between High Mass and Vespers on the first Sunday after the work is finished."

The bishop considered the offer carefully and then agreed. Work was immediately underway and everyone marvelled at the number of craftsmen on site and the quality of their work: stonemasons and metal-workers toiled for long hours to complete the spire as quickly as possible. One Saturday evening the work was completed and all the labourers disappeared as if by magic. The Devil returned to ask the bishop to inspect the work and give his approval.

"You have kept your side of the bargain well," said the bishop.

"Then you must pay the price," replied the Devil.

"It shall be done tomorrow," was the reply.

The cathedral was full the following day, and High Mass began. The Devil was waiting, eager to grab the souls he had been promised.

The service seemed to go on and on and both the congregation and the Devil were growing restless and impatient. But when the bishop at last pronounced the final words of the High Mass, he went on without a pause to continue with the next office and so on until Vespers had been recited.

And so the Devil was tricked and the cathedral had a magnificent spire.

The Devil's Bridge
(Pont Krac'h over the Aber Wrac'h)

This impressive structure of huge blocks of stone, mostly submerged at high tide, is actually a Gallo-Romano bridge.

miller on the banks of the Aber Wrac'h was fed up with the length of his journey to clients across the wide river, as there was no crossing point and he had to go up to the head of the estuary. He entered a pact with the Devil who offered to build a bridge in a single night on condition that he received the soul of whoever made the first crossing.

The miller woke up next day to find the bridge complete. Aware that the Devil was waiting eagerly on the other side, he took a sack of flour but stuffed his black cat in at the top before fastening it up. Then he heaved it onto his back and started across. About half way over, the miller stopped and put down his burden as if weary. He undid the sack and the cat shot out across the bridge, thus providing the Devil's payment.

Angry at being tricked in this way, the Devil took his revenge in later years, according to local tales, drowning any drunken stop-outs who tried to cross the bridge late at night.

The Devil's relatives

Oddly enough, the Devil has a family in some stories. These relatives are usually female, a wife or mother. In the Forêt de Quénécan on the southern shore of Lac de Guerlédan a strange rock formation is even attributed to his grand-mother. These ancient female powers may represent pagan fertility goddesses demonised by the Church. Sometimes they seem to be firmly on the side of humans against the Devil himself.

The Devil's mother[1]

When she was cast out of the area around Vannes by the arrival of Christianity, the Devil's mother was carrying two white apples in her apron. In her flight the apron tore and the apples fell to earth, rolling to a standstill to form Mané Guen.[2]

A hero was set the task of getting three hairs from the Devil's beard. He came to the Devil's house and found

---

[1] Mamm an diaoul in Breton.

[2] The apples may have a double significance, their loss symbolising that her breasts (and therefore fertility) were no longer useful, and the biblical symbolism of the apple in the Garden of Eden as a tool of the Devil is also implicit. Mané Guen = 'White Mountain' or 'Sacred Mountain'.

only his mother in. She agreed to help him and hid him in the corner. When the Devil came home hungry she cooked a mountain of crêpes to cover the smell of a Christian. When the Devil finally went to sleep, she herself stole the three hairs, gave them to the hero and smuggled him out.

The Devil thwarted

Stories of the devil being outwitted or duped by humans were naturally very popular. Often the protagonists are priests, whose job it is to get the better of evil after all, but ordinary people also have their moments of triumph.

At Briec lived a very poor couple in conditions of great hardship. Ah, they thought, as they huddled near the hearth each night, if only that old vase in the corner was full of gold. At once the Devil appeared and said he would fill the vase with gold before daybreak in exchange for their souls. After a moment's pause, they agreed. When the Devil had gone, the wife instructed her husband to cut out the bottom of the vase and hang it up in the chimney. At midnight the Devil's workers arrived with sacks of gold. But no matter how much they put into the vase it never became full. The couple sat below in the hearth, gathering up an endless stream of coins. At daybreak they were rich, and freed from their pact with the Devil.

On the banks of the Vilaine river lived a young girl who became possessed by the devil. She was taken to the priest for a ritual of exorcism and sprinkled with holy water. The devil cried out that he agreed to leave the body of the girl on condition he could enter that of the sacristan. "Fine," said the priest, "but you must leave by the mouth of the girl and enter by the backside of the sacristan." The sacristan immediately sat down on the stoop of holy water so that the devil was forced to leave the girl and then go away, because he could not pass through the holy water.

The Devil's malevolent force

The Devil, or his demons, can represent any kind of evil-doer, and the following gruesome story has nothing to do with Christianity. It is more of a regeneration legend, with trials being necessary to establish true worth deserving of reward, a symbolic death leading to a new life.

One dark and stormy night, a hero arrived at a semi-ruined château. He saw a bright light, and a woman with a flaming torch appeared to show him to a bedroom where he could sleep. At midnight three devils came to seek out the hero. They killed him, then cooked and ate the body. In the morning, a princess, with only her head visible, came to the chamber and managed to find a small bone remaining from the hero's body. This she brushed with magic ointment and the hero was resuscitated.

The next night, the devils came back. They hurled the hero against a wall until his body was completely broken. In the morning the princess, this time visible to the waist, appeared and once more restored him. On the third night, the devils cut the hero into pieces and swallowed them. But the princess managed to find a tiny piece of his nail, enough to revive the hero. At this the devils were vanquished and the hero was able to marry the princess and gain the kingdom.

Punishing bad behaviour

This unpleasant and moralistic story of the Devil as an instrument of the church comes from Haute-Bretagne.

A little girl refused any of the cherries she was carrying first to a desperate beggar and then to a poor woman. But when asked by a well-dressed man, she willingly offered them. In the church's eyes, she had freely given the Devil what she had refused to Jesus Christ and the Virgin Mary. It was a terrible error of judgement. At midnight the Devil came to her house and ate her before leaving through the keyhole!

Beware curiosity

At a crossroads near the village of Kruch, the Devil used to wait on the night of the New Moon to catch the first soul who passed. To attract men into the danger spot, he used beautiful naked she-devils, and for the women, handsome devils who whispered blandishments in their ear. The only way for a human to pass safely was with eyes closed and ears blocked with clay to avoid succumbing to these temptations. Otherwise they would be drawn into the Devil's clutches and thus down to Hell for eternity.

One of the villagers, a man called Laouig, had known about these goings-on for twenty years. One day he realised that there was a way to get up close and observe what happened without being seen, for he saw that goats passed the spot without coming to any danger. He decided to cover himself with the skin of a billy-goat and approach the spot on hands and knees. In this way he was able to pass the crossroads, but he lingered to watch the antics of the male and female devils, which attracted the attention of one of them. "Hey, billy-goat," the devil said, "This is no place for you, so get on your way or tell me why you're dawdling."

In panic, Laouig emitted a cry, and in his terror stood up to flee at a remarkable speed. This took the devil by surprise, but he instinctively hurled a curse when poor Laouig still had one foot in the magic circle of fiendish power. So it hit, but with weakened effect.

Laouig returned home, threw off the animal skin and fell into an exhausted sleep. In the morning he went about his business, but when he left the house, the villagers ran from him in fright. He was startled and went to a stone trough full of water to look at his reflection. Horrors! He had the horns of a billy-goat! At that moment a mysterious voice came to him: "Curiosity is a sin and you must be punished by sporting these horns for three moons. From now your name will be Laouig an Diaoulig (Willie the Devil)."

The hostility of the villagers drove Laouig from his home and he was never seen in the region again. The crossroads is still there, but the Devil carries out his work elsewhere.

The broken promise

young woman was engaged and promised she would never marry another. But her fiancé died and later she got married to someone else, thus breaking her solemn word. The Devil came and snatched her up into the air ready to hurl her down into hell, but something prevented him and he realised she must have some kind of talisman protecting her. He tore off her clothes and tried to find it without success. But finally he noticed in her hair a single strand of blessed silk. He removed it and was able to thrown her down into the fiery depths.

Another common theme of legend in Brittany is the exchange of babies in the cradle. This is often attributed to *korrigans* or *poulpicans*,[1] but also to the Devil himself. Such tales reflect fundamental superstitious fears of losing a child, but also may be a personification of instinctive ideas about the 'dark' and 'light' side of every human being.

ne night a baby named Médal was stolen from his cradle by the Devil, taken to a remote corner of the forest and left to die exposed. The Devil then took his place in the house to be brought up in the family. But a few days later, Médal's father was hunting in the woods and discovered the abandoned infant. He brought him home and raised him alongside the Devil-child he believed was his real son.

Later on Médal knocked down his 'brother' and suddenly the hideous figure of the Devil appeared, horns, cloven feet and all, revealing the terrible truth.

[1] See page 170.

Exorcism

Possession by evil spirits was much highlighted by certain preachers who believed that the Devil was everywhere. Madness or psychiatric disturbance was attributed to this phenomenon, in the absence of scientific knowledge to the contrary before the mid 20th century. Certain priests 'specialised' in exorcism or were regarded as having special powers to expel malignant demons and they would be called on to help sufferers disturbed in their wits, and also to deal with the tormented spirits of those who already passed over but came back to haunt the living.

The priest, the black dog and the Yeun Elez

Tadic-Coz (literally 'little old father') was a priest in Bégard, Côtes d'Armor, but he travelled around extensively and was known throughout Finistère and the Trégor. He was said to have amazing powers, including the ability to perform exorcisms and release suffering souls from torment.

One day a soldier serving in the army of Louis-Philippe[1] came home to Brittany on leave. He was from the village of Trézélan, and after being dropped by the stage-coach a few miles away, set off to walk the rest at a sprightly pace. As he was passing Méné-Bré he saw a figure approaching. It was an old priest, using his stole as a lead for the fierce black dog by his side.

"Hey, Tadic-Coz", called out the soldier. "Don't you recognise me? I'm Jobic Ann Dréz from the farm of Coatfô. You baptised me and gave me my first communion."

"Yes, of course," said the priest. "I think your mother Gaud Ar Vrân will be glad to see you back." He hesitated. "I suppose you are eager to reach the farm?"

"You bet! I'll be glad to get home. But, father, why did you ask me this?"

---

[1] This dates the story to the period 1830-1848, and it is also mentioned in the text of Anatole Le Braz that there was as yet no railway.

The old man explained that he had to take the dog to the rector of Louargat, but that he was already tired and doubted he had the strength to complete the journey. The soldier willingly offered to take the dog himself, although the beast became fractious as the lead was handed over and Tadic-Coz had to murmur a few words in Latin to calm it down. Then they parted and Jobic set off for Louargat. When he arrived he greeted the rector cheerfully and prepared to hand over his charge.

The priest smiled at him.

"Tell me, young man, did you undertake this task of your own accord?"

"Why certainly, to oblige Tadic-Coz."

"Well, I'm afraid you have not yet finished. You must go on to Belle-Isle and tell the rector I sent you."[1]

"What are you saying?" said Jobic crossly. "You're trying to make a monkey of me. Here's your dog, take it! I'm off home."

"Not so fast, young man," said the priest. "Once you have taken on such a beast you must see the task through to the end. If you let him go, the evil spirit inside him will come after you instead. Then we'll see how you like that. Just look at his eyes."

For the first time, Jobic looked closely at the dog, and saw it had most peculiar eyes, the eyes of the devil. That's a right trick old Tadic-Coz played on me, he said sourly to himself.

So Jobic went on for several hours and arrived at the presbytery in Belle-Isle. Here he was welcomed cheerfully and offered dinner and a bed for the night before he continued his journey with the dog in the morning.

With a sinking feeling, he said, "So this is not your dog either?" "No, my friend," was the reply. "You must leave early for Gurunhuel."

---

[1] Belle-Isle-en-Terre, not the island Belle-Ile.

Anger flared up in Jobic, but when he caught the crazy eyes of the dog he sunk down into a chair exhausted and gave up the fight.

The next morning he was sent on his way early, resigned to following this mad task to the end. And so it went on for several days, through Callac and Maël-Carhaix and Trébrivan, with priest after priest offering food and wine and a place to rest before sending him on his way to the next presbytery. Finally Jobic found himself in the highest hills in Brittany, the Monts d'Arrée, and arrived at the village of Commana.

And here, at last, his reception was different.

"Yes, yes," said the rector, interrupting Jobic's tale of woe. "Get yourself some cider from the kitchen. You're going to need all your strength to help with what I have to do. The beast doesn't look very obliging."

"Don't you worry," exclaimed Jobic, "if it's to be rid of that dog, I'll show you what I'm made of!"

"You just be ready when I give you the sign," said the priest. "But we must wait until the sun goes down."

When evening fell, the rector in his full vestments, summoned Jobic and warned him that he must not let go of the dog at any cost, or both men would be lost. Then they set off, the rector in front followed by Jobic and then the dog.

The night was dark and they seemed to travel across a wasteland of desolation where nothing grew. At the foot of a mountain they stopped for a moment.

"We are now entering the Yeun Elez," said the rector. "Be sure that whatever you hear, you keep your eyes front and that you hold onto that beast come what may."

They went on, the path ever more gloomy and the surroundings more bleak, black earth saturated by black marshy water.

"This is truly the entrance to Hell," thought Jobic.

They had not gone far when the black dog began to howl and struggle frenziedly to free himself. Jobic held on tightly, even though his fingers bled as the beast raged more and more violently.

Finally the rector stopped and whispered a word of warning in Jobic's ear. Then he approached the dog which made as if to bite him, but the priest with remarkable dexterity, slipped his stole around the dog's neck. The dog let out one terrible howl.

"Quick," commanded the priest urgently, "Get down on the ground and keep your face to the earth." He threw himself down and Jobic followed his example. At once he heard the noise of a body falling into water, then a huge furor of noise and movement as if the whole marsh was on fire. This lasted for half an hour, then all went silent.

"You can retrace your route now," the priest said to Jobic. "But be sure to stop at each presbytery as before and tell them you have completed the task."

Jobic needed no prompting. He set off happily, glad to have been released from his irksome experience and keen to get home. But his thoughts turned angry when he dwelt on what Tadic-Coz had put him through.

But when he finally reached the old priest, Jobic learnt an astonishing thing. The tortured soul he had led across the country in the form of a black dog was no other than his own grand-father whose spirit had haunted his relatives for several months following his death. It had taken Tadic-Coz's remarkable powers of exorcism to perform the extraordinary feat of forcing the evil spirit into the body of the dog.

So it was not unreasonable after all that Jobic had been sent on this lengthy errand of mercy before he could go home to enjoy the company of his family for what remained of his leave.

Driving the devil away from a potential victim was also a form of exorcism. Luzel recorded this example of the powers of a priest well-known as a *conjurateur*.

An old lady who was addicted to playing cards became short of partners as she wanted to play every day and night. Late one evening a stranger presented himself at the house and immediately agreed to sit down to a hand of cards with her. He produced a pile of gold coins and they began to play. The old lady won game after game to her delight, and accumulated a great stack of gold. Still they played on. But when a card was dropped on the floor, the maid bent down to pick it up and saw that the young man had cloven feet. Without saying anything she ran to the presbytery for the priest, who was one of great renown in the area for his powers of exorcism. He was still up, praying, though it was after midnight, for he had sensed someone was in need of his aid.

When he reached the house he entered very quietly on tiptoe and went into the room where the card-game was still in progress. Then he leapt at the Devil, wrapping his stole round his neck and sprinkling him with holy water. With a terrible cry, the demon disappeared, fleeing in the form of a ball of fire.

Meanwhile the old lady had fallen to the ground as if dead. The priest revived her, and after confession she went to live peacefully in a convent for the rest of her life. All the gold she had won turned into nothing more than a pile of dry leaves.

CHAPTER 10
LEGENDARY WOMEN

Women appear frequently in the great spectacle of Breton legend, but not so often in a starring role. Through the lens of religion, their individual characterisation is sacrificed to the polarisation of good and bad behaviour. They perform their functions as mothers, wives, sisters and daughters, but rarely drive their own stories for their own sakes. So we see sirens and witches, temptresses and malevolent spirits at one end of the scale and the virginal, totally pure of heart and faith at the other. Older traditions may present a more powerful and positive image.

Two tales of wicked step-mothers

The wicked step-mother motif of fairy and folk tales makes its appearance in the stories of Aude and poor Azenor, two exemplary young women seriously misjudged by their gullible menfolk, but in the latter case, suffering was recompensed by becoming the mother of a great saint…

Azenor was a beautiful and virtuous young woman, daughter of the lord whose castle was at Brest. She made a good and loving marriage to Chunaire, Count of Goëlo, and went happily to live in his territory. Soon after her father, Even, married again and Azenor's step-mother conceived a violent dislike of the girl, and determined to ensure that she did not inherit her father's wealth. Gradually she poisoned the mind of Even and Chunaire against Azenor, who was now pregnant, accusing her of the worst of crimes – infidelity – claiming she had taken a lover and shamed her husband.

Azenor was brought back to Brest by her husband and imprisoned in a tower of the château[1] whilst a court decided her fate. It was agreed that Azenor should be burnt

---

[1] This tower still bears her name to this day.

to death, but when the fire was lit beneath her it mysteriously failed to ignite. This was taken not as a sign that she should be spared, but that those responsible should take care that her death was not directly on their hands. The next plan was to seal her in a chest and throw it into the sea. This they did, and Azenor bobbed off over the waves, protected and nourished by an angel. She finally landed in Ireland where she was released from the chest and gave birth to her son, Budoc, later to be a great saint.

When the lies of her step-mother were revealed, Azenor's husband searched for her through many lands and finally discovered his wife and son in Ireland. He brought them back to Brittany, but died on the sea crossing, and Azenor soon followed him to the grave. The child was entrusted by his grand-father to Saint-Samson.

One can still see today the romantic ruined castle of Trémazan, near Landunvez on the northern coast of Finistère. It was once the home of lord Golon, a widower who had two children, a daughter Aude and son Gourguy. When their father remarried, life became very difficult for the brother and sister because of their step-mother's hostility, and after some years Gourguy decided to leave his home and try to make a new life at the court of Childebert in Paris.

Left alone, his sister, a quiet and pious girl, was more and more vulnerable to the cruelty of her step-mother, who gave her all the hardest household chores and kept potential suitors well away. The latter Aude did not mind as she had decided to dedicate her life to God through prayer and contemplation. Being sent away to a lonely retreat was intended as a punishment, but the girl was delighted at last to be able to enjoy a solitary and devout life.

One day some years later, however, a young man approached her, clearly in a state of savage anger. Just as

Aude recognised her brother and ran happily towards him, he drew his sword and struck off her head. Remorse followed swiftly as the peasants living round about the castle told him the true situation and showed him that he had fallen for the lies of his step-mother, who had led him to believe that Aude was unchaste.

Gourguy went at once to his father to beg forgiveness, ignoring the presence of his step-mother. There, as he started to explain the terrible events, Aude herself appeared, carrying her own head. She calmly placed it back on her shoulders and roundly confronted her step-mother with all her wicked behaviour. She was met with a haughty dismissal, but suddenly the evil woman was doubled over by savage stomach pains and then thrown dead to the ground by a streak of lightning.

Gourguy went to St-Pol to do penance for his misdeed, and then became a monk, taking the name Tanguy.[1]

Strong characters do emerge however from the legends, through the smokescreen of judgement, in the story of Dahut and the wiles of Viviane, legacies of an earlier pre-Christian society where women's role was less restricting. Looking back to the earliest religious traditions suggests an important emphasis on a mother goddess, symbol of fertility. This image becomes less prominent with the rise first of the warrior class (despite some evidence that Celtic women participated in battle) and later Christianity.

Celtic mythology is full of powerful women, often with magical powers, often destructive and to be feared, a reflection perhaps of the fact that tellers and authors of most tales are men. The position of women in Celtic society appears to have been on a certain level of equality with men. The Celts themselves left no written records so the evidence is fragmentary – much is pieced together from later works by potentially biased authors.

Myth and history give us strong female rulers like Meave, queen of Connaught in Ireland, and Boudicca, leader of the Iceni tribe in East

---

[1] Later he founded an abbey at Pointe-St-Mathieu, where the ruins remain today on the cliff-top.

Anglia, brutally suppressed by the Romans after an uprising in 71AD. Julius Caesar, who conquered the tribes of Gaul in the 50s BC, records the equality of property rights between men and women, and it is clear that married women managed their own possessions.

Women in Celtic society were apparently sexually freer than the later constraints of monogamy imposed by Christianity allowed.[1] They could apparently divorce and take lovers without censure or fear of legal sanction, and were not married against their will. It seems fair to say that they had a greater degree of equality than women in other societies of the time.

We have seen that women were actively involved in the early days of Christianity in western Brittany[2] and this may well reflect a prominent part in earlier religious practices where women were priestesses, seers and healers in pre-Christian society.

Pomponius Mela, a Roman geographer in the 1st century AD describes the mysterious Druid priestesses on the Île de Sein, who are both of this world and another.

On the Île de Sein is an important oracle, said to consist of nine virgin priestesses. They can conjure up tides and winds with their spells, take on the form of any animals they please and heal that which others regard as beyond all help.[3]

More evidence comes from Wales and particularly Ireland, where Celtic societies were not subject to the same Romanisation as Gaul (France), including Brittany. With the arrival of the Christianity of the Church of Rome, women were kept out of the altar area, the place of greatest mysteries of faith which could now only be transmitted through men and their interpretation.

Suppressing the ancient power and importance of women in earlier myth and legend was a task the early Church rose to swiftly. The best illustration of this can be found in the transformation of the legend

---

[1] Characters like Dahut may reflect these earlier times.

[2] See page 26.

[3] The Latin text of their powers reads: *maria ac ventos concitare carminibus; seque in quae velint animalia vertere; sanare quae apud alios insanabilia sunt.* The word 'carmen,' a song or chant becomes a spell.

of Ys[1] which becomes a tale of the well-deserved punishment of a wicked woman in the Christian tradition. Dahut's lack of responsibility, her rejection of her father's authority and the morality of the Church, symbolised by St-Guénolé, condemn her to a watery kingdom, out of the way of men.

It is worth remembering in this context that the fearsome power of the sea, so vital to the lives of many around the vast Breton coast, remains personified as a female element, and has given rise to many legends about sirens and sea-spirits.

Sea Spirits and Sirens

Ahes/Dahut

The story of Dahut is an illustration of Christian evangelistic propaganda, where her desire for a pleasure-filled life is juxtaposed by the saintly behaviour of Corentin and Guénolé. She represents sin, the reprehensible personification of a life denying God and living for the moment, for the joys of the flesh. In Christian tradition she was bound to be the scapegoat, sacrificed by her father for the greater good of virtue. But in Breton legend she is transformed into the sea goddess Ahes after her death in the water.

The legend of Ys is one of transformation – the power of the sea being significant in Breton history and legend. Other sirens of the mermaid type figure in Breton legend, seeming to follow as descendants of Ahes. They are pictured, perhaps surprisingly, on many religious buildings, sometimes with a comb and mirror to dress their long hair, sometimes with fish tails. The strange mummy-like 'bandaged' female figure at La Martyre may also be of this ilk. They are said to have the mermaid power of alluring song, which may prove dangerous to unwary fishermen. Stories of sirens are given in Chapter 6.

Caryatid at
La Martyre, Finistère

---

[1] This important Breton legend could be seen as reflecting a conflict between different forms of Christianity. See page 105.

Saints and sinners

Women are at worst the victims of male greed, jealousy or violent rage, and at best the object of political advantage in the marriage stakes, like Ste-Tréphine. Those with an unreservedly good press like the wife of St-Efflam or Ste-Yuna lived a life of total devotion to God without thought of breaking their chastity. They have to become saints themselves to gain the respect of the church.

 **ainte Yuna[1] was the sister of Saint Envel (or brothers of that name) and has a chapel dedicated to her near Loc Envel in Côtes d'Armor. She came from Britain with her brothers and each established their own hermitages, Yuna's being separated from the others by the river Guic. They agreed that devotion to worship would forbid further sibling contact, but Yuna rang her chapel bell each day so her brothers knew she was still alive, until one day ... there was only silence.**

In the Christian written tradition women may appear in legend as evil foils for saints, as in the stories of St-Ronan and St-Ké[2] where they oppose the arrival of the saints with their new religion. We see in the Lives of other saints how many struggled to interact with women, not surprisingly perhaps as priests were forbidden contact with the opposite sex. Saint Samson seems to have had particular trouble with women. He was noted for shunning their society in his early life, and an unpleasant incident from his time at the French court of Childebert in Paris describes how the king's wife tried to kill Samson in various ways, but was finally struck down with a horrible seizure and severe bleeding, which caused her death. It is a rare example in the Saints' Lives of a sinner not being forgiven and saved. Later another woman, wife of a nobleman at Dol-de-Bretagne, had it in for Samson, as this extract from one *Vita* shows. She is not even deemed worthy of a name.

---

[1] She is the patron of sabot-makers, because of her woodland associations.

[2] See page 46 and 203.

Frogerius was a benefactor of the monastery at Dol-de-Bretagne, but Frogerius' wife hated Samson and wished him and his monks only harm. At a moment when the crops stood high in the monastery fields, she instructed the boy who looked after her pigs to drive them in amongst the grain. Hearing of this, Samson rushed out to see them off and warned the boy never to do such a thing again. This made the woman angry and the very next day she gave the same order. Seeing this, Samson prayed to the Lord to protect the monastery and its possessions from harm. At once the pigs were turned into filthy, smelly goats to everyone's astonishment. Only when the woman apologised and begged pardon were they restored to their original form.

But it didn't end there. It was a strict rule that no woman was allowed into the monastery under any circumstances whatsoever. But one day the wife of Frogerius, seeing the door left open, pushed a couple of her ladies inside. They came out unscathed and so she decided to go in herself, boldly entering and even daring to walk in the cloister. But when she tried to go out again, she found she was struck blind and could not find the door. Forced to go to the guest-house building, she fell seriously ill there. Her husband rebuked her severely for her folly, but begged St-Samson to pardon her and help her plight. This he did, offering up prayers that healed her of all malady.

With the development of society, the individual ownership of land and the construction of permanent buildings, issues of property and family inheritance become more crucial. The production of legitimate heirs to guard estates and the expansion of holdings and possessions through marriage alliances both involve the stricter control of women by men, so that financial and social restrictions on behaviour become more the order of the day. It should be noted, however, that evidence exists in Brittany of a more positive situation for certain women of status. From the *Cartulaire* of the Abbey of Redon, a document from the 9th century detailing all the abbey's land-holdings, we know that noble females could hold public office in that they were responsible for order in their area through the role of *machtiern*, a sort of judicial post open to men and women. The name of Aourken, a woman who held this post at Carentoir has come down to us. The *cartulaire* also provided evidence of women buying, selling and administering their own property and acting on their own account, with a male intermediary. This gives a rather more positive picture of women's position in early medieval society than one might infer from legends alone.

Christianity certainly changed things for women. Ironically they were to become the mainstay of the church as devoted worshippers, but all the power and authority of Christianity devolved through men. Legends often reflect a negative image of women, such as that of Dahut or Morgane as self-indulgent sensualists, dangerous temptresses or evil schemers.

In the eyes of the Church, women were important practically in the context of motherhood and the sanctity/security of the family home, but in the abstract women were held at best as imperfect, and at worst dangerous and not above suspicion as some of the legends mentioned above indicate. There is always a tension between notions of motherhood and sexuality. The fact that priests were forbidden concourse with women made it easier to create a negative picture of them in legend and hagiography – with a few notable exceptions of the utmost purity, selflessness and devotion to God. St Efflam's strange marriage (p193) is an example. His wife was apparently quite prepared to give up the joys of physical union to worship God. Female martyrs were also acceptable and there are many tales of women accepting cruel deaths rather than deny their Christian faith or marry when they wished to devote themselves to God (such as in the legend of Ste-Barbe).

The cult of motherhood in the Church is represented by the ideal woman, Mary the Virgin, who became a mother without sexual intercourse. Her constant presence in church iconography and legend is a reminder of the utmost purpose of a woman in the eyes of early Christianity, miraculously pure yet fecund. It is interesting to see some portrayals of Mary on certain *calvaires* where she appears with breast exposed for feeding the baby Jesus. One of these, at La Martyre, was defaced by a prurient priest, and at Tronoën, the long flowing hair and naked breasts look rather sensual. A legend from Josselin given below gives a rare picture of a less-than-perfect Mary.

Right up until the mid-20th century, women in rural Brittany were expected to undergo a purification ceremony (*relevailles*) in church after the birth of a child, the original act of sex which caused this needing a sort of redemption. She was not accompanied by her husband who was not reckoned in need of the same purification!

Two contrasting stories of Our Lady in Josselin

Many stories tell of the appearance of Mary, mother of Christ, or Notre-Dame (Our Lady). The cult of Mary, fostered by Renaissance art, became especially important after the Counter-Reformation and almost every Breton church has statuary and an altar dedicated to the mother of God. She is particularly important as a focal point for female worshippers within the faith.

In legend, it is often the statue of Mary that plays a role in miraculous happenings. Two interesting and contrasting tales concern the town of Josselin. In one, the healing power of Notre-Dame is to the fore; in the other, she demonstrates a rather un-Christian-like vindictiveness, which has not encouraged the church to make much of the story.

Our Lady of the Brambles
(*Notre-Dame-du-Roncier*)

According to a 17th century account, which refers to a much earlier story, a peasant of Josselin found a statue of Our Lady among brambles he was clearing. He took it home, but it returned of its own accord to the previous spot. When the bishop heard of this miraculous event, he agreed to the building of a new church there – where the current one now stands. The statue also had miraculous powers of healing: the peasant's daughter, blind from birth, was given her sight on touching it. This led to a horde of

pilgrims flocking to the town in hope of cures.

The statute was burnt at the time of the Revolution, but a few charred remains were preserved in a reliquary in the base of the replacement statue made later, which is still carried today in the famous Pardon.[1]

The Barking Women of Josselin (*Les Aboyeuses*)

One day a group of women were doing their washing at the *lavoir* when they were approached by a poor wretch who asked for a drink of water.

N-Ð-du-Roncier, Josselin

They scorned the old woman and set their dogs on her, at which she turned into a gleaming vision of Our Lady, and decreed that in future the women and their daughters would bark like dogs in memory of their intolerant brutality.

It is documented in later history of the town that certain women did fall into a strange frenzy, especially during the procession of Pentecost, and made a howling sound like wild dogs. Some early examples of photographs survive of these afflicted women, examples of a curious merging of legend and real events. In 1728, three children in Josselin were seized by a strange malady that caused them to fall to the ground and bark like dogs. When their father took them to touch the statue of Our Lady in the church, they were cured.[2]

---

[1] This takes places in early September, with an evening torchlit procession followed by the main mass and procession on the next day.

* Science put such troubles down to a form of epilepsy.

It is something of an irony, considering Brittany's reputation for dominant females,[1] that in the later Catholic church there is a strong trend of female official saints, often represented in Breton churches. But Brittany does not have its own Ste-Marguerite, foot on the dragon that swallowed her, only to regurgitate the meal when she tickled its insides with her crucifix. Although a virgin, she became the patron of child-birth – women prayed to her for a delivery of the same ease with which she was eliminated from the dragon's stomach! Or the learned Ste-Catherine of Alexandria, tortured on the wheel after managing to convert eminent philosophers to Christianity.

Witches

There are many stories of witches in Breton legend, and even in the early 20th century the tradition persisted. Charles Geniaux's book on old French customs includes his meeting with the Witch of the Château at Rochefort-en-Terre and photographs of the old woman in her cloak, holding a large baton. As in many other parts of the world, there could be a slim distinction between healers or herbalists, who often provided important service in rural communities and evil spell-casters, bringing harm through malicious motives.

Ernest Renan said that if there were no accounts of witch-trials in Brittany it was perhaps because everyone practised such things!

An underwater sorceress

Two young orphans of Lannilis were devoted to each other and keen to marry, but could not afford to do so, being lowly farm labourers without prospects. One day the young man, Houarn, decided to go across the Monts d'Arrée to the south of Finistère where it was said there were riches to be had. He had heard tell of a sorceress who lived in a palace made of mother-of-pearl, and stuffed full of treasures. His beloved, Bella, was reluctant to let him go and insisted that he took some protective gifts. She had

---

[1] For an analysis and refutation of commonly held notions of a powerful Breton matriachy, see Anne Guillou's *Pour en finir avec le matriarcat Breton*.

always treasured the three items found with her in her cradle, and now presented Houarn with a knife and a little bell, keeping for herself a wooden baton. In fact these things were once the property of saints, and had great powers.

Houarn made his long journey, finally taking a boat out to the Île de Loc'h in the archipelago of the Îles Glenan, where he had been told the sorceress lived. On the shore of a lake he stepped into a little boat which at once began to move, and then turned into a white swan. In the middle of the lake, the swan plunged, taking Houarn with it, and brought him to the entrance of an under-water palace of glowing shells. Here the witch welcomed Houarn, and she was so beautiful that he was entranced and amazed by the treasures lying all around.[1] She offered him wine and he took a sip from each of the enchanted nine goblets that appeared. At once he fell deeply in love with her and declared his desire for their marriage.

To prepare a celebratory feast, the witch dipped a net into a pool and brought it up full of tiny fish which she then tipped into a hot frying pan.

"What is that noise?" Houarn asked, as strange sounds came from the cooking fish.

"There is no noise," she said, laughing, and placing a large cover over the pan.

Still he could hear what sounded like whispers and muttering. "Tell me, please, what is that noise?" he asked again. She ignored his question and began to sing a charming song as she led him to the table. She served him a golden plate of little fish and left the room to fetch more wine. He was so hungry he thought she wouldn't notice if he had just one fish, so he took out the knife Bella had given him. But as soon as he touched a fish, it turned into a little man and the same thing happened when he chose

---

[1] There is a link to the siren idea - the sorceress was said to have the powers to cause shipwrecks and then make the currents bring all the loot to her palace by an underground way.

another. Soon he had a whole plateful of these tiny figures calling out to him the warning that if he ate a fish he would become like them. The witch came back in time to hear this warning and she instantly covered Houarn with her net, turning him into a crab and throwing him into the pool to await his turn to be eaten. But as she did so, the little bell in his pocket set up the most tremendous din, so loud that by its magical power Bella heard it all that way away in Lannilis. She knew her beloved was in danger. Taking up the wooden baton, she set it in the earth and at once a young horse appeared to carry her away to the Île de Loc'h. On the way she met an old woman who warned her of the sorceress and told her to appear at the palace under the water not as herself but in disguise as a young man.

This she did, and the sorceress herself fell in love at first sight. Bella only pretended to drink the wine offered. She then expressed a desire to fish in the pool for the pretty golden fish and the sorceress could not refuse her. As soon as Bella took the net, she put it over the witch, ensnaring her and suddenly all the spells were undone and the fish returned to men. The witch also began to change shape, appearing first as an old woman, and then a fish.

So Bella regained her beloved Houarn and they took with them enough treasure to ensure a long and happy married life, inviting the entire parish of Lannilis to their wedding.

The nine sheep

Luzel records this *conte* from 1874. The witch's power to transform humans into animals recalls Circe in the Odyssey turning Odysseus' men into pigs.

Once upon a time there lived a family of ten orphans, the eldest a girl and the rest boys. They lived in a château in the middle of a wood, and whilst Levenez[1] was undisputed mistress of the household, the boys happily ranged out and about in the forest, playing and hunting.

One day they came upon a rough hut which they had never noticed before. Curious, they went up to the entrance on the pretext of asking for a drink of water. Inside to their horror they saw a terrible sight: sitting in the middle was an old woman with great long teeth and a tongue that coiled round her body. As they turned to run away, she called out to them pleasantly to come in and make her acquaintance. Reluctantly the boys entered the hut. She asked what they wanted and then provided water, fresh from her spring, in a wooden pail, fondling the boys' blond heads as each drank. Anxiously the boys thanked her and made to leave.

"Wait", she said, in a tone that brooked no resistance. "I have given you service and it must be paid for."

The eldest boy, a tall lad called Goulven, said falteringly, "We have no money, but we will get some from our sister and bring it to you tomorrow."

The old woman smiled an ugly smile.

"It's not money I want," she said, "but a husband. I'll take the eldest." Looking straight at Goulven, she asked "Will you marry me, young man?"

The boy was so shocked he did not reply at once.

"Come on now," the old woman said. "Will you take me for your wife?"

---

[1] Her name means Joy.

"I d-don't know," stammered poor Goulven. "I must ask my sister."

"Very well," she replied. "But I will come to the château tomorrow morning for your answer."

The boys went home in a state of fear and told Levenez all that had happened.

"Will I really have to marry that dreadful crone?" said Goulven in tears.

"Of course not," his sister comforted him. "I don't know what she may do to us, but we will not abandon you to this awful fate, I promise."

The next day the old woman arrived and found the brothers and their sister in the gardens.

"You know why I'm here?" she asked Levenez.

"My brother has told me everything."

"And are you keen to be my sister-in-law?"

"Indeed not. This is quite impossible."

"And why not? Do you know who I am and what I can do?"

Levenez stood firm. "I am sure you can cause me and my brothers harm but I will never agree to what you propose."

"You would be well advised to change your mind while there's still time," cried the old woman, her eyes like hot coals.

The boys trembled in fear, but their sister stood firm and calm.

"I will never change my mind," she said.

The old woman took out a magic wand and waved it in the direction of the château. At once the whole building collapsed, leaving nothing but a heap of rubble. She then turned to the boys and uttered the words of a magic formula. And they were no longer boys but nine white sheep, and the beautiful gardens of the château were transformed into nothing more than a wild heath.

To Levenez, who remained in human form, the witch said:

"Guard your sheep on this wasteland. And never tell a human soul who they are or the same fate will befall you."

She left, cackling with pleasure at the mayhem she had wrought.

Poor Levenez tended her beloved sheep with care, searching for tender grasses on the heath, stroking and petting them. She spoke to them constantly as if they could understand and little by little they managed a sort of communication, especially with Goulven who was much larger than the rest. She built a shelter for them all to huddle together in bad weather, but otherwise stayed always beside them outside, singing in her beautiful voice to keep up their spirits.

One day a young nobleman overheard this delightful sound and stopped to speak with her. He fell at once for her beauty, sincerity and humility and begged her to go to his castle with him and become his wife, but Levenez refused for the sake of her brothers. The nobleman returned again and again to see her and finally persuaded the girl to accompany him and consent to become his wife. The only condition was that she was never to be parted from her sheep.

For a time all went well. Levenez was happy in her marriage and spent her days in the gardens of the château with her nine sheep. The joy of the married couple was enhanced when she became pregnant. But little did Levenez know that her maid, also pregnant, by the château's gardener, was none other than the daughter of the old witch who had cursed her brothers, and meant her harm.

One afternoon when Levenez was strolling in the garden and stopped to look into a deep well, the maid came up behind her, lifted her legs and dropped her right down the well. She then went to her mistress' room, drew the curtains and took her place in the bed. When the nobleman came in he asked what had happened to the maid, that Levenez was all alone. He then searched all over for the servant but found nothing. Returning to his 'wife' he asked if she was feeling alright.

"No, I'm not well."

When he went to open the curtains, she asked him not to as the light hurt her eyes.

Assuming she was close to giving birth, he then asked if he could get her anything. Was she perhaps hungry?

"Yes, indeed" replied his 'wife'. "I'm very hungry. I fancy a nice bit of mutton. Have the biggest of the sheep killed and roasted at once."

"Are you sure?" said the nobleman in astonishment. "After all your care of them?"

"I assure you, nothing else will do. And make sure you pick the biggest of them all."

He went out into the garden and ordered the gardener to catch and kill the biggest sheep. But it proved quite a task as the beast ran round and round the old well. Eventually the nobleman went over to help and to his amazement heard a voice coming from the depths of the well.

"Who is there?" he demanded down the shaft.

"It is Levenez, your wife," came the faint reply.

At once he lowered the large bucket and then winched up his beloved wife ... and also the baby she had just given birth to in the well.

"We must baptise him at once," urged Levenez. "Let us go now to the church."

"But what about a godfather?" said her husband.

"I choose that sheep," she said, pointing at Goulven.

"What? Are you sure?"

"Yes, yes. Please let us go at once."

So they went, with all the sheep following close behind.

The priest, although mildly astonished by the sheep godfather, agreed and began the service. Goulven stood on his hind legs to flick the baby with water.

The second the ceremony was completed the sheep suddenly took back his original form and the young man Goulven stood before them. He was able to tell the whole story which his sister had not been able to do before.

"So these are really your brothers?" asked the priest, regarding the eight sheep in his church.

"Yes, but now the spell can be broken if you will touch each one with your stole and say a blessing."

The priest did so and all the brothers were restored to human form.

Now all that remained was to punish the guilty. The old witch and her daughter were torn apart between four horses and their remains burnt to ashes.

Levenez, her husband and her brothers lived happily ever after.

The two sorceresses of the Arthurian tales, Morgane, the half-sister of Arthur, and Viviane, Merlin's beloved, are both cunning and potentially vengeful, loving but dangerous. They personify men's fears of women's powers: even Merlin's magic is disabled by the strength of his love for Viviane and she is able to wield power over him. Morgane's reaction to her betrayal by Guyomarc'h is a potent demonstration of female stringency in the face of male weakness.[1]

Another aspect of this is the allure women can exert over men, often to the extent of death and destruction. The famous nocturnal washer-women are possibly a variation on the White Lady legend which can be found in many countries and cultures. In Brittany their stories are closely connected to the Monts d'Arrée, where the wild and eerie landscape contributes to the atmosphere of the tale. The Yeun Elez is a vast bowl of marsh, today containing a modern reservoir, but traditionally a dangerous place containing the entrance to the Celtic underworld and home to many strange creatures.

---

[1] See Chapter 8 for Arthurian legends.

The nocturnal washerwomen

The *Lavandières*, who call unwary travellers to help fold their laundered shrouds, thus luring them to a grim death by crushing their bones, were souls in torment, said by some to be undergoing punishment for killing their own children before their spirits could rest in peace.

There are a very large number of outdoor washing-places remaining in Brittany, some still in use, and these legends may reflect the importance of this everyday custom, where women gathered to perform ther tasks. There is even a *Fête des Lavoirs* each August 15th at Pontrieux, when about 50 picturesque stone and tiled lavoirs along the river are decorated and illuminated.

Long ago now there lived a man named Job Postic, who liked a drink or two. Returning home one night on a lonely road in a state of merriment he even ran into Ankou, Death's henchman and received some dire warnings, but he continued on his bumbling way until he came face to face with the fearful nocturnal washerwomen. When they saw this cheery traveller, they rushed towards him with loud cries holding out their damp shrouds and calling on him to help wring them out and get rid of the water.

He smiled obligingly. "That's not much to ask between friends, but one at a time, ladies. A man only has one pair of hands for wringing or embracing!"

He put down his walking stick and grasped the end of the sheet presented to him by one of the ghostly figures, taking care to heed the warnings he'd heard from old people and turn the fabric in the same direction as his partner. This was the only way to avoid being caught and being crushed.

But as he was wringing the shroud, other women surrounded him and to his horror he recognised his aunts and his sisters, his mother and his wife. All were wailing

"A thousand curses on he who lets his own relatives burn in hell, a thousand curses!"

They shook their dishevelled hair and cried out again "A thousand curses on him!"

Job felt his hair stand up on end; in his confusion he forgot all his previous care and began to wring the fabric the other way. Immediately the shroud caught him in a vice-like grip and he fell, crushed by the iron arms of the washerwoman...

The Laundress' Tale

When I was a very young child I first heard the strange story of the washerwomen haunting the moors by night. It was said that these women were condemned to their lonely plight as a punishment for killing their own children, the most shocking thing that I could ever have imagined. On the misty wastes they endlessly washed their piles of long white sheets, as if it were possible to cleanse a soul in such a way. But evil will out, as my mother always said, and they continued to practise their murderous instincts, ensnaring ill-fated travellers, disorientated by the darkness, in their wicked clutches, binding the helpless bodies in freshly prepared shrouds.

It was nothing more than an old wives' tale, or so I thought. I myself grew up with a thirst for cleanliness and order, although it was not easy in a single room shared by my parents, my siblings and not a few animals as well in winter time. How I hated the dust and dirt that seemed impossible to contain!

But as a young woman I was fortunate to attract the eye of Lors as I danced at St-Jean's feast under a blue June moon. His father was a weaver who had made good profits from the trade, setting his son up in a small stone farmhouse, with enough land to support a family when he had a mind to take a wife. I liked Lors' quiet manner and strong body, but above all his clean and well-stitched clothes, which spoke to me of a better, tidier life with good household linen.

So we wed, and all was as I'd hoped. I took a rare pride in my laundry, never minding the physical effort of dragging the handcart piled with clothes and sheets down the steep track to the washing-place and up again at the end of the day when my back and arms were sore from scrubbing and pounding and folding.

Within a year I fell pregnant and made a start on preparing the little shawls and dresses our first child would wear one day. The only blot on the landscape of our lives was that we had disturbing neighbours. A rough hovel stood at the end of the track that led to our well-kept little farm, and from the start we were a source of scorn and mockery to Cherm al Lonker the drunken buffoon and Chann Gloukik his drunken slut of a wife, who lived there in worse conditions than our pigs in their sty. There would have been days of work in season for Cherm and my kind husband had offered him this means of earning an honest wage, but he refused with a foul oath, preferring to spend his time at Per Tol Atao's drinking house with money scrounged or worse from who knew where.

I often walked into the village, stepping carefully to avoid the muddy cart-tracks, particularly when my condition made me restless, and each time I determined to ignore the unprovoked insults or cat-calls from either of these two pitiful creatures – for she was worse than that poor excuse of a man - as I passed.

It had been a year of bad harvests, and many were struggling more than usual to make ends meet. All remembered times of famine on the harsh land of the Monts d'Arrée, when people died for lack of food and little children succumbed quickly to disease. We were more fortunate with our well-stored supplies.

I tried to help out where I could, even taking courage to stop at my neighbours' door, where Chann dashed the bag of buckwheat from my hand and spat on the floor at my feet when I asked how they fared in those hard days. Returning home I brushed and brushed at my clothes to drive away the contaminating filth of their shack.

A reckoning was to come in a way we could never have foreseen.

My husband, too easy-going soul that he was, had a falling out with this Cherm, when his patience finally ran out and he took the good-for-nothing to task over trees cut down on our land to feed their ill-swept fireplace. There was no fight. Cherm didn't have the stomach for anything but the contents of a bottle. He shouted, swore and half-swung a punch that went nowhere. But the very next day I smelt the arrival of his dirty wife as I knelt at the washing-place. She stayed only to hiss in my ear, "I'll put a curse on you, you'll see."

I kept myself calm, thinking of the baby almost fully grown inside me. Life went on as usual, and little Naïg soon entered our world safely. I lay back on the old grain chest covered with blankets, placed near the hearth for my delivery, and held the tiny girl close, listening to her ragged breath. There seemed nothing more to desire in the world for Lors and me, but it turned out that Naïg was not an easy child to settle and often I had to hold her whilst trying to do my chores and keep the house spotless.

My milk came strongly and the little girl grew well in her first months. Her father doted on her, a good thing I daresay, but almost everyday he left the fields to come and hold his darling in his arms, cooing and singing whilst she gazed up at him in the rapture of innocence. I chided him constantly for tramping in the dirt on his boots, but he hardly heard me, engrossed in some silly baby talk that only the two of them could understand.

At night we climbed into our box-bed, a fine piece of furniture that had been a wedding gift from his parents. I felt proud each time I put my foot on the wooden step or traced the carving of our names and date of marriage with my finger – just to check no speck of dust lingered there. Lors would place the infant tenderly in her crib, hung above us, so the touch of his hand or foot could set the cradle rocking if she whimpered in the night. When I lay awake, it seemed almost crowded with the baby in our warm nest.

Life got harder, of course, as with a child there is always so much more to do. I was never afraid of hard work, but the mess a baby creates without trying depressed me as the days went on. It seemed she would never go down into her basket easily, always waiting for her dad to run in laughing and calling for his little girl. It made me angry when he woke her and all my efforts for calm and peace to get on with my chores were set at nought. And never could I have imagined how dirty babies were!

I knew it would be easier when the girl was grown but sometimes my mind drifted back to those simpler days at the washing pool and I remembered sadly my old pleasure in the white softness of our linen, and the carefully folded clothes in our chests. It was barely possible to get down there now with the child having to be carried and watched all the time. Lors sometimes took her to the fields in a sling on his back and kept her by him while he worked, a sight that others found amusing, I am sure. Only then could I breathe easily and take my time in the way I liked best.

One clear, sunny day when Lors was off at the market in Commana I determined not to waste my time but to go down to the washing-place regardless of tending to the baby. I wrapped little Naïg tightly in a shawl and placed her firmly in the crib in the box-bed, giving it a good push to get it swinging before pulling the door gently closed.

It was such a beautiful day, I lingered at my task and only returned shortly before my Lors was due back home. I came up the track with a lighter heart, but stepping over the threshold reminded me that I was not alone and some care must be given to the baby. I pulled back the door of the bed.

Often we had woken in the dawn to Naïg's snuffling cries, soon followed by gummy grins and waving fists as she saw her father's loving face ready to greet his treasure. This time, nothing but a heavy silence greeted me. The cradle was still, Naïg lay motionless as I had left her. I knew I should try to wake the child, but my mind was on preparing a meal for Lors after his long day, and doing so in peace. I pulled the shawl a little away from her face and left her there, fetching potatoes from the sack and scraping their muddy skins. It gave me satisfaction to make things clean.

Lors came in jovially, keen to be re-united with his daughter. I said she was sleeping and not to disturb her, but he went eagerly forward to steal a glimpse. There was a dreadful pause. I saw his arm reach in to touch her face and then he stood back abruptly, striking his head on the wooden frame.

"Anna, she's gone, she's gone," he wailed. "We have lost our love and all our happiness. Dear God, how could you be so cruel!" He stood paralysed with horror. I went over to him as if in a dream and looked into the crib. He was right. The child was dead.

The priest was prompt enough in carrying out his duties and soberly reminding us of God's will and purpose. There was nothing to do but soldier on, he said, and wait for His blessing to fall on us again. Meantime, he would expect to see us in the church the following day, where our sorrow could be shared.

I did not want to go. I found it hard to bear the depth of sadness in Lors' eyes, and to listen to his laments, flashes of true anger that such a gift from God could be so speedily withdrawn, mingled with the pure pain of bereavement.

Finally we dressed as best we could and stumbled along the track, thankful at least for silence as we passed the empty shack. We were late, and the church was nearly full when we arrived. The priest was about to begin the service, but beckoned us forward with a gesture of kindness, to squeeze into a pew near the front. As soon as we were settled, he began the words of the blessing.

But at that moment the heavy door crashed open and Chann burst into the church, lurching towards the priest. She stopped level with our pew and, pointing at me, called out, "Father, Father, this woman is a murderer. She smothered her baby. I saw her with my own eyes!"

A powerful silence filled the nave. The priest was visibly struggling to collect himself.

"Come, Chann, this is a terrible allegation. Why would a loving mother do such a heinous thing, child?

She turned towards the congregation with malicious glee all over her raddled face. "Jealousy" she sneered. "Her husband loved the little lass more than her do-good mother and she couldn't bear to watch him dote on the child a moment longer. She wrapped it in a cloth, I SAW HER DO IT!"

Lors half-rose, gazing at her then me, his face suffused with anger, and I heard the whisper from a pew behind, "Look, it must be true".

"Do you have proof of this awful accusation?" asked the priest soberly. But he did not succeed in cutting off the drama.

Chann moved forward and grabbed wildly at the foot of the statue on the wall behind him. Her words rang round the church. "I swear by St-Yves de Verité that I have told the truth. Let God see into her wicked soul and punish her for all her sins."

I was on my feet, turning this way and that, stunned with horror by this cruel attack. All eyes were on me. I heard the murmurings and saw not indignation at her lies but suspicion, hostility, at best pity. I gasped and ran, dragging free of Lors' attempt to stop my flight. Bursting out of the church I kept on running, knowing not where I was going or what my purpose was. When I finally stopped and flung myself to the ground, the world was dark and all my strength was gone.

I woke up to find myself in this lonely place with these dread companions of the marsh, these wild, mad women still buoyed by the energy of their crimes And here I have been ever since, tied by invisible threads, a prisoner between life and death with nothing to do but scrub and knead the eternal laundry, and dwell on far-off days....

It's almost a relief when my reverie is broken by harsh cries breaking out nearby. One of the women has seen a light in the distance moving in trepidation on the marsh. My heart sank, as the noise portended another lonely traveller facing a brutal end to his existence by simple dint of straying from the main path in the darkness. My fellow-workers were quickly all up and running, bare feet slapping on the mud, loose white garments trailing like sails before the wind.

"Over here," they called towards the flicker of light. "Come over here, you'll be safe with us!"

I shivered, remembering how Lors had come looking for me in the early days after my abrupt departure. I heard his voice calling "Anna" over the marsh, a lantern swinging from side to side in his desperate search. He must have feared I had tumbled into the marsh. I strained with every fibre of my being not to react, not to bring him towards the cruel and certain death awaiting in the arms of my grim sisters.

They heard him too and began to rise and writhe like a nest of vipers, marshalling their forces for a strike. But then the wind changed and carried off his echoing call and the prick of light vanished too.

I wonder now if my longing caused me to imagine that he searched for me or that he cared enough to risk a lost foothold in the bog.

That was long ago. Many generations have had their time since Lors and I were wed in happiness before the loss of the beloved child. Things are not always what they seem. There's another side to every story...[1]

Devil Women

It was clear, at least to the church, that women had much in common with the Devil. They were impure (menstrual bleeding), they seduced men to lead them astray and they were always seeking the upper hand. In legends a woman can be the opponent of the Devil or often his agent.

A chant from Plougastel recorded by L.M.Bodenes

Women are very clever
And many young men are caught
Without much trouble, women can even
Catch the Devil himself.

Katell Gollet

The terrible fate of Katherine 'the Lost' is graphically displayed in sculpture on the famous *calvaires* of Guimiliau and Plougastel Daoulas. Her story, which may be one invented by priests as a warning, is the ultimate deterrent tale for unruly teenagers!

Katell lived in the château of Roche-Maurice, near Landerneau, with her uncle. She was a beautiful girl, but wilful and stubborn, wanting only to dance and amuse

---

[1] Story reprinted from *The Shape of Mist: Tales of the Monts d'Arrée* by Wendy Mewes (2011).

herself rather than settle down to the sober marriage her uncle was keen to see to take her off his hands. Some said her passion for the dance was on a par with her desire for taking lovers. She refused to consider suitors unless they could dance non-stop for twelve hours: some died of exhaustion in the attempt, none succeeded.

Her uncle confined her to the castle in the hope of breaking her spirit, but the girl was undeterred and managed to

Katell Gollet, calvaire at Guimiliau, Finistère

escape. She appeared at a festival at La Martyre in the company of yet another young man. Some said she stole sacred objects of the mass from a church at her lover's bidding. He was, of course, the Devil in disguise. They began to dance and went on and on and on, dancing and dancing, and Katell, heated fiercely by the alcohol she had drunk and the passion of the music, could not seem to stop. They generated such extraordinary heat that the Devil finally appeared in his fiery person and dragged her off into the Gates of Hell.[1]

The following bizarre tale, symbolising the seductive and destructive power of women, was told by *conteur* du Laurens de la Barre (1819-1881).

Trémeur wished to become a Christian, but his father, the pagan Conomor, cut his head off. Saint Herbot put it back on with butter.[2] Trémeur was then baptised, which infuriated the Devil. He appeared in the form of an old man with a red beard, and appealed for Trémeur's help in

---

[1] Another version describes the worst of her bad behaviour in a refusal to confess her terrible sins to the priest.

[2] See page 84. He is the saint of cattle and is still honoured today by the 'Butter Pardon.'

freeing his daughter, who was being held by a terrible ogre. Trémeur obliged, cutting the ogre in half and carrying the girl off in his arms. She was said to be 'devilishly' pretty, and this exertion warmed the young man up, so the butter holding his head on began to melt. There really was a danger of him 'losing his head' for the sake of the girl. Luckily, Trémeur had the presence of mind to make the sign of the cross and suddenly the girl disappeared.

But be warned! She remains at large in the world ...

Women of mystery

The White Lady is a universal motif is legends and folktales. The colour white signifies virginity, purity and goodness, but it has also come to be the colour of ghosts, restless spirits waiting for release from their state of limbo. An aura of mystery often shrouds these stories, perhaps an aspect of the unfathomable nature of women (from man's point of view, of course).

The White Lady of Trécesson

In the year 1750 a poacher was in the grounds of the Château de Trécesson[1] one night. Hearing sounds approaching, he hid behind a tree to see who else was out in the darkness. A carriage drawn by two black horses appeared, with men carrying spades walking behind. When it stopped, the poacher was amazed to see a young woman dressed all in white and with flowers in her hair like a bride pushed out of the carriage violently and then held captive by two well-dressed men whilst the servants dug a grave. In tears she beseeched the men as her brothers, begging them not to kill her, but they said only that she had dishonoured them. She was thrown into the trench which was immediately recovered with earth. All then left.

---

[1] This handsome château built of the distinctive purplish granite of the area is near the Forêt de Paimpont (or Brocéliande). It is privately owned, but the exterior with its lake, moat and drawbridge offers an impressive sight.

The poacher was horrified at what he'd witnessed, but did not know what to do. Finally he rushed to the château and informed M. de Trécesson of what had happened. The lord was highly dubious about the story and it was not until dawn that he arrived at the spot with some of his men. They dug up the young woman, who actually opened her eyes but then died. He made extensive enquiries to find out who this young woman was, but all in vain. Finally he had her buried properly in the chapel of the château. The mystery remains – but ghostly appearances of a White Lady at the château over the years keeps the legend alive.

Two important Annes

Ste-Anne is the female patron saint and 'grand-mother' of Brittany. Mother of Mary and thus also Jesus' grand-mother, she appears not in the New Testament but in the Apocrypha. A Breton legend (of varying versions) claims her for its own. She often appears in sacred statuary in churches, shown as a tall woman with a veil covering her head, frequently teaching her little daughter Mary to read.[1]

Ste-Anne

Anne lived in the south-west of Brittany. She was married to a cruel nobleman from the Forêt de Nevet, and to her great misery had not conceived a child. An angelic visitation told her that she would one day become a mother and that the daughter she bore would in her turn become the mother of God. This gave Anne hope that her unhappiness would come to an end. One day she was walking by the sea in the Bay of Douarnenez when a boat manned by an angel in gleaming white arrived and carried her far away across the

---

[1] At Commana, the famous altarpiece of Ste-Anne pictures her in bed with the baby being washed by a midwife. In addition to the chapel at Ste-Anne-La-Palud mentioned here, there also is a celebrated shrine of Ste-Anne at Ste-Anne d'Auray in Morbihan, visited by Pope Jean-Paul II in 1996.

seas. She landed in Judaea and there began a new life, bearing a daughter, Mary.[1]

After fulfilling her grand destiny in this way, Anne was overcome by longing for the land of her birth and prayed for divine aid. Again a boat manned by the same angel (this time in black, an indication that her former husband had died) appeared and she was taken back to the shores of Brittany, landing at what is now called Ste-Anne-La-Palud in the Bay of Douarnenez. Here she was kindly welcomed and settled once again in her homeland.

Many years later a young man appeared and introduced himself as her grand-son, Jesus. He asked Anne what blessing he could give her for 'her Bretons'[2] and she asked for a sacred spring whose waters could cure all ills. Jesus struck the ground with his staff and the spring appeared. He returned to the Holy Land, but Anne remained in Brittany until she died. The locals revered her in life and were disappointed that her body disappeared when she died, leaving no relics for a shrine.

But fishermen in the bay caught no fish that day – in their nets was a stone statue of Anne. They brought it into shore where a child stepped forward from the waiting crowd to carry the statue a short distance inland towards the sacred *fontaine*. Once he put it down there no human effort could move it again, so everyone knew this was the place for a chapel to Ste-Anne to be built.[3]

---

[1] In some versions, she was already pregnant and thrown out by her cruel husband when the angel found her – but that would make a vicious and vindictive tyrant the grand-father of Christ.

[2] An obvious anachronism as the Armorican peninsula was part of the Roman empire at that time and it would be centuries before any sense of Brittany existed.

[3] This early chapel is said to have been lost when the city of Ys was flooded. A second chapel slightly inland was later submerged in drifts of sand, although its existence is recalled in the name of the road Hent santez Anna gollet (the road of lost Ste-Anne). Today a beautiful chapel to Ste-Anne stands behind the shoreline at La Palud, with an elaborate fontaine nearby. A famous Pardon or religious procession and celebration takes place here each year on the last weekend of August.

And her namesake, a medieval duchess...

Time and national desires seem to have almost merged the two figures of legendary Ste-Anne and Anne Duchess of Brittany in the late 15th century. This Anne was the last ruler of an independent Breton state before the French king François (who married Claude, daughter of Anne after the duchess' death) subsumed the duchy into the state of France in 1532. Although a well-documented historical figure, such was the popularity and media-awareness of the duchess that some of the reverence devoted to the grand-mother of Christ managed to rub off on her. She has also attracted stories that seem to belong in the realm of legend, including that of the emblematic animal, the ermine.

Once whilst travelling Anne and her entourage witnessed an ermine pursued by a pack of hounds. They watched the animal at bay turn and face certain death rather than cross a deep sea of mud and thus soil the beautiful white fur of its winter coat.[1] For this reason the Duchess ordered the hunters to spare the animal, which became her symbol. Years later on a visit to Morlaix she is said to have been presented with a frisky live ermine, from which she recoiled. "But Madam, it is your emblem," was the response of the disappointed official who had had the bright idea.

The nursery rhyme '*Duchesse en sabots*' is a later manipulation of Anne's image to fit that of last Breton ruler before the tyranny of France, a projection dear to the hearts of Breton nationalists from the late 19th century onwards.[2] It also reflects the idea of Anne's popularity with ordinary people, not unlike what we know today as the Princess Diana effect. Unsurprisingly, the idea of the sophisticated and fashionable duchess in wooden clogs (and sometimes Breton peasant headdresses) has no historical foundation.

---

[1] A similar tale is told of Conan Meriadec (see page 89) in a (false) attempt to create a pre-French origin for the heraldic use of the ermine in connection with Brittany. In fact it began with Pierre de Dreux in 1213 and was used as a ducal symbol particularly by the Montforts. In the 14th century, Jean IV inaugurated the chivalric L'Ordre de l'Hermine.

[2] The fact she was not a Breton-speaker is apparently no obstacle to this constructed image.

There was Anne de Bretagne, a duchess in sabots
Returning to her lands
In sabots, fa la la.
Ah ! Ah ! Ah !
The wooden clogs live on.

Anne became queen, with her sabots,
The Bretons were in misery, in sabots, fa la la,
Ah ! Ah ! Ah !
The wooden clogs live on.

The Bretons were in misery, with their sabots,
They no longer had a ruler, in sabots, fa la la,
Ah ! Ah ! Ah !
The wooden clogs live on.

Marion du Faouët

This woman was a real person who became a criminal, but later attained cult-like status and a positive image in oral tradition. The metamorphosis is a good example of the creation of a legend, from early hostile views to a veritable folk heroine.[1] More than that, she has come to personify something perceived as essentially Breton, in her rurality, her courage and defiance of authority and her melancholy fate. From relatively little historical evidence an elaborate personage has been constructed – as the following account suggests.

Marie-Louise Tromel (or sometimes she is given the surname Finefont) was born in 1717 near Le Faouët. Of a poor farm-labouring family, she helped scrape a living as a child through selling trinkets at markets, before trying her hand as a pick-pocket. This proved a much more lucrative skill, and by the age of 23 she was head of a gang of thieves who operated over a wide area, targeting merchants returning from trade fairs and religious pardons. As many as 80 men were under her command, including her own brothers and many fugitives. For the

---

[1] Marion's story also has the Robin Hood association, not only in name but in the lifestyle of ducking and diving to avoid capture, and stealing from the rich but not from locals.

next fifteen years they ranged over the countryside of Cornouaille executing many robberies, but apparently without undue violence. She gained a reputation for justice in the oral tradition, punishing her own men if they stepped out of line. On the other hand she is said only once to have hit a man – Pierre Douain - with her club.

Marion was a striking woman with lustrous red hair, almost a symbol of her supposed powers, like a female Samson,[1] grey eyes and a buxom figure. She was said to admit members of her band into her bed when fancy took her. Legend says she met her great love, Henri Pezron, when he saw her bathing naked in a lake at Priziac. They were to have three children together.

Marion was first arrested in 1743, but managed to escape after some time in prison, a feat that greatly added to her later reputation. She was not so lucky when she and her lover were seized a few years later. Pezron was sent to the gallows and Marion only got off with a brand of the letter V (*voleur* = thief) on her shoulder. She was also banned from her home area around Le Faouët, but seemed to take little notice of such restrictions.

The life of crime continued and she was arrested again some months later, the day after giving birth to a fourth child. Again she was spared the death penalty, but afterwards was ever on the move, seeking to keep one step ahead of the authorities from Quimper to Nantes. Finally taken for vagrancy in the latter city, she was recognised by someone from Gourin and sent back to prison in Quimper.

She is said to have been tortured by having her feet placed on a red-hot brazier in an attempt to extort names of her accomplices, but she gave nothing away and was hung in the Place St-Corentin by the cathedral in May 1755.

---

[1] A study of 1884 by Julien Trévédy described how she attended a child's baptism with her wonderful hair cut short, thus losing all her charm, as if some residual power was gone.

The elements of her later legend derive essentially from the fact that she was a woman – the first such leader known in France - with her striking red hair, her strong sexuality used to hold power over men and her reputation as a witch who wielded a magic instrument[1] and could make sleeping potions. More menacing sides are suggested by Paul-Yves Sébillot's record that the image of Marion was used as a warning to naughty children - "be quiet or she'll get you." A local proverb says "Marion Finefont has gone to the devil – do you want to go with her?" These are presumably hostile traditions derived from the nobles and merchants on whom she preyed. Her popularity and later almost veneration comes from the ordinary people.

Anatole Le Braz preserved a popular tradition that Marion's spirit still haunted her home territory, wheeling a cart of gold pieces, and calling out "Who wants some?" - but always disappearing if anyone tried to lay hand on her.

Marion du Faouët enjoys the romance of the rebel, defying conventional authority but remaining popular with the people of the area. The analogy is expanded in her later reputation as someone who targeted strangers to the area rather than thieving from locals, who used no violence in the robberies she executed – her preferred weapon was a club - who spared the poor and gave to the needy, especially during the severe famine of 1740/1.

A *gwerz* in the *Barzaz Breiz* records her:

> **Marie the redhead, Marion Tromel**
> **Marie the outlaw, the rebel**
> **Marie the sweet young thing**
> **Marion du Faouet, the beauty.**
>
> **See all the beggars,**
> **The women and children**
> **Starving and freezing:**
> **To them she brings justice.**

Many details of her life, whether true or evolved, including various emotional liaisons and children (she had four) are well-known. What

---

[1] A gimlet or auger.

Marion's glorious and sad history does reflect are the social dissatisfactions, privations of poorer people and agrarian hardships in pre-revolutionary Brittany, trends that were to lead to widespread support for the Revolution and its Republican ideals. This, together with the 1970s revival of a romanticised Breton past, also explains the later glamorization of her story. She has inspired novels, and a TV film of her exploits, starring Carole Richert and Laurent Mallet (and a range of anachronistic hand-guns), was shown in 1997, aptly summarising the romance and imaginative appeal of the tale. Popular songs of her beauty, exploits and tragic end are often performed by Breton *conteurs* and singers today.[1]

---

[1] The famous Breton folk trio Tri Yann who perform at many festivals include the song 'La Complainte de Marion du Faouët' in their repertoire.

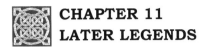

CHAPTER 11
LATER LEGENDS

Legends are not only a phenomenon of the distant past, but continue to spring up even from relatively recent history where events and characters may be well-documented. Some real events and people have nevertheless attracted an aura of legend, and some have left an air of mystery – the breeding ground of legend – around certain places even today.

Eon de l'Etoile and a strange sect

The story of Eon de l'Etoile is a curious one and merits its place here even though he was a real person.[1] Born into a noble family, Eon became a hermit in the Forêt de Brocéliande. Whether living in isolation drove him mad or mental illness was already in his make-up is impossible to say, but what followed went well beyond normal behaviour. He became delusional, believing that the word '*eum*' (he) pronounced in the expression of the Latin mass *Per eum qui venturus est judicare vivos et mortuos* (through he who will come to judge the living and the dead) referred to him personally (eum = Eon) and that he was in fact the re-incarnation of Christ himself.

Followers flocked to support him as he claimed to be the New Messiah, and he was soon at the centre of what can only be called a cult. This adulation seems to have exacerbated his personality disorders. Soon he was leading a band of malcontents on an extraordinary spree of pillage and destruction, looting churches, abbeys and châteaux over a wide area. All the spoils were brought back to the forest where it was said – in increasingly elaborate and fanciful detail - orgies and wild celebrations regularly took place. Eon fasted to extremes, going into an altered state

---

[1] His name means 'Eon of the star' because the appearance of a comet fitted his claims of being the second messiah - the equivalent of the star that marked Jesus' birth.

of consciousness and dressing up in rich ecclesiastical robes he had stolen. He began to practise sorcery, and became a master of black magic, conjuring up evil spirits and – some claimed – the Devil himself. His magic and illusions impressed the simple souls who believed fervently in his powers. His reputation spread and other branches of Eon's cult sprang up elsewhere.

But finally the Church intervened and in 1148 he was arrested, then taken to appear before the Council of Reims and respond to charges of sorcery and heresy. He defied his judges, affirming staunchly that he was the son of God. It was soon decided that Eon was not in his right mind and the decision was for lifelong incarceration in a monastery rather than death, but he died soon after in his prison. His followers were not so lucky. Many were rounded up and put to death.

It is said that his spirit still haunts the secret places of Brocéliande, for after all, near to the fountain of Barenton where he had his headquarters there is a village called Folle Pensée or 'Mad Thoughts'[1]...

Sinking of the *Cordelière*

This well-known and much written about event of 1512 has taken on a legendary twinge in the history of conflict with the English navy around Breton shores. The *Marie La Cordelière* was a state-of-the-art warship built near Morlaix at the end of the 15th century. It had already seen service in the Mediterranean, but was back in Brest at the time when English raids on the Breton coast were frequent.

On August 10th 1512 ships of the Franco-Breton fleet stationed at Brest were on the water celebrating St-Laurent's day with feasting and dancing. On board the Cordelière hundreds of people, including many women, had gathered, with all the noble families of Léon represented. Hervé de Portzmoguer was in command. His estate at

---

[1] Local tradition says that the hamlet was built with stones from Eon's former priory in the forest.

Plouarzel had been sacked in an English raid not long before.

For the pleasure of the guests it was decided to up anchor and sail along the Goulet towards its entrance on the Atlantic coast. The crew may have numbered up to six hundred, so there were probably about nine hundred people on board the Cordelière. Other ships from the fleet came along too, perhaps twenty in all.

When they reached the bay of Bertheaume, sails were seen ahead around the Pointe St-Mathieu. There was a pregnant pause as everyone craned to identify the vessels. Friend or foe? It was in fact an English fleet, commanded by Edward Howard, and including the *Mary Rose*. They appeared to outnumber the unfortunate Franco-Breton contingent.

The duty of the latter was clear: to block access to the Goulet and protect the vulnerable fleet still in harbour at Brest. There was no time to disembark all the guests as manoeuvres began rapidly and continued for up to eight hours, as long as daylight lasted.

Howard's vessel the *Mary Rose* was the first to attack the *Cordelière*, the largest ship on the opposing side, although it was not the French flagship. The *Sovereign* also approached and the *Peter Pomegranate*. As the other Franco-Breton ships suffered damage and began to withdraw, the *Cordelière* was in danger of being surrounded. It made an approach towards the *Regent*, with the intention of grappling the ships together and boarding, but the *Sovereign* continued to threaten on the other side until a canon shot took out its main mast.

Once the *Regent* and the *Cordelière* were bound together, the English ship was boarded and fierce hand to hand fighting ensued. The *Regent's* mast fell, taking many victims, and sporadic fires broke out on both vessels as the bloody chaos increased over both decks.

Suddenly there was a huge explosion. As many as two thousand men on the two ships lost their lives in that instant. Portzmoguer was hurled into the water by the blast and his heavy armour prevented any escape. The *Regent* and the *Cordelière* went together to the bottom of the sea.

As night fell, the remaining English ships made off for Southampton and the other Franco-Breton vessels returned to Brest as best they could.

What happened exactly in this deadly engagement is not known for certain. Was the fatal explosion an accident or a deliberate decision by Hervé de Portzmoguer? In subsequent literature, it has often been presented in the latter fashion, a brave action for the heroic sacrifice of his own ship in order to destroy his opponent and perhaps put an end to the engagement. It has come to be part of the Breton collective memory of heroism and patriotism in the on-going conflict with the English.

The song-writer Théodore Botrel (1868-1925) composed a song *Les gars de Morlaix* on the theme, giving the captain's words 'The sea will be my shroud, but I shall not sleep alone!'

We must not forget to tell our children
Of the twelve hundred brave men
Who went down with the Cordelière,
Dragging three thousand English with them.

An unsavoury memory of the Montfort Dukes

Gilles de Bretagne, third son of Duke Jean V of Brittany was largely brought up in England. After his father's death in 1442, Gilles was unhappy with his share of the inheritance, as his brothers seemed to fare much better than he did. François became the new duke and Pierre had control of most of the powerful Penthièvre area. He felt he should have some important lands and properties for himself and was not slow to voice these dissatisfactions.

Besides his complaints, Gilles also made himself unpopular at court by his desire to marry the attractive Françoise de Dinan, who had been engaged to one of the duke's friends.

As things between the brothers deteriorated, Gilles seized his lady love and ran off with her to the Château du Guildo.[1] But intrigues and allegations of potential rebellion flew thick and fast, with Gilles' letters protesting his innocence of wrong-doing being intercepted and altered, so that accusations of a plot against the duke and a treacherous alliance with the English were believed.

Gilles claimed to be a victim, but his brother Pierre was apparently convinced of his guilt and even favoured the death penalty. The duke's soldiers eventually arrested Gilles at the château, and he was then held prisoner at the Château of the Hardouinaye. Gilles survived attempts to starve him through the help of an old woman who brought him crusts of bread, and he failed to succumb quickly to the poison administered by his guards. He was finally murdered in his bed in April 1450, by Olivier de Méel, presumably at the behest of Duke François, who thus acquired the stigma of fratricide.

Château du Guildo

[1] The impressive ruins of this castle beside the river Arguenon near Créhen in Côtes d'Armor can be explored today.

Legend says that Gilles had a premonition of his death and managed to make confession through the bars of his prison to a man brought from the Abbaye de Boquen by the same old woman who had aided him before. Gilles swore that he was innocent of any crime against his brother and was simply a victim of his enemies' manipulations. He begged the man that, when he heard of Gilles' death, he should go to the Duke and tell him that as he had refused justice to his brother in this world, he should present himself within forty days at God's seat of Judgement.

When word got out that the unfortunate soul was dead, the man went in search of the Duke. François had just heard a mass for his dead brother's soul when the man approached and held the bridle of the duke's horse so he had to listen to Gilles' summons to the heavenly tribunal. The Duke was disturbed by the message and soon became ill. His condition worsened steadily and he died at Vannes in June 1450, forty days after his brother's death.

The Siege of Guingamp

Guingamp was the object of two famous sieges, in 1489 and again in 1591. Many versions of a popular chant concerning a siege of the town exist, recorded by among others Luzel and La Villemarqué. The memories of the two events may have become blurred over time.

After the death of Duke François II in 1488, following his disastrous defeat at the battle of St-Aubin-du-Cormier by the French and their Breton allies, the situation in Brittany was precarious. François' eldest daughter Anne was made duchess by her supporters who still hoped to keep the French from taking over the duchy. French troops tried to secure major centres throughout the region, including the town of Guingamp, which was sacked by the lord of Rohan in early 1489.

During the Wars of the League, the town was again under siege in 1591, this time by the prince de Dombes supported by many English troops determined to overthrow the ultra-Catholic Duc de Mercoeur who was rallying opposition to the Protestant king of France Henri IV.

The chant given here is that included by La Villemarqué in the *Barzaz Breiz*, about the event of 1489 and an apparent miraculous intervention which saves the city. This legend relates to the patronage of Guingamp by Notre-Dame de Bon-Secours, the 'black Madonna', still resident in the main church today.

"Porter, open this gate! The Lord of Rohan[1] is here with twelve thousand men, ready to lay siege to Guingamp."

"This gate will never be opened to you or anyone else without a direct order from the Duchess Anne, to whom this town owes allegiance.

"Shall we open this gate to a perfidious prince here with twelve thousand men ready to lay siege to Guingamp?"

"My gates are bolted, my battlements fortified; such an idea is shameful, the town of Guingamp will never be taken."

"Let them encamp here for eighteen months, the city will still not be taken. Load your canon! There! Courage! And let's see who'll regret his efforts!

Here are thirty cannonballs, thirty cannonballs to be loaded; we've plenty of gunpowder, lead and tin!"

On his way back he climbed up and was wounded by a shot, a shot fired from the camp by a man named Goazgaram.

Duchess Anne[2] then said to the wife of the gunner: "Lord God, what shall we do? Look how your poor husband is wounded!"

"Even if my husband dies, I will replace him! I know how to load his gun with fire and powder! And then we'll see!"

As she said these words, the walls were breached and the gates smashed in; the town was full of soldiers.

---

[1] The determination of Jean de Rohan, head of one of the most powerful families in Brittany, to oust the Montforts from ducal power led to his joining the French side at the Battle of St-Aubin-du-Cormier. His son François, however, fought for the duke and was killed on the battlefield.

[2] Her appearance here is figurative rather than real.

"Pretty girls for you, soldiers, gold and silver for me, all the treasures of Guingamp, and best of all, the town itself!"

Duchess Anne fell to her knees on hearing him brag like this. "Notre-Dame de Bon Secours,[1] I beg you, come to our aid!"

Duchess Anne, hearing this, ran to the church and threw herself on her knees on the cold, bare earth:

"Is this what you want, Virgin Mary! To see your house made a stable, your sacristy a wine-cellar, and your altar a dining table!"

As she was speaking a great terror swept over the town: a cannon shot had just been fired, and nine hundred men were dead;

And there was a terrible din, as houses shook and church-bells clanged tumultuously, ringing of their own accord.

"Page, little page, you are light, fit and lively, climb quickly to the flat tower and see who is making the bells sound.

Your sword is by your side; if you find anyone up there, if you find anyone ringing the bells, plunge your sword into his heart."

He went up singing, he came back down trembling. "I went up to the very top and I saw no-one.

I saw no-one there but the blessed Virgin, the blessed

Virgin and her son – truly. They are the ones sounding the bells."

The perfidious prince then said to his soldiers – "Get our horses and away! Let us leave these houses to the saints!"

---

[1] 'Bon secours' = swift or reliable aid, a common attribute of the Virgin Mary in legend.

In Brittany the advent of Republicanism at the time of the French Revolution in the late 18th century was countered in certain places by bands of royalist Catholics. These 'Chouans' loosely formed part of the movement that is probably best known for large-scale battles fought in the Vendée.

The Devil's Grotto

Deep in the granite Chaos of Huelgoat with its vast boulders bigger than houses lies the Devil's Grotto. Those who are brave enough can descend a metal ladder to venture into this grim cave above the rushing waters. Here at the time of the Revolution, a Republican soldier from Berrien took refuge when being chased by a band of Chouans. It was decidedly chilly in this underground chamber, so he kept on his cloak and large feathered hat. He then made a fire in the gloom to get warm and heat food on a toasting fork.

When his pursuers came close in their search and began to descend beneath the earth, the first man looked down and saw a burning glow, and the huge shadows of a strange creature and a pronged instrument of torture. "It's the devil," he yelled and scrambled back up to safety, fleeing from the scene with his comrades as fast as they could go.

The Battle of St-Cast

During the Seven Years War between England and France in the mid 18th century, the shores of Brittany were under constant threat of attack. After an abortive attempt on St-Malo in 1758, English troops moved west to St-Cast-le-Guildo where they hoped to re-embark. They were attacked by local troops, led by the Comte d'Aubigny, later joined by the Duc d'Aiguillon and his French army. More than 1000 English were killed, many drowned and many taken prisoner. Breton and French losses amounted to a few hundred, some now buried in the *Cimetière des Braves*. A monument where the

285

fighting took place shows a greyhound triumphing over the leopard of England.[1]

La Villemarqué's account of popular tradition about this event, given below (with a few additions for clarity), reflects a not uncommon degree of anglophobia in the search for Breton identity in the 19th century. By contrast, the solidarity of Welsh and Breton soldiers, albeit on different sides, is suggested.

It also shows that the role of the local Breton troops is elevated to minimise that of the French. The Battle of St-Cast did not have a significant effect on the outcome of the war, but it is presented as a major triumph: with its monuments and legends, a place of symbolic memory.

The Breton and the English are neighbours and yet enemies: they were put in this world to fight each other forever.

When I was sleeping the other night, the sound of a trumpet rang out in the Bois de la Salle: "The English! The English! The cursed English!"[2]

The next day when I got up I saw the English arriving, I saw their soldiers in their golden equipment and red uniforms.

When they drew up in lines on the shore, I watched as the French arrived to face them, d'Aubigny at their head, drawn sword in hand.

"Charge!" cried d'Aubigny; "none shall escape us! Courage! Come on my brave lads, charge! Follow me! And keep steady!"

The French replied with one voice to this appeal: "Follow d'Aubigny, step by step!"

D'Aubigny is described as a fine man and great fighter, covered in the blood of the English he has killed. On the battlefield he remained a calm, commanding presence, unmoved by danger.

---

[1] This was put up in 1858. Apparently the sculptor chose the greyhound/leopard ensemble without consultation. The greyhound may be in reference to the 14th century leader Charles de Blois.

[2] The Breton for English is *Saoz* = Saxon.

Then the men of Basse-Bretagne[1] arrived at the combat, singing "He who is thrice victorious, is always victorious.

At Camaret just now the English landed; they were parading on the sea, under their billowing white sails.

They fell on the shore, struck down by our shot like so many wood pigeons; of the four thousand who disembarked not a single one got back home safely.

At Guidel they landed, at Guidel in the district of Vannes, at Guidel they were dead and buried as they had been at Camaret.

In Léon[2] opposite the Green Isle once they landed too; they lost so much blood, the sea turned red.

There's not a hill or hillock in Brittany that doesn't bear their bones for the dogs and crows to fight over, for the wind and rain to whiten."

The archers on the English side, on hearing these songs, stood still in astonishment; they seemed fascinated by such words and harmonies.

"Archers of England," (said their captain) "tell me, are you so weary you must stop fighting?"

"If we stop," (was the reply), "it is not because we are weary. We are Bretons like them!"[3]

They hadn't finished speaking when (the captain called) "We are betrayed! Flee, soldiers!"

And the English ran as fast as they could to the ships, but only three of all their number escaped.

In this year 1758, the second Monday of September[4] the English were defeated in our country.

In this year, as before, they were sent on their way.

Always like hail on the sea the English swoop down on Brittany.

---

[1] i.e. Breton speakers.

[2] The area of north Finistère.

[3] It was a troop of Welshmen, who understood the Breton soldiers' song.

[4] La Villemarqué writes *de la paille blanche*, translating word for word the Breton *Gwengolo*, "white straw", which is the name of the month of September.

Some buildings have attracted legends in comparatively recent times.

Château de Combourg

The famous writer François-René de Châteaubriand (1768-1848) spent part of his childhood at this château in Ille-et-Vilaine and his work *Memoires d'Outre-Tomb* describes the sense of fear generated in himself, his mother and sister by the legends of this haunted place. He slept in the so-called Tour du Chat...

The Château de Combourg is haunted by a black cat which roams the passages at night. In medieval times this animal was regarded as the companion of the Devil, so it was common practice for a cat to be sealed up alive in a wall during building construction to ward off evil for those who were to live there. Such a mummified cat was found in the château...

Even more to be feared was the companion of the cat on its rounds, for many have heard the tap, tap, tap of a wooden leg making its way down the staircases and knocking on the doors of any occupied rooms. This strange appendage belonged to the Marquis de Coëtquen, a former owner of the château who had lost a leg in 1709 at the Battle of Malplaquet during the Wars of the Spanish Succession and later died in his bed at Combourg. Clearly, the leg lived on...

Pigeonnier de Kerscuntec

This large dovecote or pigeon-house once belonged to the 16th century Château de Cosquer which was demolished in 1975. It has been converted today to provide a viewing platform giving long views over the polders towards the sea at Combrit in south Finistère. Local legend said that the ghost of a horse appeared around here on each night of the full moon. The horse had been brought back from China in the 19th century and was supposedly buried in the pigeon-house. In 1989, remains of a small horse were dug up by workmen on the site.

Experience of an Englishman in Brittany

Thomas Adolphus Trollope was the brother of the famous novelist Anthony Trollope. He also was a writer of travelogues, history and fiction, and left a detailed account of his journey around Brittany in 1840. The book he singles out as giving him the best sense of the Bretons was Emile Souvestre's *Les derniers Bretons*, which was recently published at the time of his visit.

Trollope has this to say about the strength of popular traditions:

"Nor are the recollections and histories attached to these localities yet extinct among the people. Many of the fables of local superstition and tradition, which have in other countries been lost, or preserved only by the gleaning care of the antiquary, are here still subjects of popular belief and respect. The gigantic stones erected by their earliest ancestors for temples or for monuments, are still objects of superstitious veneration to their descendants; though in some instances the clergy have succeeded after a long struggle in attaching catholic legends to monuments intended by their authors to perpetuate the memory of far other facts and deeds. In many parts of the country, ceremonies, evidently of Pagan origin, are still observed; and it may surprise many persons as much as it did me to learn that within a hundred years there were in the Isle of Ouessant persons still professing paganism."

On his visit to Corlay, the people he met were keen to tell any foreigners local legends, starting with the underground passage leading from the castle:

The people relate a story of a traveller who came to Corlay, and having procured lights, descended into this passage, and has never been heard of from that time to this. The entrance has since been stopped up.

During the wars of the League, the castle of Corlay was seized and held for the parliament by the too celebrated Fontenelle. There is no part of Brittany in which traditionary (sic) tales of the cruelties and abominations

of this terrible chieftain are not still rife.[1] Though he remained in possession of Corlay little more than two years, the peasants still tell stories of his ravaging the country, burning the houses, carrying off young girls, etc.

Among other anecdotes they point out the spot in the midst of the ruins of the castle were, one night, when Fontenelle was giving a ball, the whole floor gave way beneath the dancers and all were precipitated into the vaults below. Most of the revellers were more or less hurt, but Fontenelle himself broke his leg, and remained lame ever after.

He was at last driven from Corlay by the Maréchal d'Aumont, Henry the Fourth's general in Brittany. When he heard that the maréchal's forces were marching against him, he sent a spy to ascertain whether they had any cannon. This man was caught and made drunk, and then paraded over and over again before four or five old guns which had no carriages, and then sent back to his master. He reported that he had seen a formidable array of artillery; and Fontenelle at once gave up the castle.

A murder mystery

The Seznec affair, as it is commonly called, refers to events in May 1923.

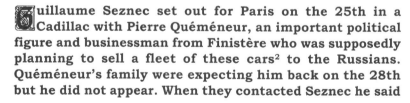

Guillaume Seznec set out for Paris on the 25th in a Cadillac with Pierre Quéméneur, an important political figure and businessman from Finistère who was supposedly planning to sell a fleet of these cars[2] to the Russians. Quéméneur's family were expecting him back on the 28th but he did not appear. When they contacted Seznec he said

---

[1] Guy Eder de la Fontenelle (1572-1602) caused an incredible amount of savage mayhem over a large part of western Brittany during his short life and was the most notorious bandit of the Wars of League in the late 16th century. He pillaged and destroyed many towns and villages, finally setting up a base on the Île Tristan at Douarnenez in 1595. He was eventually executed in Paris.

[2] The cadillacs had been left in France by the American forces after WW1.

the car had broken down and he had taken Quéméneur to the station at Dreux where he got a train to Paris.

On June 13th a telegram, apparently from Quéméneur, was sent from Le Havre,[1] saying he wouldn't be back for some days. A week later, a clerk at the station there found a suitcase which turned out to contain papers belonging to Quéméneur. Among them was a *promesse de vente* concerning the sale of the Manoir de Traou Nez, owned by Quéméneur, to Seznec at a low price. Seznec claimed that Quéméneur was in need of cash for business deals, but the supposed transaction only cast further suspicion on Seznec.

Quéméneur was never heard from again, and Seznec was eventually arrested and tried for murder, which he denied. Witnesses cast doubt on his story of having left Quéméneur at Dreux and there were alleged sightings of Seznec in Le Havre at the time the telegram was sent and the suitcase deposited.[2]

Seznec was convicted, but as there was no evidence of pre-meditation, he was sentenced to hard labour overseas. No body or murder scene were ever found.[3]

Seznec always maintained his innocence. He refused a presidential pardon in 1933 and did not return to France until after WWII. He died in 1953 as a result of a hit and run accident in Paris. His grandson Denis Seznec has worked for many years to have the conviction quashed in the courts, citing amongst other things possible corruption on the part of one of the police officers. His last attempt in 2006 was unsuccessful.

---

[1] The main port for America, leading some to speculate that Quéméneur went off to start a new life and escape financial scandals in France.

[2] One of the witnesses much later said pressure was put on her by the police to say she recognised Seznec. People who knew Quéméneur well by sight claimed to have seen him in various places after his disappearance.

[3] In 1953 after Seznec's death and his alleged delirious reference to a grave at Traou Nez, a search was made there. Apparently nothing was found, but in 1996 a descendant of one of the officers involved discovered a photograph of a skull among his papers relating to the investigation.

The heart of the mystery seems to have been the large house known as the manor of Traou Nez. This isolated and imposing building lies near the river Trieux in the commune of Plourivo. Its position and the wooded estate in which it lies once lent a curiously brooding atmosphere which only added to the tainted reputation it gathered in the Seznec affair proceedings. Although the house itself was not an issue in the trial, many people, whose testimony was never heard, believed that it may have been the scene of the crime. There were reports of shots being heard, bullets found near the house and a man in shirt sleeves seen running away ...

Some boatmen in a vessel on the river near the house at the end of May were surprised to see the remote house all lit up. They knew Quéméneur owned the place but he was rarely there. Was there perhaps a party for the wedding of the guardian's daughter? They heard shots. A woman accompanied by some men called out to them but they did not want to get involved and left. Some time later they decided to report their experience to the justice of the peace at Pontrieux, who in 1931, long after the trial, began to make his own enquiries.

He managed to date the mysterious events at the house to the night of the 27th of May. He also discovered that a man had been brought by car from Guingamp to Traou-Nez then. If it was Quéméneur and if he was killed at or near the house at that time, then Seznec could be innocent, as his own movements were known on those days. But despite the serious doubts felt by many about a miscarriage of justice, the true facts of the matter still remain an enigma today.

The Manoir de Traou Nez can now be visited in its role as the *Maison de l'Estuaire* for the Trieux river valley. A nearby halt for the steam-train *La Vapeur du Trieux* makes it a popular tourist destination for a cider and crêpe pause, accompanied by Breton music.

A cursed lighthouse

The Phare de Tévennec lies in the Raz de Sein, north of the Pointe du Raz and the island of Sein. The rock on which it was built between 1869 and 1874 had often been the scene of shipwrecks. In one a ship's captain, injured in the disaster, had been washed onto the islet but weather conditions prevented any boat reaching him and he died there a few days later. This may have been the source of the curse...

The construction of the light-house took a long time. Not only were weather and marine conditions very difficult, but the workforce were often alarmed by strange cries that seemed to ring out – "*Kerz kuit, kerz kuit!*"[1] A report from the late 19th century said the men were terrorised by all kinds of strange phenomena from demented howls of laughter to nocturnal wailing and mysterious sounds of quarrelling and fights.

When the light-house was finished it was decided that a single guardian would be appointed. The first holder of the post was Henri Porsmoguer, a Sénan.[2] He had applied despite having worked on the building and being aware of the peculiar goings-on. As soon as he moved in, things got worse. He heard loud warnings: "*Kerz kuit, kerz kuit!– Ama 'ma ma flas!*" "Go away, go away – this is my place!" He did not stick it out for long. Talking to Anatole le Braz about his experiences he claimed he had invited the ghost to have a drink with him and got beaten up for his pains! He said "I was amazed not to wake up the next morning and find my hair turned white. Fifteen days later I handed in my notice. The ghost of Tévennec well and truly put me off being a light-house keeper!"

Things fared little better for subsequent guardians, even when the authorities recognised the particular difficulties of the post and allowed first two keepers and then even married couples to reside at Tévennec. One cut himself

---

[1] "Go away" in Breton.

[2] Inhabitant of the Île de Sein.

badly and bled to death, another died in his wife's arms and she had to put his body in a salt-barrel to preserve it until help arrived. Others were said to have been driven mad by the ghostly activities and the stone cross placed on the little chapel-shaped house did little to stop the diabolic groans echoing all over the rock each night.[1]

Ile de Sein 1940

In this story, Pierre Jakez Hélias adds another dimension to the famous war-time feat when all the able-bodied men of the Île de Sein responded to General de Gaulle's appeal by sailing to England in their fishing boats to join the fight to free France.

In June 1940 the cry went up from Cap Sizun to the Île de Sein that the Germans had set foot on the Baie des Trépassés and that the mainland of Brittany was taken. The men of the island did not hesitate to leave their homes in the name of liberty and freedom. They said fond farewells to their mothers, wives and daughters and set off in a flotilla of fishing boats to join the Free French army forming in England.

That night the women lay awake. They too wanted to play their part and to follow their menfolk in the glorious enterprise of liberating their homeland.

"Oh, if only we could follow our menfolk with the island as a boat! Brittany, our hearts are breaking! How we would like to follow our menfolk to the cliffs of England, if only we could make a raft of this land here, in danger from Germans who have halted just across the way on the rocks at the edge of Finistère!"

And at that very moment, the island began to shake as the poor women lamented. All a quiver, it tore itself up from the depths of the sea. And there it was, floating, rocked by the swell, keen and buoyant, already taking leave of the Vieille lighthouse, whereat the women's shout

---

[1] The lighthouse is now being renovated and is intended to become a retreat for artists.

resounded: "Each to their oar and pull hard!" And the oars of the women of Sein toiled hard in the deep night. Brittany, our heart is breaking! And the oars of the women of Sein, at each pull, head away towards England, where their men had already landed to avoid servitude.

But when the first ray of the dawning sun fell on the island, Sein had not moved from its usual setting...

L'Arbre d'Or (Golden Tree) – a legend in the making?

The beautiful forest of Brocéliande[1] has suffered from a series of fires in the second half of the 20th century.

Two serious outbreaks in 1990, probably started intentionally, led to local resolve to take action to restore and protect the forest. A large sum of money was raised, consents of land-owners obtained and in the autumn/winter of 1991/2 volunteers undertook the massive task of planting more than 30,000 new deciduous and conifer trees.

As a symbolic statement of the resurrection, a Golden Tree (L'Arbre d'Or) was created by sculptor François Davin, who covered the bare bones of a chestnut tree from the forest in gold leaf. The tree's skeletal shape echoes the horns of a stag, particularly the one shown in a mosaic in the local church at Tréhorenteuc. It has been placed by the *Miroir aux Fées* at the entrance to the Valley of No Return, accompanied by the burnt remains of five oaks destroyed in the last fire.

The impression of this striking sight in such an evocative landscape is sure to stimulate popular imagination over the years...

L'Arbre d'Or

[1] See page 197.

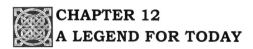

CHAPTER 12
A LEGEND FOR TODAY

YANN AR YEUN AND THE GREY LORD

It was in the days long before our own green time when the Land of Arrée trembled under the will of the Grey Lord. His impregnable castle rose above the Yeun, and it was said that this fortress harboured a malevolent energy which had reduced the marsh-dwellers and all the shades of the quickening deep to silence. Long since they had ceded the day to the Lord's determination to be master of their land, but by night, as the Grey Lord slept, the spirits of the Yeun oozed freely from the bog, follets flickering like stars over the mossy fen, lighting a deceptive way for foolish travellers.

Yann Ar Yeun bore all this with only sadness in his heart. After long roaming, this traveller with feet like the wind had settled in his chosen paradise. Here he dwelt for over a thousand years before the Grey Lord established his powers through means unknown to the land of Arrée. Formerly, on his graceful dragon-fly legs, Yann was the only one to walk safe-footed wherever he wished on moor and marsh, to speak the language of otters and beavers and to understand the cries of warblers from the marshy grasses. But in the Grey Lord's daylight, he felt his nurturing powers begin to fail the gentle plants and creatures of the bog.

By night he wandered forlornly round the Yeun, deaf to the malicious glee of the korrigans and the wheels of his cousin Ankou's cart creaking on the butter-soft paths.

One evening approaching the silent shapes of An Eured Vein he chanced to meet Laou ar Maen, the spirit of this place.

"Why so sad, old friend?" asked Laou.

"I am weary of the Grey Lord's rule," said Yann ar Yeun. "My energy is dry and brittle under his dominion. The age of peace and freedom haunts my memory."

"What can we do?" said the other. "It is always better to stay as we are, without raising ripples on the water."

Yann ar Yeun looked closely at the rugged face.

"You are truly content under the shadow of this lord who seeks even to quieten the belches of Youdig?"

The solemn Stone man slightly shook his weighty head.

"No change is good," he said. "Variety, upheaval, transformation all shake up our bones. Let us rest and enjoy our torpor, for stones live in stillness and all Eternity is set in stone. Better to endure, my friend. As things are, so let them be."

Then falling into slumber, he said finally "and that is all".

Laou slept, merging into the stones as the shadows streaked over the moor, leaving Yann ar Yeun to stride on across the vast hollow of the marsh and up the gaunt slopes of Tuchenn Gador. At the top, he came to rest on the stone seat from which he was accustomed to watch over his beloved Yeun.

Laou ar Maen's fatalistic view disturbed him. "How can I fight, with only my feeble fists", thought Yann. "But there must be a way out of the web without a clash of violence. And here I vow to find it." The scar of the grey castle of the Elez still loomed through the dusk before him, as he felt a deep passion to get rid of this sinister symbol of the Grey Lord's power stir in his belly.

Suddenly a red arc swung across the sky, cutting through the low stars like a scythe. With a hiss of steamy breath L'Aerouant appeared and fixed him with the dragon-glare[1].

"I am here, Yann ar Yeun, risen from my deep kingdom at your desire."

"What is the change you seek? To bring back goblin power to Brennilis, to make the giants jealous? What is it to be?"

He spun into the air, bending and shifting into these grotesque shapes one by one, squaring up to a fight in a blazing circle.

Yann ar Yeun waited quietly until the fireworks were over and L'Aerouant stood once again before him.

"Torment me not with your tricks, son of Fire," he said, "I've seen them a hundred times before. But tell me truly how it is possible to drive the Grey Lord from this vale and bring peace to all the creatures of the Yeun. I know that the wheel turns and the time has come, for you are here."

A flame flashed from the nostrils of the dragon. L'Aerouant swept a huge wing across the yawning bowl below towards the grey château.

"There is a stronger power than all these, which came before and will outlast any other. What you must do is call together the spirits of the place, those who ruled here long before the first human struck our soil or fished our waters."

Hope flickered in Yann ar Yeun when he heard these words and understood the message he'd received.

"You know this well, L'Aerouant, born of Fire that you are. So I will be the agent of a new age and restore the clean light to the Yeun."

Yann ar Yeun made his way down the stony track, through the scrub, his senses lifting and lurching at the

---

[1] Aerouant is imagined as the dragon on the Welsh flag.

scent of the peat. Ignoring the frustrated chatter of washerwomen by their stagnant pool, he reached the heart of the marsh and stopped. The familiar was all around, but he also felt the intake of a universal breath. Throwing out his arms towards the sky, he named and called on the primeval powers of the place.

There was a moment's silence, deeper than the forest chasm where Dahut's lovers met their death. Then from the north the trembling hills proclaimed the arrival of Earth. In the south, Fire blazed on Cleguer's Rock, while to the west Water rose in a shimmering wave. Lastly from the east a strident shriek of wind announced that Air was present. The whole world of the Yeun seemed to swell in waves and glow under the presence of these energies.

It was Earth who spoke to Yann ar Yeun:

"You have called us to rid the land of Arrée of the Grey Lord. The time has come. Though we can each destroy, today we are the vital forces of life: together we embody all the energy that is. We will proceed gently, without violence. This is how:

My brother Fire will stir in him creative energies which will guide him to respect and not abuse the natural world. Then my brother Air, on the west wind's draft, will infiltrate the Grey Lord's thoughts to send him on his way; So he will go and leave the Yeun rightly in my hands and those of my brother Water.

And you, Yann ar Yeun, return to the heights this night, then take thought once again for all that lives and flourishes in this our kingdom."

Nothing followed. Nothing but a sudden darkness and ringing silence. Yann ar Yeun knew no more where he was, but moved away by instinct and up the winding path to the top of Menez Mikel. There he slept deeply all the long reaches of darkness, until rosy-fingered dawn opened his eyes on a sea of mist filling the Yeun like a bowl of snowy porridge.

He waited in tense anticipation for the moment when the sun's rays drove off the haze, and then in total clarity he gazed and gazed towards the castle of the Grey Lord, but could see no trace, nothing beyond his beloved Yeun and what there was always to be seen - earth and water below, fire and air above...

So the Grey Lord left the valley without regret, and Earth took back its own, for nothing rises but from her matter and nothing exists for long without her will and accord. So Yann ar Yeun brought back wholeness to the land of Arrée, and once again lived amongst his marshland folk by day. And you may find him there still, if you have eyes to see beyond the limit of your sight...[1]

This story was one of the prize-winners in a competition held by the Parc naturel régionale d'Armorique in 2010. The nuclear power station in the Monts d'Arrée was the first to be built in France in the 1960s. Its location was on the edge of Lac St-Michel in the bowl of marshland called the Yeun Elez below the crests of the highest hills in Brittany. This area is one of the cradles of Breton legend. The station was decommissioned in 1985 and has been undergoing a process of dismantlement, not without its controversies.

The challenge was to create a legend, drawing on the existing traditions of the area and in a style appropriate to the genre, to explain the eventual physical disappearance of the site.

[1] © 2010 Wendy Mewes. The story was translated into French for the competition by Yves Marhic, and later published in the bi-lingual collection of short stories *The Shape of Mist* (*Lambeaux de Brume*) in 2011.

INDEX

Some single references to people and places of limited significance are omitted here.

Cover illustrations
Front: Mont St-Michel-de-Brasparts, statue of St-Hervé from Ste-Anne-La-Palud.
Back: medallions from Église St-Ronan, Locronan, Devil from Plougonven,
        author photo by Joan Cundy.